NORTHERN ONTARIO IN HISTORICAL STATISTICS, 1871–2021

D1714569

NORTHERN ONTARIO IN HISTORICAL STATISTICS, 1871–2021

Expansion, Growth, and Decline in a Hinterland-Colonial Region

David Leadbeater with Pat Marcuccio,
Charlene Faiella, Tomasz Mrozewski,
and Caitlin Richer

University of Ottawa Press
2024

Les Presses de l'Université d'Ottawa
University of Ottawa **Press**

The University of Ottawa Press (UOP) is proud to be the oldest of the francophone university presses in Canada as well as the oldest bilingual university publisher in North America. Since 1936, UOP has been enriching intellectual and cultural discourse by producing peer-reviewed and award-winning books in the humanities and social sciences, in French and in English.

www.Press.uOttawa.ca

Library and Archives Canada Cataloguing in Publication

Title: Northern Ontario in historical statistics, 1871-2021 : expansion, growth, and decline in a hinterland-colonial region / David Leadbeater, with Pat Marcuccio, Charlene Faiella, Tomasz Mrozewski, and Caitlin Richer.
Names: Leadbeater, David (Adjunct professor in economics), author.
Series: Canadian studies (Ottawa, Ontario)
Description: Series statement: Canadian studies | Includes bibliographical references and index.
Identifiers: Canadiana (print) 20240320182 | Canadiana (ebook) 20240320255 | ISBN 9780776641669 (hardcover) | ISBN 9780776641676 (softcover) | ISBN 9780776641683 (PDF) | ISBN 9780776641690 (EPUB)
Subjects: LCSH: Ontario, Northern—Population—Statistics. | LCSH: Ontario, Northern—Statistics. | LCSH: Settler colonialism—Ontario, Northern.
Classification: LCC HA747.O5 L43 2024 | DDC 317.13/1—dc23

Legal Deposit: Third Quarter 2024
Library and Archives Canada

Printed in Canada

Production Team
Copy editing   Jonathan Dore
Proofreading   Robbie McCaw
Interior layout   Michèle Blondeau
Index   Édiscript enr.
Cover design   Benoit Deneault

Cover image – Leland Bell, *Sovereignty*, acrylic on canvas, 101,6 cm × 152,4 cm, 2010.
Author's photo (back cover) – Al Castino.

The University of Ottawa Press gratefully acknowledges the support extended to its publishing list by the Government of Canada, the Canada Council for the Arts, the Ontario Arts Council, the Social Sciences and Humanities Research Council and the Canadian Federation for the Humanities and Social Sciences through the Awards to Scholarly Publications Program, and by the University of Ottawa.

Leland Bell, *Sovereignty*, acrylic on canvas, 101,6 cm × 152,4 cm, 2010.

Leland Bell/Bebaminojmat is an Anishinaabe artist from Wiikwemkoong Unceded Territory.

Table of Contents

List of Maps

List of Tables

List of Appendix Tables

Acknowledgements

This book forms part of a larger research project, the Northern Democracy Initiative. The research was based out of Laurentian University, in Sudbury, in Northern Ontario. Sudbury is on the traditional lands and resources of the Atikameksheng Anishnawbek and the Wahnapitae First Nation and under obligations of the Robinson Huron Treaty (1850).

For their excellent work in assisting the research I thank former Laurentian students Pat Marcuccio, Charlene Faiella, and Caitlin Richer, and librarian Tomasz Mrozewski.

The research has been supported in part by funding through the Social Sciences and Humanities Research Council of Canada, the Schumacher Foundation, the J.P. Bickell Foundation, and Laurentian University's Work Study Program. The research has also benefitted from practical engagement with community partners in the Timmins region, particularly the Schumacher Arts, Culture and Heritage Association and the Schumacher Historical Society; and from collaborations with filmmaker Lloyd Salomone and economist Professor Adrien Faudot. Acknowledgement is also due to Paisley Worthington for her support in copyediting and formatting the original manuscript.

The University of Ottawa Press played an important and valued role in seeing the manuscript through to publication, including in open-access form. Thanks are due in particular to the series editor, Professor Pierre Anctil, and the Press's acquisitions and production staff, including Mireille Piché, Martin Llewellyn, and Laurence Sylvain. Thanks are also due to the anonymous reviewers for their knowledgeable comments and helpful suggestions.

Last but not least, I am grateful to Kate and Jane Leadbeater for their brightness and understanding, and to Monique Beaudoin for her special support and our many conversations about Franco-Ontarian community development.

CHAPTER 1

INTRODUCTION

The aim of this book is to provide an overview of major population, employment, social composition, and urban concentration trends since 1871 in the region now called Northern Ontario (or Nord de l'Ontario). Special attention is given to the pattern of decline in population and employment that has been occurring in recent decades, not only as a whole, but also at the district and community levels. This book raises some structural issues of economic development underlying employment and distributional disparities, and also discusses certain measurement issues, particularly related to economic dependency. More detailed analysis of the economic conditions of decline is beyond the present task. Nor is the focus on immediate policy issues but rather on contributing to a deeper empirical basis for policy discussion. To heighten the importance of the larger trends treated here for policy, such as the recent decades of decline, this book refers to some aspects of current dominant policy thinking, such as the province's *Growth Plan for Northern Ontario* (2011) and some publications of the provincially funded Northern Policy Institute.

The early development of Northern Ontario occurred in the context of a vast Canadian colonial expansion in territory and settlement westward and northward, particularly following Canadian transcontinental railway development from the 1880s.[1] As established at Confederation (1867), the then province of Ontario occupied a smaller territory than today, of about 263,000 km^2 above the St. Lawrence River and Lakes

Map 1.1. Ontario in 1867 (left) and in 1912 (right).
Source: Archives of Ontario 2012-23. *Economic Atlas of Ontario/Atlas économique de l'Ontario*, W. G. Dean, Editor/Directeur; G. J. Mathews, Cartographer/Cartographe. University of Toronto Press (1969), for the Government of Ontario.

Ontario, Erie, Huron, and Superior (see Map 1.1). But by 1912, when Ontario's boundaries reached their current limits, the province had more than tripled its size, to over 900,000 km^2, most being through settler-colonial expansion into Northern Ontario.[2]

This territorial and settlement expansion was based mainly in southern Ontario and grew out of its earlier colonization. Northern Ontario came to cover approximately 87% of the land area of Ontario (see Table 2.2). Typical of colonial place-naming patterns, the area was also called "New Ontario" (or "Nouvel-Ontario"). This book uses the term "Northern Ontario" (or "Nord de l'Ontario") reflecting more current common terms.

The definition of Northern Ontario has been a matter of contention. For purposes of the present volume, we need to address particularly the issue of the southeastern boundary, which has been imposed in different forms for purposes of governmental administration and programs, and never negotiated with Indigenous peoples. There is wide acceptance that today Northern Ontario includes at least nine *territorial districts*: Algoma, Cochrane, Kenora, Manitoulin, Nipissing, Rainy River, Sudbury, Thunder Bay, and Timiskaming. For official statistical purposes, these unincorporated districts are also *census divisions*, except for Sudbury, which has been divided into two census divisions (Sudbury District and Greater Sudbury), thus making ten census divisions (see Map 1.2).[3] This ten-census-division definition of Northern Ontario is fairly consistent with much popular discussion, which takes the southernmost boundary to be the westward-flowing French River, from its mouth on Lake Huron (in Georgian Bay) through to Lake Nipissing, and then to the eastward-flowing Mattawa River from North Bay through to Mattawa on the Ottawa River.

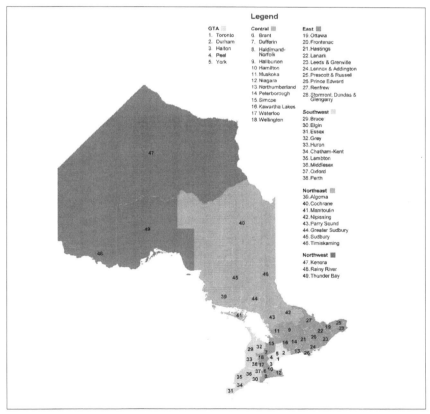

Legend

GTA	Central	East
1. Toronto	6. Brant	19. Ottawa
2. Durham	7. Dufferin	20. Frontenac
3. Halton	8. Haldimand-Norfolk	21. Hastings
4. Peel	9. Haliburton	22. Lanark
5. York	10. Hamilton	23. Leeds & Grenville
	11. Muskoka	24. Lennox & Addington
	12. Niagara	25. Prescott & Russell
	13. Northumberland	26. Prince Edward
	14. Peterborough	27. Renfrew
	15. Simcoe	28. Stormont, Dundas & Glengarry
	16. Kawartha Lakes	
	17. Waterloo	**Southwest**
	18. Wellington	29. Bruce
		30. Elgin
		31. Essex
		32. Grey
		33. Huron
		34. Chatham-Kent
		35. Lambton
		36. Middlesex
		37. Oxford
		38. Perth
		Northeast
		39. Algoma
		40. Cochrane
		41. Manitoulin
		42. Nipissing
		43. Parry Sound
		44. Greater Sudbury
		45. Sudbury
		46. Timiskaming
		Northwest
		47. Kenora
		48. Rainy River
		49. Thunder Bay

Map 1.2. Ontario Census Divisions.
Source: Ontario Ministry of Finance 2020.

However, the provincial and federal governments have expanded definitions of Northern Ontario. Currently, the Ontario provincial government also includes Parry Sound (district and census division), which makes eleven census divisions, while the federal government also includes Muskoka (district municipality and census division) and Parry Sound, which makes twelve census divisions.[4] In this book we focus on the narrower, ten-census-division area, although at points we also provide data on the Parry Sound or Muskoka census divisions.[5] When we make use of Statistics Canada's two *economic regions* categories (Northeast and Northwest)—categories which are followed by the Ontario Ministry of Finance's population projections—the Parry Sound census division (but not the Muskoka census division) is included within the Northeast economic region (Ontario Ministry of Finance 2020).

The present volume depends heavily on the use of official statistics, which carries problems related to the colonial background of Northern Ontario, which we discuss in chapter 2. It is important to note at the outset that major issues exist in the content and framing of the data from Statistics Canada; of its predecessor organization, the Dominion Bureau of Statistics; and of earlier census activities first centred in the federal Department of Agriculture, which was also involved directly in colonization and settlement activities. Official statistics play a powerful role not only in social science but also in their public policy role as "the guide of government" (Dominion Bureau of Statistics 1919). Although statistical data can play a vital role in social and scientific progress, the official statistics on Northern Ontario contain biases and weaknesses that reflect colonial as well as dominant class, racial, and gender orientations, and the policy priorities of the time. The Canadian government's pursuit of the assimilation of Indigenous peoples and the elimination of independent Indigenous cultures through the residential school system is now widely recognized as cultural genocide. The colonial outlook was also present at both the general level of the censuses as well as in specialized administrative data for enforcing the reserve system. As Neu and Therrien (2003, 23) observe, the Canadian government made use of accounting mechanisms in multiple "manipulations", including "the determination of reserve size; the membership-registration of tribes and bands; the movement of individuals from territory to territory; the 'giving' of annuities and tight budgetary controls over land transactions; the buying of tools, the selling of goods, the acquiring and exchange of provisions; and legislated interference in inheritances and family wills."

DECOLONIZATION AND ITS HINTERLAND-COLONIAL CONTEXT

The perspective of this study, one supported by a wealth of evidence and experience, is of Northern Ontario as a hinterland-colonial region. For Northern Ontario, the colonial structure of development has been well-known and deeply experienced by Indigenous peoples, and it has also been discussed by non-Indigenous social and labour activists, academics, and in some local business circles. However, the continuing colonial structure of Northern development plays little explicit analytical role in official governmental discussions and policy, reflecting a general problem noted by Habib (1984) of "studying a colonial economy—without perceiving colonialism."[6]

The hinterland-colonial conditions of Northern Ontario are not only about the past; they continue to be reproduced today. The economic structure of the region continues to be a subordinate capitalist hinterland, a back country (or *l'arrière-pays*) dependent on primary resource extraction and transportation corridors overwhelmingly subject to outside ownership and control of its lands and industries (Leadbeater 2018). For First Nations peoples, the conditions are indeed colonial, whether in the reserve system, the Indian Act, thwarted land rights, or unfulfilled sovereignty. For the non–First Nations population, the conditions can be characterized as semi-colonial or neo-colonial in the sense that there is external economic control but certain limited forms of political representation, in parliament, provincial legislature, and municipalities. The political structure has never come close to autonomy, let alone to formal provincial independence, as occurred when Saskatchewan and Alberta were created from the historical North-West Territories.[7]

As understood here, *decolonization* is the process of ending colonial rule and all elements of political, social, and economic oppression, exploitation, and inequality against Indigenous and colonized populations. Though the term has an earlier history, its widespread use grew out of a broad international movement in the second half of the twentieth century.[8] The general direction of the movement for decolonization is marked in several actions of the United Nations, including from the principle "equal rights and self-determination of peoples" enunciated in the UN Charter (1945) to establishing the Special Committee on Decolonization (C-24) in 1961, the "International Decade for the Eradication of Colonialism" of the 1990s (and two further decades), and the UN Declaration on the Rights of Indigenous Peoples (UNDRIP) of 2007. About the many years of shared Indigenous struggle behind the achievement of UNDRIP, James (Sa'ke'j) Youngblood Henderson wrote that diverse Indigenous peoples "shared concerns about the territorial appropriations of their homelands, about cultural and cognitive imperialism, and the exploitation by colonial and decolonized Eurocentric states" (2008, 11).

While there exist differing approaches and emphases in the movement for decolonization, a part of the decolonization process as suggested here should include identifying and rectifying problems in official statistics. This is not simply a narrow technical matter to be left to the upper reaches of state administration. Crucially, decolonizing changes to Canadian official statistics must be negotiated based on full consultation with and consent of Indigenous peoples as sovereign equals. There will need to be a recognition of how official statistics have not only reflected but also supported colonial objectives. There will also need to be clarity in data collection and presentation about the sovereignty of Indigenous peoples and the ownership, control, and use of Indigenous lands and resources. Most persisting problems of official statistics raised in this study stem from not recognizing openly the sovereign status of Indigenous peoples and the dispossession of Indigenous lands and resources.[9] As Thomas King (2012) observed: "The issue that came ashore with the French and the English and the Spanish, the issue that was the raison d'être for each of the colonies, the issue that has made its way from coast to coast to coast and is with us today, the issue that has never changed, never varied, never faltered in its resolve is the issue of land. The issue has always been land."

Consequently, parts of the present volume address specific problems in the official statistics, as a contribution towards decolonizing changes in official statistics. Our view is that a critical focus on understanding context and identifying various biases and limitations can help contribute to overcoming past problems. In this way, statistical evidence and analysis can become a more substantial aid to decolonization and social change, while also contributing to a deeper understanding of the conditions of the non-Indigenous population and hinterland regions.[10] This said, we recognize that the study's reliance on the existing official statistics carries a continuing hazard— even while acknowledging limitations and biases—of reproducing colonial and neo-colonial perspectives. The study, then, is provisional, but we hope nonetheless it will be another step along a path towards a deeper statistical picture of Northern Ontario that fully recognizes its colonial and hinterland character. As more work is done on data and analysis that fills gaps and shifts biases, there can also be a reformulating shift—even a revolution in thinking—not only of the statistical depiction of Indigenous peoples, territories, and conditions but also more generally on hinterland conditions and colonial structural problems in development.

The hinterland-colonial condition of Northern Ontario, in Ontario and in Canada, is not about a static land or geography but about a political-economic relationship set in place by settler colonialism. That relationship has evolved, but still within exploitative structures based primarily on extraterritorial ownership, control, and use of land and resources. The period studied here, though long (150 years) is intended to cover aspects of the era of settler colonialism as it developed through that period. A larger discussion of colonialism in Northern Ontario (including its earlier mercantile form, from regional contact in the early 1600s and earlier impacts) would need to extend at least another 250 years and to go well beyond the present focus on census materials.

The 2021 census year should not be considered as a conclusion of the 150-year era, let alone of the structural conditions that settler colonialism produced. Nor is 2021 necessarily the best year to conclude the study; it is simply the most recent census year. In fact, the 2021 census year poses special questions due to impacts of the COVID-19 pandemic. Most censuses have their particular conditions, though some are more disturbing of general patterns, such as the Second World War's impact on the 1941 census. The COVID-19 pandemic might turn out to be the special situation of the 2021 census. At the time of writing, evidence and analysis is increasing to show sharp declines in employment, lockdown-related polarization in work and income conditions, and much increased population movement across provinces and out of major metropolitan centres.[11] For Northern Ontario, such COVID-19 conditions might be relevant, for instance, to population increases in certain areas at the same time as declines in employment. It will take time and research to see if COVID-19 related patterns and movements continue or reverse, and whether they mark a substantial break with past trends.

For the present book, work began before the local onset of COVID-19 in early 2020 and the financial crisis and disastrous bankruptcy-driven proceedings at Laurentian University, unleashed on February 1, 2021. For reasons of work disruption and expected availability of 2021 census data, the completion of the research for this book was delayed so that newly available 2021 census data could be incorporated in the extended historical tables. However, given the uncertainty about how COVID-19 might have affected the 2021 data, for tables based on comparisons with a single recent census year we have continued to use 2016 census data instead.

NOTES

1. The railways were the most centralized, large-scale industrial force on the forefront of colonial expansion, especially the transcontinental railways, or what became the CPR (Canadian Pacific Railway) and the CN (Canadian National Railway). Both the federal and provincial governments aggressively supported railway expansion, through direct public construction and operation, as well as through privatization of public assets, cash subsidies, land grants, and financial guarantees to private corporations. While construction began in 1875 at Fort William (now Thunder Bay) on a railway to Winnipeg, it was not until 1885 that the CPR completed the trunk line across Northern Ontario and west to the Pacific coast. Two decades later, the federal government built the National Transcontinental Railway, which crossed Northern Ontario to the north of the CPR and later became a part of the transcontinental CN. For a geography of the transcontinental and other lines, see Andreae (1997).

2. A review of Ontario's boundary changes is provided by the Archives of Ontario (2012-23). Most of the area of Northern Ontario in its post-contact history was part of Rupert's Land under the Hudson's Bay Company (HBC), the English-chartered private monopoly trading company established in 1670. After the newly confederated colonies that formed Canada in 1867 took over HBC territory in 1870, Rupert's Land became the major part of the Canadian state's North-West Territories. The Ontario boundary was provisionally extended north and west into this area in 1874. In 1879 the federal government created a separate territorial District of Keewatin out of southern portions of the North-West Territories running through Quebec, Ontario, and Manitoba (Nicolson 1953). In 1889, as partial resolution of a boundary dispute with Manitoba, the federal government established Ontario's boundary west and north to the Albany River, which included the disputed Kenora area. In 1905, the District of Keewatin was dissolved and its area incorporated into the North-West (currently Northwest) Territories. Finally, in 1912, the boundaries of Ontario were extended to their present limits, north to Hudson Bay and west to the current boundary with Manitoba. The expansion is detailed in chapter 2 and Table 2.2.

3. Following the forced amalgamation that formed the Regional Municipality of Sudbury in 1971, Statistics Canada divided the district into two census divisions, creating one for the Regional Municipality of Sudbury (and subsequently Greater Sudbury) and the other for the remaining area as the Sudbury District.

4. The provincial government's Northern Ontario Heritage Fund Corporation (NOHFC), which requires an administrative jurisdiction for its funding eligibility, defines Northern Ontario to include Parry Sound District and all of the Nipissing District, but not Muskoka (NOHFC website FAQs). This is also the geography of the McGuinty Liberal (provincial) government's *Growth Plan for Northern Ontario* (Ontario 2011, 2005). In contrast, "designated service area" for the federal regional development agency FedNor (https://fednor.gc.ca/eic/site/fednor-fednor.nsf/eng/fn03338.html) and the Trudeau Liberal (federal) government's *Prosperity and Growth Strategy for Northern Ontario* (FedNor 2017) include the Muskoka District Municipality (Muskoka District). However, in Statistics Canada's geography for economic regions, the Northeast Economic Region includes Parry Sound and Nipissing but not Muskoka, which is considered part of the Muskoka-Kawarthas Economic Region (Statistics Canada 2016b).

5. In this approach, the Parry Sound and Muskoka census divisions are both considered "cottage country" and part of Central Ontario, or a sub-region within Southern Ontario. Nipissing District is a mixed boundary district whose district seat (North Bay) and population is predominantly in the narrowly defined Northern Ontario, but whose district includes a southern area whose largest part is Algonquin Provincial Park.

6. Such scholarly critiques are seen also, for example, in Dunbar-Ortiz (2014, ch. 1), Blaut (1993), and Anderson (1983, ch. 10).

7. Saskatchewan and Alberta achieved provincial status in 1905, but the federal government retained control of Crown lands and natural resources under the Dominion Lands Act (1872) until transferring them to the two provinces in 1930. Manitoba achieved provincial status much earlier, in 1870, in the wake of the Red River Resistance. The province originally had a much smaller area and the federal government also retained control of ungranted land and resources (unlike the first provinces of Ontario, Quebec, New Brunswick, and Nova Scotia). Manitoba's boundaries reached their present extent in 1912, while the federal government did not transfer Dominion lands and resources to the province until 1930.

8. A brief background to decolonization, including the term, is Shepard (2015). See also Manuel and Posluns (2019), Manuel and Derrickson (2017), Ness and Cope (2016), Coulthard (2014), Tuck and Yang (2012), Anghie (2005), Hall (2003, ch. 3), Adams (1989), Campbell (1973), Cardinal (1969), Nkrumah (1965, ch. 2). In the present context, the movement for decolonization is understood to include the struggles against colonialism of Indigenous peoples in settler-colonial states such as Canada and the United States, as well as the anti-colonial and national

liberation struggles for independence from colonial rule such as were prominent in the period in Africa and Asia.

9. Yet in signing on to the UNDRIP the Canadian government recognized at least in words not only that "Indigenous peoples have the right to self-determination" (Article 3) but also, among other important rights, that "Indigenous peoples have the right to the lands, territories and resources which they have traditionally owned, occupied or otherwise used or acquired" (Article 26.1) (United Nations 2008).

10. Edward Said (1994, 209) observed: "The slow and often bitterly disputed recovery of geographical territory which is at the heart of decolonization is preceded—as empire had been—by the charting of cultural territory."

11. For instance, Toronto was the only major city in Canada with a population drop in 2020–2021 (Bruce 2022); contributing factors included relatively high housing prices and affordability, "re-evaluation of life and living spaces," and "going home" to family (Davis 2022), as well as "pandemic restriction severity" and "telework adoption" (Desormeaux 2022). Research in the United States has also indicated a spike in out-migration from major metropolitan areas ("flight from density"), though much affected by demographic factors and not necessarily as a reversal of long-term trends (Frey 2022); some research has observed that U.S. out-migration was "disproportionately younger, whiter, and wealthier" (Coven, Gupta, and Yao 2023). Much earlier Canadian census-based research from the 1930s shows that employment crises can also lead to class-of-worker and dependency shifts together with out-migration, such as occurred when the employment crisis of the Great Depression led many urban workers to return to farms (MacLean et al. 1942, 269; Marsh 1940, 283, 290).

CHAPTER 2

THE COLONIAL NORTH OF ONTARIO AND OFFICIAL STATISTICS

The past century and a half of population and labour force changes in Northern Ontario reflect profoundly the area's foundational colonial conditions. For millennia, this land had been inhabited, worked, and enjoyed by Indigenous peoples. Settler colonialism involved the claiming of Indigenous territories, enforcing of external state control, displacing of Indigenous peoples, natural resource exploitation, and settling of large numbers of people generally from Southern Ontario, Quebec, and European places and European descent into the territories (Leadbeater 2018). As a result of colonization, Indigenous peoples were dispossessed, concentrated into small reserves, impoverished, subjugated as sovereign peoples, and today are still thwarted in their land and democratic national rights, and denied equality in economic and social conditions. This colonial condition and its reflections in official statistics are the focus of this chapter.

Map 2.1 represents the areas in Canada covered by treaties, where they exist, between colonial state authorities and Indigenous peoples. Treaties generally predated extensive colonial settlement and resource exploitation in the affected territories. As the provincial political boundaries and administrative divisions were established— without negotiation with, or consent of, Indigenous peoples—they commonly crossed and divided both treaty territories and traditional Indigenous lands.[1] This occurred in Northern Ontario, which covers six treaty areas. The southern boundary of Northern Ontario divided the Robinson-Huron Treaty (1850) area. The northwestern boundary of Northern Ontario divided the lands subject to Treaty 3 (1873) and Treaty 5 (1875). Treaty 9 (1905–1906) divided traditional Abitibi (Abitibiwinni) territory across the Ontario–Quebec boundary, reflecting provincial pressures in the treaty process.[2]

Based on the six treaty territories as currently recognized, Table 2.1 shows the land areas taken within and outside Ontario's present boundaries, and the land areas left as "Indian Reserves."[3] Approximately 75% of Treaty 3 and 6% of Treaty 5 is now in (Northern) Ontario, while most of the traditional territories are now in Manitoba.

Northern Ontario has 173 reserves.[4] The reserve areas are non-contiguous and in total constitute only a tiny fraction—less than 1%— of the treaty areas. The reserve areas are also Crown land as defined in the Indian Act.[5] The Treaty 3 area includes the "half-breed adhesion" of 1875 initiated by Métis people in the area of Rainy Lake.

The colonial conditions of Northern Ontario are still obscured in official statistics. Important Statistics Canada surveys simply exclude explicit recognition and statistical equality of Indigenous territories, both reserves and traditional Indigenous lands. For example, even after many decades, the monthly Labour Force Survey (LFS) still excludes "persons living on reserves and other Aboriginal settlements in the Provinces."[6] Lumped together with certain other exclusions ("full-time members of the Canadian Armed Forces, the institutional-ized population, and households in extremely remote areas with very

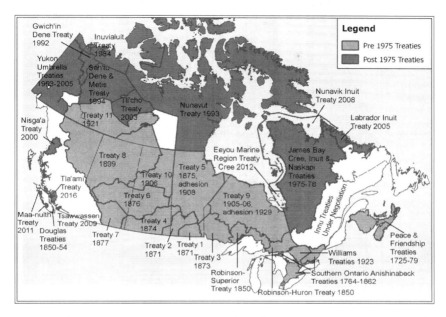

Map 2.1. The Historic treaties (pre-1975) and Modern treaties (post-1975) in Canada (Southern Chiefs' Organization 2018; Canada 2018; Leadbeater 2018).
Source: See Table Notes and Data Sources.

low population density"), Statistics Canada minimizes the exclusion, noting the groups together total 2% of the Canadian population aged 15 years and over, so presumably not of statistical consequence. The exclusion is justified as follows: "Indian reserves have historically been excluded from the LFS due to the serious challenges in contacting and interviewing potential respondents, with many of them living in remote locations not easily accessible to LFS interviewers given the short data collection period each month, and the large effort and cost associated with traveling to these locations" (Statistics Canada 2013, 19). This group exclusion of First Nations is asserted despite the fact that many reserves are at relatively close distances, or even adjacent, to many included survey areas.

For the *Census of Canada*, which is obligated legally to cover the populations of the provinces of Canada, the statistics have not been

Table 2.1. Treaty and reserve areas in Northern Ontario, 2016.

Treaties present in Northern Ontario	Treaty areas taken (km²)	Treaty areas within current Ontario boundaries (km²)	Treaty areas in Ontario left as reserves (km²)	Reserve areas in Northern Ontario as % of Northern Ontario treaty areas	Reserve areas in Northern Ontario as % of all land in Ontario (908,699.33 km²)
Manitoulin Island Treaty 94 (1862)	2,339.86	2,339.86	514.10	21.97	0.06
Robinson-Superior Treaty (1850)	43,252.80	43,252.80	226.98	0.52	0.02
Robinson-Huron Treaty (1850)	92,462.60	92,462.60	1,735.72	1.88	0.19
Treaty 3 (1873)	142,449.35	107,168.74	1,400.77	1.31	0.15
Treaty 5 (1875 and 1909 Adhesion)	345,504.41	19,542.70	303.67	1.55	0.03
Treaty 9 (1905–06 and 1909 Adhesion)	589,419.21	582,087.31	3,404.38	0.58	0.37
Totals	1,215,428.23	846,854.01	7,585.62	0.90	0.83

Northern Ontario Districts (inc. Parry Sound)	District area (km²)	Treaty areas in Ontario left as reserves (km²)	Reserve area as % of district area	Reserve areas in Northern Ontario as % of all land in Ontario (908,699.33 km²)
Algoma	48,814.88	738.85	1.51	0.08
Cochrane	141,268.51	758.73	0.54	0.08
Kenora	407,268.65	3,343.33	0.82	0.37
Manitoulin	3,107.23	717.30	23.08	0.08
Nipissing	17,103.78	263.51	1.54	0.03
Parry Sound	9,326.48	409.89	4.39	0.05
Rainy River	15,486.75	363.47	2.35	0.04
Greater Sudbury CD	3,239.02	10.36	0.32	0.00
Sudbury	40,204.77	364.30	0.91	0.04
Timiskaming	13,303.30	41.59	0.31	0.00
Thunder Bay	103,722.82	574.29	0.55	0.06
Totals	802,846.19	7,585.62	0.94	0.83

Source: See Table Notes and Data Sources.

so bluntly exclusionary, but the census too has long been beset by systemic colonial and racial bias.[7] The 2016 Census made a significant step forward with its Aboriginal Population Profile data to include "Historic treaty areas" (Statistics Canada 2018a).[8] However, despite the Aboriginal Population Profile reporting data for many variables, one still finds no data on the size of the treaty areas (km^2) or linked maps, as exist for other geographical entities.[9] Nor does one find regional or provincial aggregates for First Nations or Métis settlement areas so that the small size of the Indigenous land base relative to the treaty areas can be quantified and readily seen. In effect, treaty and reserve areas still do not have an established statistical status comparable to that of census divisions or census subdivisions (municipalities),[10] much less provinces or national entities.

The current situation is that Indigenous reserve populations and land are treated as census subdivisions (CSDs) or as equivalent to municipalities, while the official term "Indian reserve (IRI)" continues to be used, though it is not listed as a defined term in the Census Dictionary.[11] Ongoing resistance to federal policies and colonial conditions is reflected in a number of First Nations refusals and non-cooperation in the official censuses. Statistics Canada has reported that for Canada "incompletely enumerated reserves and settlements" totalled 63 in 2021, compared to 14 in 2016 and 31 in 2011. Most of the incomplete enumerations were reported in recent censuses as "permission not given."[12] In the 2021 census, Statistics Canada commented that health and safety regulations due to COVID-19 and natural events like forest fires "contributed to the incomplete enumeration." Refusals for political reasons are not addressed, nor does Statistics Canada offer a comparable assessment of COVID-19 or natural impacts on non-Indigenous CSDs.

Such a continuing colonial legacy leads to interconnected biases in the collection and presentation of data. First, there is an erasure of the status of First Nations as sovereign populations and territories. This political bias is most evident in Statistics Canada's hierarchy of geographies. First Nations and their treaty areas and current reserves are not treated as high-level or prioritized political categories even akin to provinces and territories, indeed, hardly as municipalities (census subdivisions). Although Statistics Canada has counted 1.67 million persons (in the 2016 Census) as having an "Aboriginal identity," identity data do not address the national character of Indigenous peoples, particularly their treaty or constituent constitutional status, nor the lands and resources areas, let alone marginalized economic conditions. Quantitatively, the 1.67 million count of self-identified Indigenous persons, which is larger than the population of six of the provinces and all three territories, could suggest a more respected status in official statistics. However, Statistics Canada publications still do not use even an Indigenous identity variable in crucial work, such as on wealth and income distribution, which might shift societal perspectives by revealing the consequences to a population subject to historic dispossession.[13] This said, the argument here is as much qualitative and legal as quantitative, particularly given the large number of individual First Nations and the process of colonial division, diaspora, and assimilation to which Indigenous peoples have been subjected.

The colonial bias on the political status of First Nations in official statistics is interwoven with other biases that reinforce colonial perceptions and policies, particularly views of metropolitan centrality versus remoteness, and larger urban concentration versus smaller scale or rural areas. Colonization concentrated and segregated Indigenous peoples on small reserves away from urban centres and generally the most immediately valuable land and resources.[14] While colonial settlement and resource exploitation continued to encroach on and violate even meagre treaty terms, the colonial biases also continued in the contrasts between "homeland" versus "frontier"—who was central and who was remote or distant—and between large-scale, urban concentration, which was viewed as superior, versus small-scale settlement or dispersion. It is in this context that the bias in official statistics of erasing 2% (or more) of the population as of negligible impact plays such a negative role, because it implies quantitative and qualitative comparability with other non-Indigenous populations across geographies. It denies the importance in society as a whole of dispossession or extreme impoverishment; it leaves out of view the material conditions of systemic segregation and oppression of Indigenous populations. It also prevents a more nuanced discussion and understanding of not only the dispossession and harms of colonialism but also the resilience and successes of Indigenous peoples despite the impact of colonialism and structural racism.

More important from the standpoint of analysis, the lack of attention to colonialism leads to avoiding discussion of major structural issues and, in particular, to problematizing Indigenous peoples themselves and their geographical locations as reasons for the ravages of colonialism and its continued reproduction. Neither the term itself nor anything closely resembling a recognition of the problem of colonial structures appears in Ontario's official *Growth Plan for Northern Ontario* (Ontario 2011). More serious analyses of Northern Ontario are also affected. In a significant research study for the Panel on the Role of Government in Ontario, three respected researchers attempted to identify characteristics of "communities at risk" in "peripheral" regions.[15] The study presents an ahistorical typology of negative structural characteristics that increase risk. The characteristics include small size, physical isolation, lack of economic diversification, weak economic base and employment opportunities, high costs, limited public and private services, lack of attractiveness to investors and in-migrants, and harsh climate. It also includes, "in some regions and countries, a large native population" (Slack, Bourne, and Gertler 2003, 6–8). All of the characteristics on their own are problematic, but the last should be alarming. Whether intended or not, an obvious inference from the last simplistic association is that the presence of Indigenous peoples in itself increases risk, or that hinterland regions are prone to difficulty in part because of higher proportions of Indigenous people. Such an implied association or correlation, with its

Table 2.2. Population, land, and census divisions (CDs) of Ontario, Northern and Southern, census dates, 1871–2021.

Census date	Ontario			Southern Ontario				Northern Ontario			
	Population	No. of CDs	Land area (km2)	Population	No. of CDs	Average population per CD	Average land area per CD (km2)	Population	No. of CDs	Average population per CD	Average land area per CD (km2)
2021	14,223,942	49	892,411.8	13,481,332	39	345,675	2,928.6	742,610	10	74,261	77,819.5
2016	13,448,494	49	908,699.3	12,711,178	39	325,928	2,953.3	737,316	10	73,732	79,352.0
2011	12,851,821	49	908,607.7	12,118,805	39	310,739	2,952.7	733,016	10	73,302	79,345.2
2006	12,160,282	49	907,573.8	11,414,910	39	292,690	2,933.3	745,372	10	74,537	79,317.4
2001	11,410,046	49	907,655.6	10,663,268	39	273,417	2,935.9	746,778	10	74,678	79,315.6
1996	10,753,573	49	916,733.7	9,967,203	39	255,569	2,984.1	786,370	10	78,637	80,035.5
1991	10,084,885	49	916,733.7	9,300,858	39	238,484	2,984.1	784,027	10	78,403	72,759.6
1986	9,101,694	49	916,733.7	8,337,382	39	213,779	2,984.1	764,312	10	76,431	80,035.5
1981	8,625,107	53	916,733.7	7,839,059	43	182,304	2,706.5	786,048	10	78,605	80,035.5
1976	8,264,465	53	917,434.0	7,479,978	43	173,953	2,702.4	784,487	10	78,449	80,123.2
1971	7,703,106	54	917,434.6	6,926,601	45	153,924	2,582.3	776,505	9	86,278	89,025.8

Census date	Ontario			Southern Ontario				Northern Ontario			
	Population	No. of CDs	Land area (km2)	Population	No. of CDs	Average population per CD	Average land area per CD (km2)	Population	No. of CDs	Average population per CD	Average land area per CD (km2)
1966	6,960,870	54	891,194.8	6,221,158	45	138,248	2,627.8	739,712	9	82,190	88,472.9
1961	6,236,092	54	891,194.8	5,513,918	45	122,532	2,627.7	722,174	9	80,242	91,405.4
1956	5,404,933	54	864,629.3	4,776,826	45	106,152	2,378.2	628,107	9	69,790	91,405.4
1951	4,597,542	54	940,896.7	4,061,148	45	90,248	2,627.7	536,394	9	59,599	91,405.4
1941	3,787,655	54	940,896.7	3,331,644	45	74,037	2,627.7	456,011	9	50,668	91,405.4
1931	3,431,683	56	940,896.7	3,071,575	46	66,773	2,570.6	360,108	10	36,011	82,264.8
1921	2,933,662	54	947,625.5	2,666,762	46	57,973	2,551.9	266,900	8	33,363	103,779.6
1911	2,523,274	85	675,630.0	2,308,515	81	28,500	2,728.5	214,759	4	53,690	113,654.7
1901	2,182,947	89	571,114.5	2,082,546	87	23,937	1,330.6	100,401	2	50,201	227,677.8
1891	2,114,321	89	568,891.3	2,059,445	87	23,672	1,345.4	54,876	2	27,438	225,921.0
1881	1,923,228	84	263,473.0	1,902,908	83	22,927	1,828.5	20,320	1	20,320	111,707.0
1871	1,620,851	90	263,440.8	1,612,985	85	18,976	1,452.0	7,866	5	1,573	28,003.7

Note: The census of 1921 was the first in which Ontario's boundaries reached their full extent. Though the boundaries have not changed since, the areas measured between censuses may vary due to measurement changes, particularly "geometry shifts" (Statistics Canada 2021, "Land area").

Source: See Table Notes and Data Sources.

suggestion of causality, is methodologically flawed and damaging in its representation of Indigenous persons and of Northern conditions. Nowhere does the study mention colonialism or how colonial structures might be related to other claimed structural characteristics for risk. The issue here is not about identifying structural characteristics *per se*, but *which* particular characteristics are explored. In this example, Indigenous population number was reported as a risk factor without any inquiry given to the region's colonial characteristics such as structural racism or segregation, Indigenous dispossession, land and resource rights, the reserve system, or resource-export dependency.

In this context, when examining the population and territorial changes in Northern Ontario in Table 2.2, one is examining basic patterns of a vast expansion of settler colonialism. By the First World War (1914–1918), Northern Ontario had about a quarter of a million settlers, overwhelmingly from other parts of Ontario and to a lesser extent Quebec, in a territory of over 830,000 km², or about 88% of the province's land mass (as of 1912). The colonization of new areas slowed in the interwar years, though there were still occasional local expansions in the post–Second World War decades, particularly around mining booms such as those associated with Elliot Lake and Marathon (Hemlo).

Comparing Northern and Southern Ontario, one can also see divergences in population and areas in Table 2.2 by looking at changes in the population numbers and territorial sizes of census divisions.[16] The numbers and sizes of census division changed as populations and administrative capacity increased; new census divisions were added or consolidated and boundaries were re-drawn. Census divisions correspond generally to "counties" for Southern Ontario and to "districts" for Northern Ontario. In Northern Ontario, the number of census divisions/districts briefly reached 10 by 1931, with an average population of 36,011 per census division, compared to an average population of 66,773 per census division/county in Southern Ontario. While having slightly more than half the population of Southern census divisions, Northern census divisions on average occupied

32 times more land than the Southern census divisions. By the 1980s, several Northern census divisions reached population peaks and, by the 1990s, population decline became generalized for Northern Ontario. In 1996 the average of the ten census divisions since 1976 reached a peak census population of 78,637, compared to 255,569 in the still-growing census divisions of Southern Ontario; by this point, the average Northern census division area was about 27 times larger than the average Southern census division. In 2021 the average census division population in Northern Ontario was still smaller, at 74,261, while in Southern Ontario it had increased to 345,675, and the average Northern census division area was still 27 times larger.

Like the federally established reserve system, the provincially established territorial district system reflects a colonial administrative impetus. In the evolution of official government statistics, most geographical definitions (such as census divisions) have followed closely, if not directly corresponded with, pre-existing or anticipated political definitions, such as province, municipality, county—and district.[17] The government of Ontario established the colonial districts for state administration, including the enforcement of laws and regulations, taxation, and the control of lands, transportation, and natural resources (provincial powers under the British North America Act and the Canadian Constitution). The districts contained cities, towns, improvement districts, villages, and townships as incorporated political entities under provincial municipal legislation, and they also physically contained Indian Reserves under federal jurisdiction. However, unlike counties in Southern Ontario, Northern districts were not themselves incorporated with councils and elected representatives, whether as single-tier municipalities or regional municipalities.

So Northern districts also typically have massive areas without incorporated municipalities, characterized as "unorganized territories," which have been controlled directly by the province.[18] These unorganized territories do not include Indian Reserves, which are under federal control. For example, as of 2016, 88.5% of the area of the

Table 2.3. Provincial unorganized territories in Northern Ontario, 2016.

	District/CD total		Unorganized CSDs		Unorganized total		Percent of district/CD	
	Population	Area (km²)	Population	Area (km²)	Population	Area (km²)	Population	Area (km²)
Algoma District	114,094	48,814.88			5,739	44,127.64	5.0	90.4
Algoma, Unorganized, North Part			5,739	44,084.16				
Algoma, Unorganized, South East Part			0	43.48				
Cochrane District	79,682	141,268.51			2,875	132,343.04	3.6	93.7
Cochrane, Unorganized, North Part			2,865	131,735.62				
Cochrane, Unorganized, South East Part			10	53.44				
Cochrane, Unorganized, South West Part			0	553.98				
Kenora District	65,533	407,268.65			6,737	400,813.46	10.3	98.4
Kenora, Unorganized			6,737	400,813.46				
Manitoulin District	13,255	3,107.23			169	407.67	1.3	13.1
Manitoulin, Unorganized, West Part			169	407.67				
Nipissing District	83,150	17,103.78			1,887	10,465.54	2.3	61.2
Nipissing, Unorganized, North Part			1,784	3,755.32				
Nipissing, Unorganized, South Part			103	6,710.22				
Rainy River District	20,110	15,486.75			1,385	12,257.65	6.9	79.1
Rainy River, Unorganized			1,385	12,257.65				

	District/CD total		Unorganized CSDs		Unorganized total		Percent of district/CD	
	Population	Area (km²)	Population	Area (km²)	Population	Area (km²)	Population	Area (km²)
Sudbury District	21,546	40,204.77			2,755	35,595.62	12.8	88.5
Sudbury, Unorganized, North Part			2,755	35,595.62				
Greater Sudbury CD	161,647	3,239.02			0	0.00	0	0
Thunder Bay District	146,048	103,722.82			5,872	97,009.80	4.0	93.5
Thunder Bay, Unorganized			5,872	97,009.80				
Timiskaming District	32,251	13,303.13			3,262	10,490.45	10.1	78.9
Timiskaming, Unorganized, East Part			5	249.63				
Timiskaming, Unorganized, West Part			3,257	10,240.82				
Northern Ontario	737,316	793,519.54			30,681	743,510.87	4.2	93.7
Bordering CDs								
Parry Sound District	42,824	9,326.48			2,330	2,881.46	5.4	30.9
Parry Sound, Unorganized, Centre Part			2,143	2,698.17				
Parry Sound, Unorganized, North East Part			187	183.29				
Muskoka District Municipality	60,599	3,940.48			0	0.00	0	0

Note: CD abbreviates "Census division" and CSD abbreviates "Census subdivision".

Source: See Table Notes and Data Sources Table 2.2 for 2016.

District of Sudbury (separate from Greater Sudbury) is unorganized territory with 2,755 people directly under the provincial government. In addition, outside this unorganized territory, five First Nations are under the federal government.[19]

In terms of total magnitude, Table 2.3 shows that about 93.7% of the land area of Northern Ontario is unorganized, containing 30,681 persons or about 4.2% of the Northern Ontario population.[20] Land in the unorganized territories is generally provincial Crown land (state owned). About 95% of the land in Northern Ontario is Crown land, managed mostly by the Ontario Ministry of Natural Resources and Forests, while most land in Southern Ontario is privately owned.[21] Apart from the reserve system, Northern Ontario has relatively little federal Crown land for national parks or other federal purposes.

Table 2.4 presents the census enumeration counts for the Indigenous peoples in Northern Ontario with special attention to the decades until 1971. As already noted, the official censuses, especially in earlier decades, are not a complete or fully reliable estimate of Indigenous populations. Besides limitations and biases in the administration of the enumeration, which were even more challenged in newer areas of colonial contact, there were significant changes in definitions and their applications (Goldmann and Delic 2014).

There is also a larger and changing context to the official census population counts that needs note. As discussed by the Royal Commission on Aboriginal Peoples, estimates of pre-contact Indigenous populations are being subjected to increased scrutiny, and earlier estimates are changing, generally towards higher numbers.[22] The Commission took a widely accepted estimate for Canada to be "500,000 for the Indigenous population at the time of initial sustained contact with Europeans." When viewed against the 1876 census estimate for the entire Indigenous population of 102,358 for Canada, this suggests, even if this and other early census estimates were undercounts, that the post-Confederation Indigenous population was far lower than the pre-contact Indigenous population—reflecting the devastating effects of colonialism.[23] There is evidence, for example, that colonial advance had brought smallpox to the Sault Ste. Marie area as early as 1670, and that early mining destroyed hunting lands in the 1840s.[24] These lower levels of the Indigenous population continued. Indeed, further declines occurred for some decades and in various Indigenous nations over an extended period. The Commission noted that "it would take more than 100 years—until the early 1980s—before the size of the Aboriginal population [again] reached the 500,000 mark."

The general population pattern described by the Commission is consistent with patterns in Northern Ontario (Table 2.4), although further research needs to be done.[25] The table is based on census reports of "Indian" populations by census division, particularly data from the census questions on the "origins of the people" or "ethnic origin." These Indian (including Inuit) counts are not tied to on-reserve or treaty status. For Northern Ontario, there are colonial and racial hierarchies and bias in the censuses, coupled with problems of distance and communications, that suggest the published numbers are likely minimum counts. As well, the population counts presented here grew in part due to the expansion of Ontario's boundaries, at least until 1921, which was the first census with Ontario at its present boundaries. Hence there was less growth in the Indian population than suggested in the table. When data were collected for Métis people ("half-breed" or "breed" in several censuses) these are reported in the table; however, these counts are themselves highly problematic.[26] The focus of the table is on data for the Indian populations because they provide a more consistent basis for observing the long-term trend of Indigenous population change and its geographical distribution.

A brief explanation is needed about the initial counts. The first post-Confederation census, of 1871 (vol. 1, table 3), counted 12,978 "Indians" and 2 "Half Breeds," only 0.8% in total of the entire then-defined Province of Ontario. The counts were larger in Northern census districts, numbering 3,935, or 50.0% of the census population of 7,866, for Algoma (East, Centre, and West), Manitoulin, and Nipissing (North); this suggests the settler population was about 3,931.

Table 2.4. Indigenous populations in Northern Ontario as enumerated by the Census of Canada, census dates, 1871, 1881, 1901–1971, 2016.

	1871	1881	1901	1911	1921	1931	1941	1951	1961	1971	2016
Canada											
Census "Indian" population	23,037	108,547	127,941	105,611	113,724	128,890	125,521	165,607	220,121	295,215	1,604,700
Total census population	3,485,781	4,324,810	5,371,315	7,206,643	8,787,949	10,376,785	11,506,655	14,009,429	18,238,247	21,568,310	35,151,728
Percent population counted as "Indian"	0.7	2.5	2.4	1.5	1.3	1.2	1.1	1.2	1.2	1.4	4.6
Average annual change in "Indian" population between censuses (%)		37.1	0.9	-1.7	0.8	1.3	-0.3	3.2	3.3	3.4	
Ontario											
Census "Indian" population	12,978	15,325	19,671	23,044	26,654	30,368	30,339	37,388	48,074	62,415	393,375
Métis persons, if a category	2		5,003				4,069				137,485
Indigenous population enumerated	12,980	15,325	24,674	23,044	26,654	30,368	34,408	37,370	48,074	62,415	518,300
Total census population	1,620,851	1,923,228	2,182,947	2,523,274	2,933,662	3,431,683	3,787,655	4,597,542	6,236,092	7,703,105	13,448,494
Percent "Indian"	0.8	0.8	0.9	0.9	0.9	0.9	0.8	0.8	0.8	0.8	2.9
Ontario "Indian" pop. % of Canada "Indian" pop.	56.3	14.1	15.4	21.8	23.4	23.6	24.2	22.6	21.8	21.1	24.5

	1871	1881	1901	1911	1921	1931	1941	1951	1961	1971	2016
Average annual change in "Indian" population between censuses (%)		1.8	1.4	1.7	1.6	1.4	0.0	2.3	2.9	3.0	
Northern Ontario											
Census "Indian" population	3,934	4,678	8,599	11,359	14,262	16,384	16,238	20,134	25,943	30,550	102,850
Métis persons if category	[1]		3,614				2,380				36,385
Indigenous population enumerated	3,935	4,678	12,213	11,359	14,262	16,384	18,618	20,134	25,943	30,550	136,320
Total census population	7,866	20,320	100,401	214,759	266,900	360,108	456,011	536,394	722,174	776,515	737,316
Percent "Indian"	50.0	23.0	8.6	5.3	5.3	4.5	3.6	3.8	3.6	3.9	13.9
Northern "Indian" % of Ont. "Indian"	30.3	30.5	43.7	49.3	53.5	54.0	53.5	53.9	54.0	48.9	26.1
Average annual change in "Indian" population between censuses (%)		1.7	4.2	3.2	2.6	1.5	-0.1	2.4	2.9	1.8	
Northern Ontario including Muskoka & Parry Sound CDs											
Census "Indian" population	4,242	5,068	9,084	11,986	14,963	17,199	17,302	21,104	27,062	31,730	108,200
Métis persons if category	[1]		3,951				2,498				38,395

Table 2.4. Indigenous populations in Northern Ontario as enumerated by the Census of Canada, census dates, 1871, 1881, 1901–1971, 2016.

	1871	1881	1901	1911	1921	1931	1941	1951	1961	1971	2016
Indigenous population enumerated	4,243	5,068	13,035	11,986	14,963	17,199	19,800	21,104	27,062	31,730	143,515
Total census population	14,785	47,524	134,075	262,539	313,361	406,984	507,929	588,478	778,511	838,695	840,739
Percent "Indian"	28.7	10.7	6.8	4.6	4.8	4.2	3.4	3.6	3.5	3.8	12.9
Northern "Indian" % of Ont. "Indian"	32.7	33.1	46.2	52.0	56.1	56.6	57.0	56.5	56.3	50.8	27.5
Average annual change (%)		1.7	4.0	3.2	2.5	1.5	0.1	2.2	2.8	1.7	
Northern Ontario area (km²)	140,0185	111,707.0	455,355.6	454,619.0	830,235.4	822,648.2	822,648.2	822,648.2	822,648.2	822,648.6	822,648.6
"Indian" persons enumerated / km²	0.028	0.042	0.019	0.025	0.017	0.020	0.020	0.024	0.032	0.037	0.125

Source: See Table Notes and Data Sources.

However, these counts of the Indigenous population are probably low, especially for the large Algoma and Nipissing districts. The counts also exclude areas further north, which were not in Ontario but then part of the North-West Territories. In 1876, the census authorities published estimates of "tribes" in both northern districts of the then Province of Ontario and further north: 8,637 covering northeast areas of the "Algonquins, Potowatamis, northern tribes, etc" and 9,000 covering northwest areas of the "The Salteaux, Maskégons, and other tribes."[27] Using this officially published source, one would estimate a total Indigenous population of 17,637 for Northern Ontario in the area closer to its present size. This Indigenous population would be 4.5 times larger than the 3,931 settler population counted in the 1871 Census.[28] Anthropologist Charles Bishop (1994) puts the northern Algonquian population at contact at somewhat over 8,000 (5,000 Ojibwa, 3,000 Cree, and 600 others), which gives more plausibility to the magnitude of the official estimates for northeastern areas.[29]

The census-defined counts of "Indian" peoples in Northern Ontario districts show relatively little change over an extended period, and there were absolute as well as relative declines in some decades, most notably in the 1930s, and likely around the years of the First World War. If one takes into account the census areas covered, from 1871 to 1921 there was generally a decline in the Indian population count per km^2 (from 0.028 to 0.017). That is, the Indian population in Ontario fell in relation to Ontario's territory. This is consistent both with undercounting and declines in the Indigenous population as well as with the common assumption that the more "remote" areas acquired by Ontario had fewer Indians. It was during these decades that the economic fracturing of Indigenous lands and the segregation of Indigenous peoples was enforced. Alongside this were the policies forcing assimilation and, most prominently, the residential school system, characterized by the Truth and Reconciliation Commission of Canada and by Canada's Supreme Court Chief Justice Beverley McLachlin as a "cultural genocide."[30] Northern Ontario had

16 of the 18 residential schools in Ontario identified by the Truth and Reconciliation Commission of Canada.[31]

Evidently, as settler colonization proceeded, the First Nations population declined relative to the increasing settler population. If one takes the census counts of "Indian" persons within the then-existing boundaries of Northern Ontario (excluding the Muskoka and Parry Sound Districts), the 1871 census count was 3,934, or half of the official census population. By 1901 the count was 8,599 but that now represented just 8.6% of the census population. By 1931, the count was 16,384 and 4.5% of the census population. It was not until at least the 1960s that one sees substantial increases in the measured Indian percentage of the Northern Ontario population. Further, while the proportion of the Indian census population in Ontario relative to Canada remained around 20–25% after 1911, the proportion in Northern Ontario relative to the whole province might have shifted substantially. While the Northern Ontario Indian population as a percentage of the Ontario Indian population was 30.3% in 1871 and 30.5% in 1881, it increased to 43.7% in 1901, then to around 54% in 1921 to 1961. In the following censuses, the Northern Ontario proportion of Indigenous persons fell, to about 26% in the 2016 census count (based on "Aboriginal identity," which is all the more significant given that the 2016 figure includes Métis populations).

While the Indigenous population has been growing, we will see that the increases have not yet been large enough to balance out the non-Indigenous Northern Ontario population decline. Long-term, demographic analyses have been showing that Indigenous populations are also experiencing a demographic transition through lower birth rates. In the shorter term, a portion of Indigenous people will migrate in response to declining economic conditions.[32] Population stability or, more likely, continuing decline depends much on employment and related economic conditions in Northern Ontario, which are central to understanding the relative and absolute decline of the Northern

Ontario population, particularly through job losses and population out-migration.

This overview of the settlement of Northern Ontario has discussed key foundational colonial elements that continue to be reproduced to this day. These elements can be seen in the Canadian censuses of population and other official statistics despite various colonial and racial biases in the collection and presentation of the data. First, the Canadian authorities took ownership and control of Indigenous homelands in Northern Ontario under six treaties and concentrated Indigenous peoples into small, non-contiguous reserves amounting to less than 1% of traditional Indigenous homelands. Today the reserves under the federal reserve system number about 173 in Northern Ontario out of 209 in Ontario.

Second, the settler population expanded across the region with provincial administration under a system of territorial districts. The district system was one of direct provincial control, unlike the county system in Southern Ontario, which allowed for municipal-level representation and incorporation. The number and size of districts in Northern Ontario have varied but rose overall in number to 10 today, compared to 49 counties in Southern Ontario. The total Northern Ontario population and average district populations in Northern Ontario rose to peaks between 1976 and 1996. The 2021 census shows an average Northern district population of about 74,000 with an average land area of about 78,000 km^2. The average Northern district or census division population is about 21% of that for Southern census divisions while the average Northern district area is nearly 27 times that of Southern census divisions.

Third, though mass colonization led to rural and urban settlement under private settler ownership, most land in Northern Ontario has been owned as Crown land and controlled directly by the province as "unorganized territories." As of 2016 nearly 94% of Northern Ontario land remained as "unorganized territories," in which the population of over 30,000 persons represented about 4.2% of the Northern Ontario population.

Fourth, the Indigenous population of Northern Ontario was not only dispossessed and displaced but probably suffered absolute declines during several decades from 1881 to 1941. The Indigenous population share in Northern Ontario also declined throughout these decades, as the non-Indigenous population rose. The officially counted "Indian" population of about half of the total Northern Ontario population in 1871 fell to 3.6% in 1941 and did not see substantial relative increases until after the 1960s. In 2016, a comparable count reached around 14%.

NOTES

1. The colonial disregard for Indigenous peoples in extending boundaries is illustrated in the case of the northwest boundary of Ontario by the racist positions of the Mowat Liberal government in the infamous 1885–88 case, *St. Catherine's Milling v. The Queen* (Dickason 2006, 259–262).
2. See Morrison (1986). Treaty 9, or the James Bay Treaty, had a signing process at the HBC post located on the Quebec side of Lake Abitibi. The Wahgoshig First Nation residing near Matheson comes from Abitibi people on the Ontario side, while the Abitibiwinni First Nation residing mainly at Pikogan comes from the Quebec side. Treaty 9 in some older maps has a triangular area extending into northeast Manitoba. This was considered an error (Long 2010, 87–89) and is not part of current treaty maps.
3. The data have been compiled by Charlene Faiella based on the Indian Land Registry and the Indigenous and Northern Affairs website, treaty maps of Ontario, and the First Nations Land Registry System (pursuant to the federal First Nations Land Management Act, 1999). We would like to acknowledge the First Nations staff who assisted us in clarifying and confirming often seemingly contradictory information found on different government websites. We would also like to acknowledge the suggestions of Dr. Darrel Manitowabi, now of the Northern Ontario School of Medicine, for sources in this research. We acknowledge too the GIS support of Ally Perron of the Laurentian University Library.
4. There are a total of 210 reserves in Ontario (Southern Ontario has 37). This count of reserves is higher than that published by Statistics Canada, which reported a total of 143 for Ontario (2021 Census Dictionary table 1.5). The total reported here for Northern Ontario and Ontario as a whole includes

current reserve lands (not abandoned) as identified in the Indian Land Registry System. This includes reserve lands provided by the federal government that are uninhabitable, such as swampland or under water, and illustrates further the record of colonial treatment by Canadian authorities of Indigenous peoples.

5. In the Indian Act (R.S.C., 1985, c. I-5) a reserve is defined as "a tract of land, the legal title to which is vested in Her Majesty, that has been set apart by Her Majesty for the use and benefit of a band."

6. From "Labour Force Survey: Detailed information for November 2019" on the target population (Statistics Canada 2019a).

7. See Hamilton, Mitchinson, and Marshall (2007); Curtis (2001); and Greer and Radforth (1992). Such bias is apparent in the evolution of the analytical classifications and hierarchies associated with questions of ethnic origin, race, and religion (as discussed here in chapter 4). In terms of enumeration practices on the ground, there is significant anecdotal evidence of undercounting through enumerator bias and difficulties with language, distance, and resistance, as well as the use of indirect estimates through the HBC and Indian agents, all of which point to undercounting of Indigenous persons. This said, in the early censuses, there existed a general expectation that Indigenous peoples would either be assimilated or die out as a population. Thus, the issue did not loom as large for the state-building authorities as the population magnitudes and clashes, in particular, of English versus French and Protestant versus Catholic. Further, "Indians" could not vote until 1960, so their being counted did not suffer from the additional incentive or disincentive of partisan bias. Curtis (2001, 193) suggests of early censuses that "attempts to count aboriginal peoples were mainly about creating a complete inventory of colonial resources"; this is consistent with viewing census development as part of state building and administration.

8. This was a more notable step forward after the setback suffered in the previous 2011 Census, which was forced by the Harper Conservative government to eliminate the mandatory long form of the census questionnaire, thereby removing especially data on economic and social conditions of First Nations, rural areas, and small towns.

9. It might be said that the treaty and reserve boundaries are contested. Indeed, they are, and subject to many legal challenges. But so too are the boundaries of municipalities and other geographies subject to controversy, challenges, change, and revision. Agreed formats can be negotiated to indicate the official federal or interim status of boundaries if under challenge.

10. Census division: "Group of neighbouring municipalities joined together for the purposes of regional planning and managing common services (such as police or ambulance services). These groupings are established under laws in effect in certain provinces of Canada. Census division (CD) is the general term for provincially legislated areas (such as county, municipalité régionale de comté

and regional district) or their equivalents. In other provinces and the territories where laws do not provide for such areas, Statistics Canada defines equivalent areas for statistical reporting purposes in cooperation with these provinces and territories. Census divisions are intermediate geographic areas between the province/territory level and the municipality (census subdivision)" (Statistics Canada 2018b).

11. Statistics Canada (2021). "Census subdivision (CSD) is the general term for municipalities (as determined by provincial/territorial legislation) or areas treated as municipal equivalents for statistical purposes (e.g., Indian reserves, Indian settlements and unorganized territories). Municipal status is defined by laws in effect in each province and territory in Canada."

12. Statistics Canada (2022, appendix 1.5, 2016, appendix 1.2). For Ontario as a whole in 2021, 10 of 13 were "permission not given" while 3 were "dwelling enumeration could not be completed."

13. For example, a typical Statistics Canada distributional study like Uppal and LaRochelle-Côté (2015) provides data by province or region, age grouping, education, family type, and immigrant status, but nothing related to Indigenous identity, let alone reserve geography.

14. For example, a key pressure for the Robinson-Huron treaty (1850) came from mineral exploration and copper mining at Bruce Mines, though further mining pressure diminished soon after, until after the railway juggernaut beginning in the 1880s. While the initial pressure for colonial land encroachment was not uniform in its tempo or geographical fronts, generally expanding colonial settlement and resource exploitation ratcheted up further pressures for encroachment and resource exploitation against Indigenous peoples. Even small concessions agreed by colonial authorities in treaty negotiations, such as on reserve dimensions, were later reduced and controverted. See, for example, Marlatt (2004) on initial surveys under the Robinson-Huron Treaty.

15. Slack, Bourne, and Gertler (2003, 3–16). The study considered the risk to be about "potential economic dislocation and demographic decline," but there was no precise or operational discussion of its meaning or measurement. Aspects of the structural characteristics are discussed critically in Leadbeater (2014).

16. We would like to acknowledge the assistance of reference staff at Statistics Canada's library in Ottawa in finding supplementary population and area documentation on the early censuses used here.

17. As statistical knowledge has advanced, some geographical definitions have been modified in ways that go beyond political criteria to statistical criteria that have greater consistency for purposes of comparison and analysis. Such is the census metropolitan area (CMA), which is based on consistent definitions of key elements such as a minimum population (at least 100,000) and population density (at least 400 residents per square kilometre), and an urban commuter shed (or

labour market) demarcated through a consistent set of rules. This definition does not necessarily correspond to the boundaries of a politically established city. For a detailed description of the CMA, see Statistics Canada 2018b.

18. According to the Ontario Municipal Act (2001, S.O. 2001, c. 25), "'unorganized territory' means a geographic area without municipal organization; ('territoire non érigé en municipalité')." Ontario provincial parks are not under the Ontario Ministry of Municipal Affairs but under the Ontario Ministry of the Environment, Conservation and Parks.

19. The colonial gaze continues to influence public sources such as Wikipedia: "The overwhelming majority of the district (about 92%) is unincorporated and part of Unorganized North Sudbury District. With the exception of Chapleau, all of the district's incorporated municipalities are found in the area immediately surrounding the city of Greater Sudbury to the west, east and south. North of the Greater Sudbury area, the district is sparsely populated; between Sudbury and Chapleau, only unincorporated settlements, ghost towns and small First Nations reserves are found."

20. For more on Northern Ontario's unorganized territories and municipal structure, see Nickerson (1992), Hallsworth (1985), Saarinen (1985), Weller (1980).

21. The Ontario government reports that about 87% of Ontario is Crown land, most of which is in Northern Ontario. The 87% is made up of 77% under the Public Lands Act and 10% managed as provincial parks and conservations reserves. The Crown lands include "shore lands and the beds of most lakes and rivers" (https://www.ontario.ca/page/crown-land-management).

22. Royal Commission on Aboriginal Peoples (1996, vol. 1, 20–22). For further discussion of issues in population estimates see Kerr, Guimond, and Norris (2003), and Goldmann and Delic (2014).

23. The Commission emphasized disease as well as armed violence and starvation as major factors: "The diseases brought to North America by Europeans from the late 1400s onward, diseases to which the Indigenous inhabitants had little resistance, had an enormous impact on Aboriginal population levels. During the 200 to 300 years of contact, diseases such as smallpox, tuberculosis, influenza, scarlet fever and measles reduced the population drastically. Armed hostilities and starvation also claimed many lives." Scholars are giving increased attention to socio-economic determinants and colonialism itself in the transmission and impact of disease; for example, Hick (2019) and Czyzewski (2011). The historian Roxanne Dunbar-Ortiz ties disease and alcohol abuse directly to European colonial domination driven by "invasion, warfare, and material acquisitiveness," and is critical of some U.S. historians for disease narratives that do not adequately address socio-economic factors (2014). Long after early contact the destructive effects on Indigenous health continued such as in the "horrific rates of TB deaths in residential schools" (Heffernan, Ferrara, and Long 2022, 811). In the

case of tuberculosis, Hoeppner and Marciniuk (2000) have questioned whether it was an "imported disease," arguing that endemic tuberculosis was "almost certainly" present among Indigenous peoples in Canada before European contact: "However, the social changes that resulted from contact with these traders created the conditions that converted endemic TB into epidemic TB."

24. See Daschuk (2013) and Chute (1998, especially 108–124). See also Pepperell et al. (2011).

25. The "Indian" data for Canada reported in Table 3 for 1881 to 1961 are the same as those reported by the Commission in its Figure 2.2 (Royal Commission on Aboriginal Peoples 1996, vol. 1).

26. See, for example, Goldmann and Delic (2014) and Hamilton, Mitchinson, and Marshall (2007). For Métis people, who emerged in identifiable communities out of the material conditions of the fur trade, there has been a long and continuing struggle for recognition. Debates on the Métis ethnogenesis continue (Bouchard et al. 2020). Major steps were achieved in the Canadian Constitution Act, 1982 (Section 35), and the historic *R. v. Powley* case of 1993–2003, which originated near Sault Ste. Marie as a struggle over Indigenous hunting rights (UBC First Nations and Indigenous Studies 2009). Efforts by the Métis Nation of Ontario for recognition and rights has led so far to identifying seven historic Métis communities in or near Northern Ontario: Rainy River/Lake of the Woods; Northern Lake Superior; Abitibi Inland; Sault Ste. Marie and Environs; Killarney and Environs; Georgian Bay and Environs; Mattawa/Ottawa River (Métis Nation of Ontario 2020).

27. Statistics Canada (2000). Although the 1871 map documenting the areas estimated overlaps with Northern census districts in Ontario, the estimates were largely not by the usual form of census enumeration: "The information has been drawn from the Census of 1871, from the writings and notes of the missionaries; from reports, works and memoirs published at different periods, and from details received, *viva voce*, from persons who have been in intimate relations with these clans."

28. The estimate of 17,637 (8,637 + 9,000) excludes the 3,935 Indigenous persons enumerated within the five Northern census districts in order to avoid possible concerns about double counting.

29. Bishop (1994, 631) also states that "The Assiniboine population, present within northwestern Ontario, cannot be estimated." Bishop used a method based on subsistence capacities and population densities.

30. Truth and Reconciliation Commission of Canada (2015, Introduction), Fine (2015). See also MacDonald (2015).

31. The residential schools in Ontario listed by the Truth and Reconciliation Commission of Canada (2015, 358–359) were in the following locations: Brantford, Chapleau, Cristal Lake, Fort Albany, Fort Frances, Fort William, Kenora,

Kenora/Shoal Lake, McIntosh, Moose Factory Island, Muncey, Poplar Hill, Sault Ste. Marie (2), Sioux Lookout, Spanish (2), and Stirland Lake.

32. Indigenous population mobility is discussed in Clatworthy and Norris (2014). Recent population projections and the declining trend in Indigenous birth rates is observed in Verma (2014) and Romaniuk (2014, figure 1.1).

CHAPTER 3

GENERAL POPULATION INCREASE AND DECLINE SINCE 1871

The settlement of Northern Ontario occurred over three main expansion phases before the current (fourth) phase of population decline. The first phase, which was the most rapid and extensive, occurred in the pre–First World War decades, with the population more than doubling each decade from 1871 to 1911, except the 1890s (Table 3.1). The second phase, covering the First World War and inter-war decades, saw continuing increase though at a reduced rate, in the range of 25–35% each decade, which was still higher than the rate of population increase in Southern Ontario. In 1941, Northern Ontario reached its peak census share of the Ontario population of 12.0%, or around 456,000 persons.

In the third, post-Second World War phase, population growth continued from the 1940s to the 1970s, but at a somewhat lower and declining rate, apart from the boom decade of the 1950s. Individual settlement projects still continued, particularly with resource finds

Table 3.1. Population change in Ontario, Northern and Southern, by decennial census dates, 1871–2021.

Census year	Ontario			Southern Ontario				Northern Ontario			
	Population	Pop. change between censuses (persons)	Pop. change between censuses (%)	Population	Pop. change between censuses (persons)	Pop. change between censuses (%)	Southern Ontario as % of Ontario	Population	Pop. change between censuses (persons)	Pop. change between censuses (%)	Northern Ontario as % of Ontario
2021	14,223,942	1,372,121	10.7	13,481,332	1,362,527	11.2	94.8	742,610	9,594	1.3	5.2
2011	12,851,821	1,441,775	12.6	12,118,805	1,455,537	13.7	94.3	733,016	-13,762	-1.8	5.7
2001	11,410,046	1,325,161	13.1	10,663,268	1,362,410	14.6	93.5	746,778	-37,249	-4.8	6.5
1991	10,084,885	1,459,778	16.9	9,300,858	1,461,799	18.6	92.2	784,027	-2,021	-0.3	7.8
1981	8,625,107	922,001	12.0	7,839,059	912,458	13.2	90.9	786,048	9,543	1.2	9.1
1971	7,703,106	1,467,014	23.5	6,926,601	1,412,683	25.6	89.9	776,505	54,331	7.5	10.1
1961	6,236,092	1,638,550	35.6	5,513,918	1,452,770	35.8	88.4	722,174	185,780	34.6	11.6
1951	4,597,542	809,887	21.4	4,061,148	729,504	21.9	88.3	536,394	80,383	17.6	11.7
1941	3,787,655	355,972	10.4	3,331,644	260,069	8.5	88.0	456,011	95,903	26.6	12.0
1931	3,431,683	498,021	17.0	3,071,575	334,979	12.2	89.5	360,108	92,720	34.7	10.5
1921	2,933,662	410,388	16.3	2,736,596	428,081	18.5	93.3	266,900	52,141	24.3	9.1
1911	2,523,274	340,327	15.6	2,308,515	225,969	10.9	91.5	214,759	114,358	113.9	8.5
1901	2,182,947	68,626	3.2	2,082,546	23,101	1.1	95.4	100,401	45,525	83.0	4.6
1891	2,114,321	191,093	9.9	2,059,445	156,537	8.2	97.4	54,876	34,556	170.1	2.6
1881	1,923,228	302,377	18.7	1,902,908	289,923	18.0	98.9	20,320	12,454	158.3	1.1
1871	1,620,851			1,612,985			99.5	7,866			0.5

Notes: See Table 2.2.

and associated transportation infrastructure, such as those related to the uranium boom around Elliot Lake in the 1950s. However, in these decades the rate of population growth was lower than in Southern Ontario and, by 1981, the Northern share of Ontario's population had fallen to 9.1%, from a high of 12.0% forty years earlier.

From the 1980s the Northern Ontario population plateaued and declined. There were both absolute declines as well as a continuing relative decline. In terms of the decennial census data shown in Table 3.1, there were absolute declines of -0.3% in the 1980s, -4.8% in the 1990s, and -1.8% in the 2000s, followed by an increase in the 2010s. In terms of quinquennial (5-year) census data (Tables 2.2 and 5.1), peak populations for Northern Ontario occurred not only in 1981 but also in 1996, both at around 786,000. As will be discussed later (in chapter 5), this plateau for Northern Ontario's aggregate population reflects the fact that while most Northern districts had a pattern of population growth and decline, the individual district patterns have differed considerably; in particular, some peaked earlier and some later.

Relative to Ontario's population, the Northern Ontario share continued to fall sharply, from 9.1% in 1981 to 5.2% in 2021. The Ontario Ministry of Finance has recently projected that the north's share of Ontario's 2046 population will be down to about 4.3%—even assuming conditions of significant absolute population growth for Northern Ontario.[1]

This present phase, then, is one of general regional decline both relative to Southern Ontario and, in many areas and years, absolute declines, bringing a long and difficult end to the once optimistic colonial project of New Ontario. As argued elsewhere, Northern Ontario has not had sustained growth in employment or even population stability, as a consequence of its colonial and neocolonial development conditions (Leadbeater 2018). The colonial north was developed primarily for transportation corridors and to exploit natural resources, especially its rich minerals and forests, as a resource-export-dependent hinterland. The north never achieved a balanced and self-sustained industrialization, nor did it achieve a provincial status or similar state organization that could have moderated or counteracted its colonial conditions, as occurred in the Prairie provinces. As the post-Second World War growth boom in Ontario and Canada slowed and ushered in the oil and currency crises of the 1970s, globalization, and "the great slowdown" in economic growth, Northern Ontario was hit hard by massive employment declines in its core extractive industries, mining and forestry, and their related value-added manufacturing, particularly with the downsizing and closure of refineries and mills.[2] Northern Ontario also experienced slow declines in agriculture and rail transportation, and some private services: finance, insurance, and real estate; information and culture; and accommodation and food services. As a result, there was increased employment reliance on the public sector and, though there were public interventions to staunch employment decline through relocating certain provincial and federal operations to Northern Ontario, the public sector itself became subjected to privatization, cuts, and weakened public service provision as part of a shift to neoliberal government policies and fiscal austerity. This was most evident in employment losses in direct public services and in education, especially following the 2008 financial crisis. These accumulating conditions led to Northern Ontario's present phase of general decline in employment and labour conditions, both absolute and relative to metropolitan Southern Ontario, particularly the Greater Toronto Area and Ottawa. In such conditions, the size of population has become a lagging indicator of Northern Ontario's employment and labour conditions and its vulnerability to out-migration.

The fact that Northern Ontario has had a long-term decline in population is fairly well known and might even elicit some empirical consensus. However, the question of the causes of the decline, and how decline is framed for policy purposes, is more contentious. Absent from provincial and federal government policies and regional development institutions are explanations that centre on colonial development structures, resource-export dependency, and weakened democracy in local government and associated educational, media, and cultural institutions. This failing is illustrated in some recent studies from the Ontario government-funded Northern Policy Institute (NPI), particularly recent policy-oriented analyses of the population decline. Table 3.2 reports the components of population change in Northeast and Northwest Ontario economic regions from 2001/02 to 2016/17.

In work for the Northern Policy Institute, Moazzami (2015) and Zefi (2018) focus on a few truncated observations to explain the decline in population and to raise concerns about future labour supply. Their argument suggests that birth rates (fertility rates) in Northern Ontario are below the replacement level necessary for natural increase of the population. Hence, for any increase in population, Northern Ontario depends more on migration from within Ontario, other provinces, and from other countries (immigration), than on natural growth. But Ontario and interprovincial migration patterns do not indicate a net influx to Northern Ontario; at least since 2001, "more people are leaving than are coming into the region" (Zefi 2018, 6). As for immigration, there are some differences in assessments. Moazzami (2015, 10) observes immigration flows as being net negative for 2001–2011, while Zefi (2018) asserts "international migration has been positive."[3] Despite the positive immigration trend, this influx of residents is not sufficient to counteract population aging. Thus, it is claimed, Northern Ontario faces a looming problem of dependency, when a decreasing working-age population will not be sufficient to support an increasing non-working (and largely older) population. For Northern Policy Institute CEO Charles Cirtwill (2015), regions with populations that are aging beyond a threshold dependency ratio of 1 (one or more dependent persons per working-age person) have reached "unsustainability."[4] The NPI argument then jumps to policy, advocating increased immigration to avoid rising dependency.

Table 3.2. Components of population change, Northeast and Northwest Ontario, annual, 2001/02–2016/17.

	2001/02	2002/03	2003/04	2004/05	2005/06	2006/07	2007/08	2008/09	2009/10	2010/11	2011/12	2012/13	2013/14	2014/15	2015/16	2016/17	Sum of net changes
Northeast Ontario																	
Net natural change	-67	-304	-443	-702	-556	-201	-213	-181	86	-578	20	-325	-532	-674	-808	-882	-6,360
Births (+)	4,928	4,782	4,792	4,552	4,667	4,985	5,147	5,265	5,329	5,091	5,357	5,276	5,298	5,348	5,413	5,530	
Deaths (-)	-4,995	-5,086	-5,235	-5,254	-5,223	-5,186	-5,360	-5,446	-5,243	-5,669	-5,337	-5,601	-5,830	-6,022	-6,221	-6,412	
Net immigration change	-581	16	-151	54	-236	-42	82	-12	196	25	-67	74	-33	86	67	-10	-532
Immigrants (+)	419	429	404	462	388	386	359	314	430	274	355	390	404	354	432	357	
Emigrants (-)	-1,000	-413	-555	-408	-624	-428	-277	-326	-234	-249	-422	-316	-437	-268	-365	-367	
Net migration change	-3,306	-1,907	-707	-94	-205	-676	-631	-2,144	-1,761	-1,439	-1,124	-998	-2,057	-2,084	-1,265	-771	-21,169
Net interprovincial migration (+)	-632	-503	-397	-567	-909	-778	-595	-999	-910	-799	-805	-842	-1,224	-1,015	-303	188	
Net intraprovincial migration (+)	-2,674	-1,404	-310	473	704	102	-36	-1,145	-851	-640	-319	-156	-833	-1,069	-962	-959	
Net permanent residents	-3,954	-2,195	-1,301	-742	-997	-919	-762	-2,337	-1,479	-1,992	-1,171	-1,249	-2,622	-2,672	-2,006	-1,663	-28,061
Net non-permanent residents	107	139	30	4	745	17	103	161	127	688	308	225	132	34	405	845	
Residual deviation	998	1,042	1,135	1,301	755	357	379	408	489	222	:	:	:	:	:	:	:

Northwest Ontario

Net natural change	613	574	482	381	506	509	502	593	557	363	451	524	434	386	340	314	7,529
Births (+)	2,721	2,629	2,606	2,540	2,642	2,569	2,569	2,644	2,662	2,655	2,665	2,733	2,707	2,732	2,765	2,824	
Deaths (-)	-2,108	-2,055	-2,124	-2,159	-2,136	-2,060	-2,067	-2,051	-2,105	-2,292	-2,214	-2,209	-2,273	-2,346	-2,425	-2,510	
Net immigration change	-371	5	-89	-86	-121	-148	39	59	101	95	-133	25	28	-182	8	-27	-797
Immigrants (+)	131	234	265	240	157	224	218	199	186	169	148	211	177	136	189	154	
Emigrants (-)	-502	-229	-354	-326	-278	-372	-179	-140	-85	-74	-281	-186	-149	-318	-181	-181	
Net migration change	-1,677	-1,016	-1,450	-1,945	-2,695	-2,836	-1,604	-1,119	-915	-485	-509	-657	-912	-1,094	-611	-188	-19,713
Net interprovincial migration (+)	-642	-330	-709	-1,234	-1,846	-2,164	-1,147	-920	-580	-380	-607	-571	-659	-610	-263	159	
Net intraprovincial migration (+)	-1,035	-686	-741	-711	-849	-672	-457	-199	-335	-105	98	-86	-253	-484	-348	-347	
Net permanent residents	-1,435	-437	-1,057	-1,650	-2,310	-2,475	-1,063	-467	-257	-27	-191	-108	-450	-890	-263	99	-12,981
Net non-permanent residents	67	90	17	5	295	12	61	94	68	-321	90	78	37	7	130	274	
Residual deviation	1,050	1,046	1,049	1,087	658	-233	-212	-175	-98	647	:	:	:	:	:	:	
Northern Ontario																	
Net non-permanent residents	-5,389	-2,632	-2,358	-2,392	-3,307	-3,394	-1,825	-2,804	-1,736	-2,019	-1,362	-1,357	-3,072	-3,562	-2,269	-1,564	-41,042

Notes: Northeast and Northwest Ontario here refer to Statistics Canada's Northeast and Northwest Economic Regions; Northern Ontario comprises these two Economic Regions. "Emigrants" data in this table are the sum of permanent plus temporary emigrants, minus returned emigrants. The ".." means not available.
Source: Statistics Canada 2019c.

There are several issues with the NPI work but what seems not in question is evidence of a long-term decline in the population of Northern Ontario, particularly for the non-Indigenous population. At the outset, it needs to be noted that, by itself, population decline is not necessarily a bad thing and, from an environmental perspective, it might be seen as positive. However, in the context of a capitalist economy, particularly for a *subordinate* region like Northern Ontario, absolute population decline typically reflects economic decline, including reduced income, reduced local demand conditions, increased impoverishment, and negative health impacts (Leadbeater 2014). Hence, in this chapter and the book as a whole, we look more closely at several claims about population, including the issue of demographic dependency, and we question whether an analysis narrowed to demography and labour supply conditions can actually offer a firm basis for policy.

Let us consider the three main factors accounting for population change, in turn: fertility rates, mortality rates, and migration, including immigration.

FERTILITY RATES

The starting point of the NPI analysis, that the birth or fertility rate is below replacement levels, is not a new observation and has long been discussed in literature on the demographic transition. For Canada the total fertility rate first fell below the replacement level of 2.1 in 1972 (Malenfant et al. 2007; Bélanger 2006). More significant here is that *relative* to Southern Ontario, the Northern Ontario fertility rate is actually higher. As Moazzami notes for 2011, total fertility rates in Northeastern and Northwestern Ontario were "1.60 and 1.77, respectively, with the higher rate in Northwestern Ontario reflecting the relatively greater share of Aboriginals in the subregion's population" (2015, 11). Moazzami also notes that the average total fertility rate for Ontario is 1.55 and for Canada is 1.60; women in Northern Ontario have more children than the average, as well as earlier in life. Further, higher total fertility rates occur widely in Northern Ontario. The Ontario Ministry of Finance (2018) reports that in 2014 the highest fertility rate in Ontario was actually in the Sudbury District, at 2.47, well above the replacement level. More research is needed on Indigenous fertility rates and their contribution to average fertility rates in Northern Ontario. This should include social determinants of fertility and issues of reproductive health, infant mortality, and pre-term birth (Morency, Caron-Malenfant, and Daignault 2018). However, a more realistic approach to Northern fertility conditions needs to begin by recognizing first that there is no major or new problem with below-replacement fertility levels, and that Northern levels are higher relative to Southern Ontario. Such an approach would also better acknowledge the contribution Northern women and families already make in often difficult conditions to raising the next generations.

MORTALITY RATES

The NPI analysis is marked by a lack of discussion of the other component of "natural" change in population, mortality (or death) rates. Death rates are not a beloved topic in boosterist narratives of Northern Ontario, but they deserve much greater attention even if reframed in terms of life expectancies. Substantial evidence indicates that aggregate death rates in Northern Ontario are higher than in Southern Ontario, a reality that is probably driven by known social determinants of health including industrial conditions and inequality (Nagarajan 2008). As Table 3.3 indicates, the average life expectancy at birth was 82.6 for Ontario (80.5 for males, 84.6 for females) and 84.5 for Toronto (81.6 for males, 87.2 for females); this compares with 79.6 for Northeast Ontario (77.2 for males, 82.1 for females) and 78.1 for Northwest Ontario (76.1 for males, 80.2 for females).[5] This alone shows that mortality is higher in Northern Ontario by three or more years for men (compared to the average for Ontario) and by two or more years for women. Consequently, with both fertility rates and mortality rates tending to be higher in Northern Ontario, one would expect that relative to Southern Ontario, there could be less of a tendency towards higher ages and dependency.

Table 3.3. Life expectancy at birth, by sex, Ontario, Toronto, and Northern Ontario regions, 2015–2017.

| | 2015–2017 (three-year average) | | |
	All	**Males**	**Females**
Ontario	82.6	80.5	84.6
Local Health Integration Networks			
Toronto Central Health Integration Network	84.5	81.6	87.2
North East Health Integration Network	79.6	77.2	82.1
North West Health Integration Network	78.1	76.1	80.2

Source: Statistics Canada 2019b.

MIGRATION

When it comes to migration, Northern Ontario in recent decades has had long-term net outflows to Southern Ontario and to other provinces. The loss of younger persons from communities is well-known in Northern Ontario; older persons have also left.[6] Two general observations about these losses need to be noted here: first, migration movements are less stable and can change direction more rapidly than natural changes in population, particularly in response to a deterioration in local or regional employment conditions relative to those in Southern Ontario or elsewhere. Second, in terms of magnitudes, net out-migration has a much larger importance for population stability or growth, particularly as natural population growth has slowed and turned negative. As for immigration, it is well-known that immigration is also more variable than population and subject to changes, particularly in government policy; as well, like domestic migration, the long-term pattern with immigration flows is that they too tend towards major employment growth centres (Yoshida and Ramos 2013). Turning again to the demographic data in Table 3.2, one can observe for the Northeast Ontario economic region that natural population change has been negative since at least 2001/02 in all but two years. For Northwest Ontario, population change over the same period was positive, though slightly declining, which led to a net overall natural increase for Northern Ontario of 1,169 for the 16-year period.[7] However, in the last four years of the period beginning in 2013/14, the negative natural population change in the Northeast combined with the diminished natural growth rate in the Northwest led to a situation where natural population change in Northern Ontario as a whole turned negative.

Table 3.2 also indicates that both the Northeast and Northwest economic regions experienced net out-migration in every year of the period, though in somewhat diminished numbers in later years. In the out-migration, the Northeast losses were divided almost evenly between those to Southern Ontario and those to other provinces. For the Northwest, roughly one-third left to Southern Ontario while two-thirds went to other provinces. Although the migration losses in later years of the period lessened, we cannot say at present whether this suggests a long-term trend or a shorter-term variation that could be reversed. What needs emphasis here is that the *accumulated* net outflows of population for the period, even if current employment conditions were to stabilize, were large, possibly over 41,000, and due mostly to domestic out-migration.

Further, in terms of immigration, the data from Table 3.2 are consistent with Moazzami's observation of overall net negative flows. The extent to which such population losses can be mitigated by further immigration, or whether this should be a policy priority, is not something to be addressed here. However, later chapters of this book examine the systematically lower *employment–population rates*, and consider how these and other data reflect the existence of a large, unused labour supply in Northern Ontario.

Reviewing Northern Ontario's population change over the census years from 1871 to 2021, one can see three phases of at first extremely rapid, then slowing, increases until the 1970s. From the 1980s began a phase where the population plateaued at around 786,000 and then declined. Relative to the total population for Ontario, Northern Ontario's population reached a peak share of 12.0% in 1941 then declined (even when absolute numbers rose) throughout the following censuses to 5.2% in 2021. Population changes have been affected by employment conditions in the context of colonial and neocolonial development, yet recent analyses continue to downplay and ignore the employment conditions and related hinterland-colonial development structures. Demographic analyses by the NPI have blamed declining population primarily on low fertility rates, yet the below-replacement fertility levels existed much earlier and, in any case, Northern Ontario has generally higher fertility levels than Southern Ontario. At the same time, such analyses avoid serious discussion of the north's higher mortality rates and the causes and consequences of long-term net out-migration and generally lower population to employment rates.

NOTE

1. Ontario Ministry of Finance 2023, table A. The 4.3% is made up of 3.1% for the Northeast and 1.2% for the Northwest. The ministry's projections are narrowly demographic, or determined by trends for births, deaths, and net migration; the projections are not connected directly to employment projections or other economic conditions which have major effects on net migration flows. The ministry itself recognizes the crucial aspect of net migration in their projections: "In the past, Northern Ontario's positive natural increase offset part of the losses it experienced through net migration. However, while the North has recently seen modest net migration gains, its natural increase has turned negative." Further, the ministry's projection for 2022–2046 was based on its "reference" scenario growth of 43.6% for Ontario, while it considered 62.4% as a "high-growth"

scenario and 26.0% as a "low-growth" scenario. Even by the ministry's reference scenario of significant population growth, eight census divisions in the Northern economic regions were expected to have 0–15% population increases and only Greater Sudbury, Manitoulin, and Parry Sound were expected to have 15–30% increases. A scenario assuming lower population growth would likely reduce the projections into a negative range, such as occurred in the ministry's preceding pre-COVID-19 projection (2018), which foresaw for the Northern economic regions "a slight decrease of 2.1%, from 797,000 in 2017 to 780,000 by 2041."

2. For the three decades after 1987, using data from Statistics Canada's Labour Force Survey, see, for example, Leadbeater 2018, table 5.3.

3. Moazzami (2015, 10–11) calculates net immigration loss for 2001–2011 at -30,565 for Northeastern Ontario and -15,820 for Northwestern Ontario. Zefi (2018, 5) is apparently referring to the longer period from 2001 to 2018, though the basis of the calculation is unclear. From the observation of net positive immigration flows, Zefi (2018, 6) advocates: "To build on this trend, the region should continue to showcase employment opportunities, economic and social supports, and a sense of community, since these are among the things newcomers tend to look for when deciding to migrate to Canada (El-Assal and Goucher 2017, 26). Accordingly, a Northern Newcomer Strategy would help to promote this trend by giving communities the tools and resources they need to further grow their population." See also Cirtwill (2015).

4. The ratio used here is more accurately called an age dependency ratio or demographic dependency ratio. It is the ratio of the number of dependent persons defined by age (such as 0–14 years and 65 and over) relative to the number of non-dependents defined typically as persons of working age (15–64 years). The dependency ratio can also be expressed in percentage terms by multiplying by 100; that is, the dependency ratio or level of 1 (to 1) could be indicated as 100%. Dependency ratios are discussed further in chapter 5.

5. These data are three-year averages for 2015–2017, from the Ontario Local Health Integration Network, the Toronto Central Health Integration Network, the North East Health Integration Network, and the North West Health Integration Network respectively (Statistics Canada 2019b).

6. See, for example, Southcott (2002), Bouchard, Girard, and Laflamme (2013), and Robichaud (2013). On an overview of rural and small-town migration patterns in Canada, see Rothwell et al. (2002).

7. Net natural change of -6,360 in the Northeast plus 7,529 in the Northwest gives the 1,169 overall Northern Ontario natural change.

CHAPTER 4

SOURCE POPULATIONS AND SOCIAL COMPOSITION IN THE SETTLEMENT AND EVOLUTION OF NORTHERN ONTARIO

C olonial settlement in Northern Ontario was deeply affected by national and linguistic divisions and rivalry within the newly confederated Canada, primarily between English- and French-speaking populations. The census data discussed here are relevant to understanding these relations and their consequences, from issues of language rights, schooling, and religion to interprovincial rivalries and provincial–federal conflicts. Here we look in particular at four dimensions of the source populations and social composition of Northern Ontario: birthplace, sex and marital status, national origins, and languages.

The early post-Confederation censuses took place in the context of what has been called "nation building" or "nation making," which was also rising in some European and colonial countries in the late-nineteenth century.[1] In this national development of the new Canadian federal state, the census authorities had both immediate practical motivations as well as broader concerns about allegiance, societal cohesion, and national identification in the federal state. The former included allocating parliamentary representation and public spending. For instance, part of the high priority given to collecting data on religious affiliation related to its role in allocating school funding (Curtis 2001, chapter 5). The latter concerns can be seen especially in the evolution of census questions on birthplace, nationality, and language use, and their relation to questions on sex and family conditions. Other questions, particularly related to religious affiliation, immigration, and citizenship status, also reflected official national concerns, though they receive less attention here.

Given the initial context of Ontario–Quebec rivalry in northward and westward expansion and the settlement of Northern Ontario, it is useful at the outset to highlight the approximate sizes of the English and French populations. By the time of the first census of Canada in 1871, Ontario was larger than Quebec in terms of population: about 1.6 million relative to 1.2 million, or 46.5% relative to 34.2% of the population of the then four provinces. Quebec still had by far the largest land area, nearly twice the size of Ontario and about half of Canada. As well, Montreal was by far the largest city (at a population of 107,225), with Quebec City second (59,699), while Toronto was then third (56,092) and Ottawa seventh (21,545). However, of the then 20 Canadian cities and towns over 5,000 in population, the more rapidly growing Ontario had 12 compared to 4 for Quebec (Census of 1871, vol. I, table VI). In terms of nationality, the census counted the Quebec population as about 78% of French origin compared to about 5% for Ontario. It can be noted too, due to the then strongly intertwined relation of national origin and religion, that the census counted the Quebec population as about 86% Catholic while Ontario was overwhelmingly protestant and about 17% Catholic.[2]

By contrast, Northern Ontario in 1871, before the impact of large-scale railway construction, was far smaller in population, under 8,000 (as noted in chapter 2). Nor did Northern Ontario have a major population centre. Its largest colonial settlement in 1871 was Bruce Mines, with a population of 1,298. All other centres, including the then second largest, Sault Ste. Marie, were under a thousand persons.[3] We will see that Northern Ontario also differed from Southern Ontario in having a relatively larger French presence, especially in rural and small-town areas in the northeast. As well, Northern Ontario's religious affiliations were less protestant than those in Southern Ontario and the census counted relatively larger numbers with Indigenous religious affiliations.[4] The 1871 census reported that a majority of the population in Nipissing (North) and Manitoulin districts were Catholics, while in the Algoma districts, Catholics were the single largest denomination.

Of the four data series discussed here, birthplace data was collected in colonial Upper Canada in the pre-Confederation censuses of 1851 and 1861, then continued in the post-Confederation censuses for the province of Ontario from 1871 onward. Birthplace was associated with allegiance and later citizenship, in the sense that the place of birth suggested a territory and sovereign to whose laws or allegiance those enumerated were subject or identified.[5] Second, and also collected from 1851 onward, were vital statistics including sex and marital status (or "conjugal condition" as it came to be titled in 1871). These data were central to settlement concerns about population growth and dependency; they also were used when cross-tabulated with nationality data to analyze relative growth and dependency among English, French, and immigrant subpopulations. Third, beginning in 1871, the census authorities introduced a direct question on national origin—"Origins of the People" or, in French, "Population par Nationalités."[6] This line of questioning, later to be characterized as "racial" origin and "ethnic" origin, would become the most contested and criticized, particularly in the decades following the Second World War.[7] Lastly, in 1901, the census authorities asked directly about languages spoken.[8] For instance, their introduction to the 1901 Census expressed concerns about the assimilation of foreigners and the extent to which French Canadians knew English (vol. I, viii):

> In a country peopled with so many foreign elements as Canada, it is desirable to know if they are being absorbed and unified, as may appear by their acquirement of one or other of the official languages. And as English is now in a very large degree the language of commerce throughout the world, it is also desirable to ascertain to what extent citizens of French origin are able to speak it in addition to their own.

During their evolution, these lines of census inquiry were interlaced with conceptions and classifications of colonial, racial, and patriarchal hierarchy and superiority. Official census materials have not only received such influences but reproduced them, shaping dominant understandings of Northern Ontario, not least in subordinating and diminishing Indigenous peoples and lands. So it is important to discuss some of these influences in the organization of census data with special attention to data on national origin.

To begin, the pre-Confederation 1851 and 1861 censuses had an embedded colonial and racial hierarchy, though less of the "British" imperial hierarchy than would appear later. In the personal census reports "by origin" (birthplace) for Upper Canada (Ontario), the first columns were ordered as England and Wales, then Scotland, then Ireland, then "Natives of Canada" which was subdivided by, first, "Not of French Origin" and, second, "French Origin." There followed columns for the United States, then for English colonies (Nova Scotia and Prince Edward Island, New Brunswick, Newfoundland, West Indies, and East Indies), then groupings for seven to nine continental European countries, a grouping for Guernsey, Jersey, and other British Islands, and a residual for all other places. This ordering was not by frequency (numbers reported) nor by alphabetical order in English (or French), but reflected the primacy of the English colonial power. Unlike later censuses there was not yet a grouping of England, Ireland, Scotland, and Wales as "British Isles" or "British." Further and most notably, the table added two columns, one for "Coloured Persons" and, lastly, one for "Indians."⁹

The introduction of national origin in 1871 and 1881 enabled counts for English and French origins that were not evident from birthplace alone and could be used to make inferences about language, among other things. For instance, a birthplace in England or France might suggest one is "English" or "French," but that would not necessarily imply a particular national identification or language for persons with birthplaces in Ontario or Quebec. Remarkably, both the 1871 and 1881 censuses reported their national counts simply in alphabetical order, not by frequency nor by imperial status nor with a grouping labelled as "British." The 1881 census (Vol. I, Table III) arrayed 18 nationalities in alphabetical order (by English) beginning with "African," then Chinese in second place, English and French in fourth and fifth places, and "Indian" in eighth place, while all others were of European origin including Welsh at the end.

However, in 1891 the count for national origins was dropped, except for French Canadian, while birthplace of respondents was kept and birthplace of their parents was added. The census authorities at the time thought "the division into native [born] Canadians and Canadians not native was more suitable to our present status than ... according to the races from which we originally spring" (Census of 1891, Bulletin No. 11). Reflecting their settler outlook, the census authorities explained:

> The two great sub-divisions, from a Census stand-point, are, 1st, those born within the country and 2nd, those who have not that honour. ...
>
> The first are sub-divided into: (a) French-speaking Canadians and (b) all others. This sub-division is made because it is the great fact

of Canada's population that it is bi-lingual, and accurate statements respecting this great fact are necessary for many practical purposes.

The second great fact is that Canada has, as a component part of its population, a non-native element. Of what is that element composed? To answer that question, the non-native element is sub-divided into, (a) those born in different portions of the Empire of which Canada is a part; (b) foreign-born.

The absence of a question on national origin was short lived. It came back in 1901, but with more amplified concerns about allegiance and assimilation—and explicit use of "race" and "racial origin." First, the census authorities separated nationality from national origin, ally-ing the former with citizenship while the latter was pushed toward racial origin. "Nationality" in this context was identified with alle-giance or citizenship either by birth or by naturalization. This included recognizing "Canadian" as a nationality. The 1901 Census Table of "Nationalities" (Vol. I, Table XII) arrayed 19 named nationalities in alphabetical order (by English) beginning with "American (U.S.)," end-ing with "Turkish," and including "Canadian."[10] There was no column for "Indian" (Indigenous persons). Second, the 1901 Census introduced counts of the "Origins of the People" ("Population par origines") framed as racial origin, where "origin refers to the race or tribe to which a per-son belongs or from which he is descended" (vol. I, xxiii). This change was much more than simply renaming English and French populations or nations as two "races." It involved a colonial and racial ranking of populations: listed first was "British" (English, Irish, Scotch, Others), then French, then nine "Other European" origins, then at the bottom, in order, Half-Breeds (Métis), Indian (Sauvage), Chinese and Japanese (Chinoise et Japonaise); and Negro (Nègre) (vol. I, table XI).

The intensified influence of biologically based racism is evident in the census classification process throughout the early 1900s, and would continue at least until the Second World War. In the 1901 Census (Vol. I, xviii), the census authorities adopted a four-race classification:

The races of men will be designated by the use of "w" for white, "r" for red, "b" for black and "y" for yellow. The whites are, of course, the Caucasian race, the reds are the American Indian, the blacks are the African or negro, and the yellows are the Mongolian (Japanese and Chinese).

For the "white" population, the racial line of descent was to be traced through the father, while for Indigenous peoples it was traced through the mother. To be classed as white, racial purity was paramount: "But only pure whites will be classed as whites; the children begotten of marriages between whites and any one of the other races will be classed as red, black or yellow, as the case may be, irrespective of the degree of colour" (1901 Census, vol. I, xviii).

Nonetheless, most pre-existing national-origin categories continued to be used (English, Irish, French, Chinese, Italian, etc.), while Canadian and American continued to be excluded as origins. The colonial-racial influence is visible in how the national origins were grouped and ranked. Indeed, the colonial and racial views increased even more explicitly in the interwar censuses. While the 1911 census had the primary category of "British" origins, followed by French, then German, the remaining origins were alphabetized (by English) including "Indian" and "Negro." For 1921, the census authorities made a much sharper hierarchy of "British races" (English, Irish, Scotch, Other), followed by "European races" (French, then nine named or grouped nationalities in alphabetical order, and Other), then "Asiatic races" (Chinese, Hindu, Japanese, Turkish, Syrian, Armenian), and, at the bottom, "Indian" then "Negro" (vol. I, table 22).

These interwar censuses show a more elaborated discussion of the concept of race and its application. The census authorities in 1921 and 1931 were well aware of "race" understood primarily as biological or about "physical kinship."[11] In a 1921 census study, the census authorities stepped back a little to argue that race "had acquired a cultural as well as a biological implication" and that the biological aspect was of "minor importance" for the census: "Even in such cases as Scottish and Irish, where it is well known that distinct [biological] strains exist, the cultural consideration is predominant" (Dominion Bureau of Statistics 1929, 12). They also suggested for practical census-collection purposes that the term "stock" (English stock, French stock, Italian stock, etc.) could convey "the sum total of the biological and cultural characteristics which distinguish such groups from others" (Dominion Bureau of Statistics 1929, 13). The public policy area apparently most motivating their concern was immigration, particularly how racial "stocks" were more or less "assimilable" and the issue of "non-assimilating peoples" (Census of 1921, "Origins," 14–15):

> Certain peoples readily intermarry with the native English and French stock in Canada and are easily assimilated in other respects. The larger the amount of intermarriage the greater is the number, for example, with part English blood who are classified as of Swedish origin and vice versa. As the fusion proceeds the social behaviour of the two groups becomes more and more alike. However, even when the two peoples have merged biologically and socially, the origin data perform a practical function in tracing the progress of the assimilative process and finally demonstrating that assimilation has taken place.
>
> There are other peoples like the South, Eastern and Central Europeans who are less successful in adapting themselves to Canadian social and legal institutions. The problem of assimilating such people is a difficult one.

For the 1931 census, during the Great Depression, the census authorities similarly advanced a racialized approach to "origin" both in its conceptualization and in its presentation. They also discussed long-standing concerns about English dominance relative to the numbers of those with French origins (Vol. XIII, Chapter I), through introducing a view of Anglo-Saxonism. At the time, according to 1931 census counts by racial origin, the "French stock" (at 28.2% of the population) in Canada had come to exceed the "English stock" (at 26.4%). As the census authorities wrote, "This does not mean, of course, that the French outnumber the Anglo-Saxons as a group." Combining those of English, Irish, Scottish, and Welsh descent as a group, there were "only" 54 French to their 100, while acknowledging that since 1921, "the [French] proportion has been increasing."

In the 1951 Census (Vol. I, xvi) the language of racial origin was dropped and reference was made to "a person's origin or cultural group" though origin continued to be traced through the father. A change was made for the origin of those with "mixed Indian and white parentage" to be "Native Indian" if living on reserve, but through the father if living off reserve (Vol. I, xvii), and not "Half-breed" as done in the 1941 Census. Nonetheless, the reporting structures still carried the weight of the colonial and Eurocentric past in their order: British origins, Other European origins (French plus 20 others); Asiatic origins (2); Other origins (Native Indian and Eskimo, Negro).

In the 1961 and 1971 censuses, the "origin" terminology changed to "ethnic or cultural group." Again, origin was traced through the father, and attachment was queried as: "To what ethnic or cultural group did you or your ancestor (on the male side) belong on coming to this continent?" Finally, in 1981, the restriction of following the male line was dropped, and census respondents were allowed multiple responses for their ethnic origin. As well, options for self-identification, introduced in 1971, were increased. This said, the census still queried the ethnic or cultural group in terms of the respondent's ancestors "on first coming to this continent." In these terms, "Canadian" as a response was still not considered valid or reported as a category. A write-in of Franco-Ontarian (or Franco-Ontarien) was deemed a single French ethnic origin.[12]

In more recent censuses, the shift has continued to self-identification and a loosening of response restrictions for the ethnic-origin question. The 1991 census put a greater emphasis on self-identified "roots" or ancestors, without reference to coming to the continent. In 1996 the census authorities allowed for Aboriginal-origin responses, and also introduced a separate question on Aboriginal identity. They also introduced a separate question on "visible minority groups." Perhaps most numerically dramatic in its consequences, "Canadian" (or "Canadien") was allowed as a valid response—and became the largest single ethnic origin reported.

Such changes, including greatly expanded and less Eurocentric lists of possible ethnic-origin responses, have reduced the comparability of ethnic-origin data in later censuses with earlier ones. The census authorities have noted such issues of interpretation.[13] At the same time, they have also noted the importance of the data in supporting the Canadian Multiculturalism Act (1988) and the Canadian Charter of Rights and Freedoms (1982) (Statistics Canada 2020a, 4). A question largely still to be addressed by Statistics Canada is to what extent these and related data can become important in the decolonization of Northern Ontario and other hinterland-colonial regions.

We will now look at some of these data classes in more detail.

BIRTHPLACES

In terms of origins by birthplace, Table 4.1 shows that throughout the decades from 1871 to 2021 both Northern Ontario and Southern Ontario had populations born mostly in Ontario (including Northern Ontario itself). At first, in 1871, Northern Ontario relative to Southern Ontario had a higher proportion of its population born in the province (74.2% compared to 69.8%). This suggests, due to the rapidity and scale of increases in the settler population in the early decades, that most of the new settler population in Northern Ontario came from Southern Ontario. However, the censuses have not provided subprovincial data on birthplaces (such as by census division), so further research including other sources would be needed to quantify and confirm when the population reached levels of majority self-reproduction within the Northern Ontario districts. By the end of the period, in 2021, the province-born share was even higher in Northern Ontario (84.0%) relative to Southern Ontario (58.7%). The most common birthplace outside Ontario but within Canada was Quebec, in both Northern Ontario and Southern Ontario, though it was relatively much larger in Northern Ontario.

For Northern Ontario, the most common birthplaces outside Canada during the early decades of confederation were in the British Isles followed by the United States (for example, in 1871, 10.5% and 7.5% respectively). There were some early increases in the British Isles–born share, but overall both the British Isles–born and U.S.-born shares declined in later decades (to 0.8% and 0.9% respectively in 2021). However, the share of birthplaces from continental Europe (such as Italy, Finland, and eastern European countries) increased, to over or around 10% from 1911 to 1961, after which they declined to 2.5% in 2021. For Southern Ontario, birthplaces in the British Isles were even more prevalent (in 1871, 22.8%) though their share too declined (in 2021, to 1.9%). The share of persons with U.S. birthplaces was initially lower in Southern Ontario (2.7% in 1871) but also declined overall (to 1.1% in 2021). Of greater importance in Southern Ontario, particularly after the 1960s, was the much larger shares of birthplaces from continental European, Asian, and other countries.

While the Ontario-born share of the Northern Ontario population increased over the period, there were significant changes during each of the different phases of population growth. During the first and most rapid phase of population growth, from 1871 to 1911, the leading share of population growth by birthplace was Quebec, with a share peak of 11.4% in 1901. This was followed closely by a major increase in the population of persons with continental European birthplaces, peaking at 14.8% in 1911. As a result, the share of the Ontario-born population generally declined in the decades of most rapid growth, from 74.2% in 1871 to 57.4% in 1911.

In later post-1911 phases of slowing and declining population growth in Northern Ontario, the general birthplace pattern was one

Table 4.1. Birthplaces of the population, Northern Ontario and Southern Ontario, decennial census dates, 1871–2021.

	1871	1881	1891	1901	1911	1921	1931	1941	1951	1961	1971	1981	1991	2001	2011	2021
Northern Ontario population reported	7,917	20,320	54,876	100,401	214,759	266,903	360,108	456,011	536,394	722,174	776,505	779,170	776,115	738,465	717,475	729,700
Born in (persons)																
Canada	6,424	16,084	45,860	83,951	150,392	201,579	268,841	366,799	449,881	607,429	680,175	698,180	711,720	685,455	671,795	675,115
Ontario (inc. Northern Ontario)	5,878	15,315	38,481	70,166	123,350	166,865	223,119	301,982	365,831	503,524	571,230	598,395	616,645	605,950	602,260	613,270
Quebec	380	497	6,057	11,459	22,614	27,954	32,273	33,981	40,732	48,149						21,015
Other Canada	166	272	1,322	2,326	4,428	6,760	13,449	30,836	43,318	55,756						40,830
British Isles / UK 1951-	830	3,009	5,955	7,426	21,096	26,135	29,407	27,147	24,665	26,036	20,230	16,220	11,495	8,385	6,835	5,755
England, Wales	477	1,390	2,932	4,156	13,965	17,983	19,806	18,010	16,844	17,557						
Ireland/ Northern Ireland 1951-	184	687	1,450	1,512	2,217	2,199	2,328	2,191	1,245	1,256						
Scotland	169	932	1,573	1,758	4,914	5,953	7,273	6,946	6,576	7,223						
Other British Possessions	4	12	40	122	1,902	693	866	920	327	776						
United States	593	667	1,574	3,053	8,515	9,774	9,677	9,683	8,587	8,747	8,745	8,460	6,645	5,610	5,375	6,570
Other European countries	57	324	1,203	5,229	31,857	27,577	50,076	50,326	51,835	77,539	62,300	50,180	39,400	31,700	23,070	17,925
Other countries	0	24	205	115	972	1,121	1,218	1,091	1,099	1,647	5,060	6,130	5,740	6,445	8,370	24,345

	1871	1881	1891	1901	1911	1921	1931	1941	1951	1961	1971	1981	1991	2001	2011	2021
Asian countries	n/a	n/a	9	90	900	1,025	1,157	999	964	1,321	2,695	3,890	3,475	3,775	4,900	15,655
Other Americas, Africa, Oceana	n/a	n/a	n/a	25	72	96	61	92	135	326	2,365	2,240	2,265	2,670	3,470	8,690
Not given, at sea/non-permanent 1991-	9	200	39	505	25	24	23	45	-	-	-	-	1,115	885	2,005	0
Born in (%)	100	100	100	100	100	100	100	100	100	100	100	100	100	100	100	100
Canada	81.1	79.2	83.6	83.6	70.0	75.5	74.7	80.4	83.9	84.1	87.6	89.6	91.7	92.8	93.6	92.5
Ontario (inc. Northern Ontario)	74.2	75.4	70.1	69.9	57.4	62.5	62.0	66.2	68.2	69.7	73.6	76.8	79.5	82.1	83.9	84.0
Quebec	4.8	2.4	11.0	11.4	10.5	10.5	9.0	7.5	7.6	6.7						2.9
Other Canada	2.1	1.3	2.4	2.3	2.1	2.5	3.7	6.8	8.1	7.7						5.6
British Isles / UK 1951-	10.5	14.8	10.9	7.4	9.8	9.8	8.2	6.0	4.6	3.6	2.6	2.1	1.5	1.1	1.0	0.8
England, Wales	6.0	6.8	5.3	4.1	6.5	6.7	5.5	3.9	3.1	2.4						
Ireland/Northern Ireland 1951-	2.3	3.4	2.6	1.5	1.0	0.8	0.6	0.5	0.2	0.2						
Scotland	2.1	4.6	2.9	1.8	2.3	2.2	2.0	1.5	1.2	1.0						
Other British Possessions	0.1	0.1	0.1	0.1	0.9	0.3	0.2	0.2	0.1	0.1						
United States	7.5	3.3	2.9	3.0	4.0	3.7	2.7	2.1	1.6	1.2	1.1	1.1	0.9	0.8	0.7	0.9
Other European countries	0.7	1.6	2.2	5.2	14.8	10.3	13.9	11.0	9.7	10.7	8.0	6.4	5.1	4.3	3.2	(cont)

Table 4.1. Birthplaces of the population, Northern Ontario and Southern Ontario, decennial census dates, 1871–2021.

	1871	1881	1891	1901	1911	1921	1931	1941	1951	1961	1971	1981	1991	2001	2011	2021
Other countries	0.0	0.1	0.4	0.1	0.5	0.4	0.3	0.2	0.2	0.2	0.7	0.8	0.7	0.9	1.2	3.3
Asian countries	n/a	n/a	0.0	0.1	0.4	0.4	0.3	0.2	0.2	0.2	0.3	0.5	0.4	0.5	0.7	2.1
Other Americas, Africa, Oceana	n/a	n/a	n/a	0.0	0.0	0.0	0.0	0.0	0.0	0.0	0.3	0.3	0.3	0.4	0.5	1.2
Not given, at sea/non-permanent 1991-	0.1	1.0	0.1	0.5	0.0	0.0	0.0	0.0	-	-	-	-	0.1	0.1	0.3	0.0
Southern Ontario population reported	1,612,934	1,902,908	2,059,445	2,082,546	2,308,515	2,666,759	3,071,575	3,331,644	4,061,148	5,513,918	6,926,600	7,755,095	9,200,940	10,547,085	11,934,315	13,302,050
Born in (persons)																
Canada	1,172,086	1,477,425	1,662,842	1,774,836	1,865,053	2,090,400	2,358,557	2,687,574	3,297,696	4,275,506	5,315,535	5,810,335	6,769,995	7,479,405	8,234,205	8,630,840
Ontario (inc. Northern Ontario)	1,125,456	1,420,332	1,601,650	1,714,594	1,808,376	2,008,500	2,255,779	2,533,735	2,971,762	3,801,764	4,638,645	5,045,310	5,837,995	6,560,585	7,313,850	7,805,855
Quebec	40,096	49,910	52,715	50,317	42,169	53,755	60,133	70,270	113,402	148,062						299,645
Other Canada	6,534	7,183	8,477	9,925	14,508	28,145	42,645	83,569	212,532	325,680						525,340
British Isles / UK 1951-	367,039	348,289	319,489	232,055	326,618	422,284	482,759	408,402	407,969	474,076	497,265	480,315	397,380	334,515	285,105	251,435
England, Wales	123,585	137,641	148,369	117,350	218,638	299,345	322,853	275,877	282,607	321,281						
Ireland/Northern Ireland 1951-	152,816	129,407	102,536	66,582	47,918	43,052	50,086	40,085	29,089	34,857						

	1871	1881	1891	1901	1911	1921	1931	1941	1951	1961	1971	1981	1991	2001	2011	2021
Scotland	90,638	81,241	68,584	48,123	60,062	79,849	109,820	92,440	96,273	117,938						
Other British Possessions	2,595	2,594	3,553	2,800	9,052	10,185	13,312	12,676	8,777	23,963						
United States	42,813	44,787	41,128	41,122	47,159	60,955	62,848	62,164	63,716	72,716	92,695	100,860	91,490	92,580	109,665	151,310
Other European countries	25,444	26,272	27,492	25,702	55,110	75,477	145,023	152,512	271,454	645,056	856,990	897,305	923,985	961,410	890,995	840,035
Other countries	1,090	1,274	2,571	1,692	5,151	7,202	8,873	8,004	11,536	22,601	164,115	466,280	893,045	1,589,435	2,281,945	3,428,390
Asian countries	n/a	n/a	88	1,217	4,488	6,457	8,165	7,142	9,493	17,314	68,420	239,020	519,215	1,058,160	1,612,430	2,507,270
Other Americas, Africa, Oceana	n/a	n/a	n/a	475	663	745	708	862	2,043	5,287	95,695	227,260	373,830	531,275	669,515	921,120
Not given, at sea/non-permanent 1991-	1,867	2,267	2,370	4,339	372	256	203	312					125,050	89,730	132,420	45
Born in (%)	100	100	100	100	100	100	100	100	100	100	100	100	100	100	100	100
Canada	72.7	77.6	80.7	85.2	80.8	78.4	76.8	80.7	81.2	77.5	76.7	74.9	73.6	70.9	69.0	64.9
Ontario (inc. Northern Ontario)	69.8	74.6	77.8	82.3	78.3	75.3	73.4	76.1	73.2	68.9	67.0	65.1	63.4	62.2	61.3	58.7
Quebec	2.5	2.6	2.6	2.4	1.8	2.0	2.0	2.1	2.8	2.7						2.3
Other Canada	0.4	0.4	0.4	0.5	0.6	1.1	1.4	2.5	5.2	5.9						3.9
British Isles / UK 1951-	22.8	18.3	15.5	11.1	14.1	15.8	15.7	12.3	10.0	8.6	7.2	6.2	4.3	3.2	2.4	1.9
England, Wales	7.7	7.2	7.2	5.6	9.5	11.2	10.5	8.3	7.0	5.8						

(cont)

Table 4.1: Birthplaces of the population, Northern Ontario and Southern Ontario, decennial census dates, 1871–2021.

	1871	1881	1891	1901	1911	1921	1931	1941	1951	1961	1971	1981	1991	2001	2011	2021
Ireland/ Northern Ireland 1951-	9.5	6.8	5.0	3.2	2.1	1.6	1.6	1.2	0.7	0.6						
Scotland	5.6	4.3	3.3	2.3	2.6	3.0	3.6	2.8	2.4	2.1						
Other British Possessions	0.2	0.1	0.2	0.1	0.4	0.4	0.4	0.4	0.2	0.4						
United States	2.7	2.4	2.0	2.0	2.0	2.3	2.0	1.9	1.6	1.3	1.3	1.3	1.0	0.9	0.9	1.1
Other European countries	1.6	1.4	1.3	1.2	2.4	2.8	4.7	4.6	6.7	11.7	12.4	11.6	10.0	9.1	7.5	6.3
Other countries	0.1	0.1	0.1	0.1	0.2	0.3	0.3	0.2	0.3	0.4	2.4	6.0	9.7	15.1	19.1	25.8
Asian countries	n/a	n/a	0.0	0.1	0.2	0.2	0.3	0.2	0.2	0.3	1.0	3.1	5.6	10.0	13.5	18.8
Other Americas, Africa, Oceana	n/a	n/a	n/a	0.0	0.0	0.0	0.0	0.0	0.1	0.1	1.4	2.9	4.1	5.0	5.6	6.9
Not given, at sea/ non-permanent 1991-	0.1	0.1	0.1	0.2	0.0	0.0	0.0	0.0	0.0	0.0	0.0	0.0	1.4	0.9	1.1	0.0

Source: See Table Notes and Data Sources.

of a gradually increasing share born in Ontario (including the north itself) and in other parts of Canada. While the Ontario-born share rose in 2021 to 84.0%, the Canada-born share rose to 92.5%. In line with this, the general pattern included an overall decline in the share for those with birthplaces outside Canada, particularly in the British Isles, the United States, and continental Europe (in 2021, to 0.8%, 0.9%, and 2.5% respectively). Unlike Southern Ontario, there was only a small increase in the numbers of persons from Asia (2.1% in 2021) or other countries in Africa, the Americas, or Oceania (1.2%).

SEX AND MARITAL STATUS

The data for sex in Table 4.2 and elsewhere in the book are based on the census categories for sex, except for 2021. From 1871 to 2016, the census counts for sex, male and female, were conceived as binary, typically biological, categories. As of the 2021 census Statistics Canada began shifting to the use of "gender" rather than "sex" as the default variable in its social statistics.[14] The introduction of gender in the 2021 census was an historic conceptual change. The 2021 census continued to collect data on sex, though modified in the census questionnaire to assigned sex at birth: "what was your sex at birth?" At the same time, the census introduced a new partially open-ended question for gender: "what is your gender?" (Statistics Canada 2023, 20, 23). Census gender data for 2021 is now reported for the population 15 and over in five categories for Canada, the provinces, territories, and census metropolitan areas, though not for most subprovincial levels, which is most of Northern Ontario. Those categories are: cisgender men, cisgender women, transgender men, transgender women, non-binary persons.[15] As well, Statistics Canada introduced two composite gender categories, "men+" and "women+," as aggregations of the five primary gender categories, and it provided the data for subprovincial levels as well as the higher geographical levels. In terms of historical comparability, Statistics Canada considers that the use of men+ and women+ gender data for 2021 together with data for male and female sex data for previous censuses in data tables and analyses "will not result in a significant impact on historical trends, given the small size of the transgender and non-binary populations."[16]

The hinterland-colonial context of Northern Ontario has been reflected in major changes in the sex composition of the population. Periods of rapid growth in settlement, especially around mining, forestry, and transportation, were associated with higher numbers of males relative to females. As shown in Table 4.2, during the most rapid period of population growth, from 1871 to 1911, the male share rose from 53.9 to 61.7%, while the female share declined from 46.1 to 38.3%, even as the total numbers were growing for both males and females. Indeed, 1911 marked the peak male share and lowest female share in all 15 decades surveyed. From the low point in 1911, the female share tended to increase though it did not reach the more typical condition of 50% or over until 1991 and later censuses. By contrast, Southern Ontario throughout had no comparable gap in male–female shares. By 1901, Southern Ontario already had a female share over 50%. The female share then dipped slightly and hovered around half until after the Second World War when, in all censuses, the female numbers were higher than the male numbers.

Examining the sex composition of the population in Northern Ontario also casts a clearer light on overall population decline after the 1970s. The male population reached a census peak in 1971 of 399,000 after which it declined by nearly 8% to 368,200 in 2021. However, the female population reached a census peak in 1991 of 393,675 then declined by nearly 5% to 374,400 in 2021. Hence, between the 1980s and 1990s, not only did the total population plateau in Northern Ontario but the female share also reached more than 50% in 1991, achieving for the first time overall a more typical sex composition.

It deserves note that patterns of national and racial segregation, discrimination, and exclusion have affected sex composition. This

Table 4.2. Population by sex in Northern Ontario and Southern Ontario, decennial census dates, 1871–2021.

	1871	1881	1891	1901	1911	1921	1931	1941	1951	1961	1971	1981	1991	2001	2011	2021
Northern Ontario																
Total population reported	7,866	20,320	54,876	100,401	214,759	266,900	360,108	456,032	536,394	722,174	776,505	786,060	784,025	746,770	733,015	742,600
Males	4,237	11,138	30,566	58,477	132,463	148,315	201,866	249,647	287,838	378,672	399,000	396,260	390,350	367,165	360,515	368,200
Females	3,629	9,182	24,310	41,924	82,296	118,585	158,242	206,385	248,556	343,502	377,505	389,800	393,675	379,615	372,510	374,400
Male–female shares (%)																
Total population reported	100	100	100	100.0	100.0	100	100	100	100	100	100	100	100	100	100	100
Males	53.9	54.8	55.7	58.2	61.7	55.6	56.1	54.7	53.7	52.4	51.4	50.4	49.8	49.2	49.2	49.6
Females	46.1	45.2	44.3	41.8	38.3	44.4	43.9	45.3	46.3	47.6	48.6	49.6	50.2	50.8	50.8	50.4
Southern Ontario																
Total population reported	1,612,985	1,902,908	2,059,445	2,082,546	2,308,515	2,666,762	3,071,575	3,331,623	4,061,148	5,513,918	6,926,605	7,839,045	9,300,860	10,663,280	12,118,805	13,481,345
Males	824,353	965,332	1,038,921	1,038,163	1,166,827	1,333,575	1,546,978	1,671,554	2,026,332	2,755,856	3,441,910	3,850,525	4,562,730	5,209,890	5,902,625	6,602,655
Females	788,632	937,576	1,020,524	1,044,383	1,141,688	1,333,187	1,524,597	1,660,069	2,034,816	2,758,062	3,484,695	3,988,520	4,738,130	5,453,375	6,216,175	6,878,685
Male–female shares (%)																
Total population reported	100	100	100	100	100.0	100	100	100	100	100	100	100	100	100	100	100
Males	51.1	50.7	50.4	49.9	50.5	50.0	50.4	50.2	49.9	50.0	49.7	49.1	49.1	48.9	48.7	49.0
Females	48.9	49.3	49.6	50.1	49.5	50.0	49.6	49.8	50.1	50.0	50.3	50.9	50.9	51.1	51.3	51.0

Source: See Table Notes and Data Sources.

was evident even in earlier decades of rapid expansion and relatively higher labour demand. For instance, in 1911, at the time of the highest male and lowest female population shares in Northern Ontario, most settler groups by nationality had much lower female population shares than in Southern Ontario, including dominant national groups. The national-racial hierarchy in settlement, and whether the settlement came at an earlier or later stage, had their effects.

Taking 1911 census data on national origin, Table 4.3 shows that within the general 38.3% female share in Northern Ontario, the early and dominant English, Irish, Scottish, and French national settler groups had about 41–42% female shares in Northern Ontario, compared to 49–51% in Southern Ontario. Some later settler groups, such as the Italian and Polish, had much lower female shares within Northern Ontario, 16.8% and 16.3% respectively, as well as relative to Southern Ontario, 27.2% and 36.7% respectively. Those facing the sharpest exclusionary pressures in immigration—both legislated and non-formal—had the most extreme lower female shares, particularly those of Chinese backgrounds (2.3% in Northern Ontario and 3.8% in Southern Ontario) but also some of eastern European backgrounds.

In contrast, the census data available on Indigenous peoples suggest a more balanced female share. For 1911 in Northern Ontario a reported 49.5% of "Indian" peoples were females—the highest share. This compared to 47.7% in Southern Ontario.

In terms of reported marital status, Northern Ontario in 1871 had a somewhat higher initial level of married persons, particularly for females, than Southern Ontario, but in 1881 and subsequent decades Southern Ontario had a higher level of married persons (Table 4.4). For Northern Ontario, the total number of married persons, both male and female, rose to a peak in 1981 then declined absolutely by 26.5% until 2021. In terms of the percentage of the total population married, the long-term trend rose from 32.2% in 1871 to a peak of 46.7% in 1981, then declined progressively to 36.3% in 2021.

Table 4.3. Census of 1911 national origin categories by sex, Northern Ontario and Southern Ontario.

	Northern Ontario				Southern Ontario			
	persons	male	female	female %	persons	male	female	female %
British	109,128	64,069	45,059	41.3	1,817,971	910,971	907,000	49.9
English	42,963	25,098	17,865	41.6	841,469	430,031	411,438	48.9
Irish	34,646	20,419	14,227	41.1	573,491	281,788	291,703	50.9
Scotch	30,773	18,084	12,689	41.2	394,100	194,450	199,650	50.7
Other	746	468	278	37.3	8,911	4,702	4,209	47.2
French	45,355	26,490	18,865	41.6	157,087	79,586	77,501	49.3
German	6,505	3,781	2,724	41.9	185,815	92,882	92,933	50.0
Austro-Hungarian	7,286	6,081	1,205	16.5	4,485	3,471	1,014	22.6
Belgian	105	76	29	27.6	528	350	178	33.7
Bulgarian and Rumanian	451	436	15	3.3	1,032	968	64	6.2
Chinese	394	385	9	2.3	2,372	2,283	89	3.8
Dutch	790	456	334	42.3	34,222	17,289	16,933	49.5
Finnish	7,836	5,412	2,424	30.9	783	411	372	47.5
Greek	248	223	25	10.1	1,056	947	109	10.3
"Hindu" [South Asian]	0	0	0		17	9	8	47.1
"Indian"	11,359	5,739	5,620	49.5	11,685	6,111	5,574	47.7
Italian	7,638	6,353	1,285	16.8	13,627	9,921	3,706	27.2
Japanese	3	3	0	0.0	32	26	6	18.8
Jewish	1,289	747	542	42.0	25,726	13,516	12,210	47.5
"Negro" [African]	61	41	20	32.8	6,686	3,442	3,244	48.5
Polish	3,269	2,736	533	16.3	7,333	4,641	2,692	36.7
Russian	2,331	2,217	114	4.9	1,668	1,149	519	31.1
Scandinavian	5,497	3,638	1,859	33.8	2,753	1,538	1,215	44.1
Swiss	252	171	81	32.1	1,678	866	812	48.4
Turkish	280	162	118	42.1	1,474	1,283	191	13.0
Other	888	602	286	32.2	3,542	1,979	1,563	44.1
Unspecified	3,794	2,645	1,149	30.3	26,943	13,188	13,755	51.1
Total	214,759	132,463	82,296	38.3	2,308,515	1,166,827	1,141,688	49.5

Notes: The terms and order for each national origin are those used by the 1911 Census. The "Austro-Hungarian" category included Austrian, Bukovian, Galician, Hungarian, and Ruthenian national origins. *Source:* See Table Notes and Data Sources, Table 4.5 for 1911, also in Census Vol. II, Tables X and XII.

Table 4.4. Population by marital status and sex in Northern Ontario and Southern Ontario, decennial census dates, 1871–2021.

	1871	1881	1891	1901	1911	1921	1931	1941	1951	1961	1971	1981	1991	2001	2011	2021
Northern ontario																
Total population reported	7,866	20,320	54,876	100,401	214,759	266,900	360,108	456,032	536,394	722,174	776,505	786,060	784,025	746,770	733,015	742,600
Males	4,237	11,138	30,566	58,477	132,463	148,315	201,866	249,647	287,838	378,672	399,000	396,260	390,350	367,165	360,515	368,200
Females	3,629	9,182	24,310	41,924	82,296	118,585	158,242	206,385	248,556	343,502	377,505	389,800	393,675	379,615	372,510	374,400
By marital status																
Married	2,535	6,505	18,125	31,115	75,805	99,167	138,418	187,111	239,021	314,050	345,285	366,705	343,990	313,925	292,190	269,395
Males	1,281	3,308	9,308	17,630	43,337	52,545	74,480	97,275	122,665	159,235	173,510	183,735		156,975	146,020	134,465
Females	1,254	3,197	8,817	13,485	32,468	46,622	63,938	89,836	116,356	154,815	171,765	182,955		156,935	146,165	134,935
Widowed	337	586	1,459	1,839	5,296	8,127	11,274	15,284	18,905	24,520	30,010	36,795	43,305	45,130	43,850	47,415
Males	114	223	674	702	2,353	3,556	4,987	6,071	6,579	7,292	6,805	7,000		8,630	9,110	11,675
Females	223	363	785	1,137	2,943	4,571	6,287	9,213	12,326	17,228	23,185	29,790		36,485	34,750	35,730
Divorced				9	21	191	197	442	913	2,350	5,115	11,605	31,585	40,905	34,070	54,245
Males				4	15	94	134	258	480	1,116	2,620	5,365		19,130	15,480	25,315
Females				5	6	97	63	184	433	1,234	2,515	6,240		21,765	18,590	28,950
Separated								3,467				16,135	19,780	23,590	21,070	26,755
Males								1,760				7,705		10,950	9,715	12,420
Females								1,707				8,425		12,655	11,365	14,330

	1871	1881	1891	1901	1911	1921	1931	1941	1951	1961	1971	1981	1991	2001	2011	2021
Living common law														53,440	99,120	83,220
Males														26,580	49,460	41,405
Females														26,855	49,645	41,805
Marital status (% of pop.)																
Married	32.2	32.0	33.0	31.0	35.3	37.2	38.4	41.0	44.6	43.5	44.5	46.7	43.9	42.0	39.9	36.3
Males	30.2	29.7	30.5	30.1	32.7	35.4	36.9	39.0	42.6	42.1	43.5	46.4		42.8	40.5	36.5
Females	34.6	34.8	36.3	32.2	39.5	39.3	40.4	43.5	46.8	45.1	45.5	46.9		41.3	39.2	36.0
Widowed	4.3	2.9	2.7	1.8	2.5	3.0	3.1	3.4	3.5	3.4	3.9	4.7	5.5	6.0	6.0	6.4
Males	2.7	2.0	2.2	1.2	1.8	2.4	2.5	2.4	2.3	1.9	1.7	1.8		2.4	2.5	3.2
Females	6.1	4.0	3.2	2.7	3.6	3.9	4.0	4.5	5.0	5.0	6.1	7.6		9.6	9.3	9.5
Divorced				-	-	0.1	0.1	0.1	0.2	0.3	0.7	1.5	4.0	5.5	4.6	7.3
Males				-	-	0.1	0.1	0.1	0.2	0.3	0.7	1.4		5.2	4.3	6.9
Females				-	-	0.1	-	0.1	0.2	0.4	0.7	1.6		5.7	5.0	7.7
Separated								0.8				2.1	2.5	3.2	2.9	3.6
Males								0.7				1.9		3.0	2.7	3.4
Females								0.8				2.2		3.3	3.1	3.8
Living common law														7.2	13.5	11.2
Males														7.2	13.7	11.2
Females														7.1	13.3	11.2

(cont)

Table 4.4. Population by marital status and sex in Northern Ontario and Southern Ontario, decennial census dates, 1871–2021.

	1871	1881	1891	1901	1911	1921	1931	1941	1951	1961	1971	1981	1991	2001	2011	2021
Southern Ontario																
Total population reported	1,612,985	1,902,908	2,059,445	2,082,546	2,308,515	2,666,762	3,071,575	3,331,623	4,061,148	5,513,918	6,926,605	7,839,045	9,300,860	10,663,280	12,118,805	13,481,345
Males	824,353	965,332	1,038,921	1,038,163	1,166,827	1,333,575	1,546,978	1,671,554	2,026,332	2,755,856	3,441,910	3,850,525	4,562,730	5,209,890	5,902,625	6,602,655
Females	788,632	937,576	1,020,524	1,044,383	1,141,688	1,333,187	1,524,597	1,660,069	2,034,816	2,758,062	3,484,695	3,988,520	4,738,130	5,453,375	6,216,175	6,878,685
By marital status																
Married	505,662	612,532	687,733	740,330	885,031	1,097,537	1,296,005	1,490,510	2,000,596	2,628,463	3,300,575	3,776,100	4,187,875	4,673,170	5,075,210	5,468,995
Males	253,061	306,253	343,752	370,148	449,313	554,641	656,711	753,821	1,001,772	1,313,606	1,647,710	1,890,705		2,294,000	2,535,300	2,732,360
Females	252,601	306,279	343,981	370,182	435,718	542,896	639,294	736,689	998,824	1,314,857	1,652,870	1,885,415		2,289,190	2,539,910	2,736,630
Widowed	52,635	70,739	86,608	99,072	106,675	134,086	159,789	187,657	222,138	267,247	328,220	399,645	477,095	533,015	570,030	638,010
Males	16,440	21,966	27,104	30,293	31,211	39,398	47,236	54,139	57,392	61,465	61,535	65,620		96,585	108,870	138,355
Females	36,195	48,773	59,504	68,779	75,464	94,679	112,553	133,518	164,746	205,782	266,710	334,030		436,450	461,155	499,670
Divorced				220	395	2,313	1,889	4,714	11,521	19,426	64,980	156,325	389,100	556,690	559,660	861,830
Males				105	174	1,041	937	2,033	4,286	7,432	25,595	59,650		230,695	215,680	352,060
Females				115	221	1,272	952	2,681	7,235	11,994	39,360	96,675		326,005	343,980	509,750
Separated					1,141			28,677				177,925	221,660	287,790	298,735	362,460
Males					485			12,345				76,835		125,125	124,075	156,700
Females					656			16,332				101,100		162,650	174,650	205,765

	1871	1881	1891	1901	1911	1921	1931	1941	1951	1961	1971	1981	1991	2001	2011	2021
Living common law														531,065	692,090	948,120
Males														267,135	348,160	476,260
Females														263,935	343,945	471,865
Marital status (% of pop.)																
Married	31.3	32.2	33.4	35.5	38.3	41.2	42.2	44.7	49.3	47.7	47.7	48.2	45.0	43.8	41.9	40.6
Males	30.7	31.7	33.1	35.7	38.5	41.6	42.5	45.1	49.4	47.7	47.9	49.1		44.0	43.0	41.4
Females	32.0	32.7	33.7	35.4	38.2	40.7	41.9	44.4	49.1	47.7	47.4	47.3		42.0	40.9	39.8
Widowed	3.3	3.7	4.2	4.8	4.6	5.0	5.2	5.6	5.5	4.8	4.7	5.1	5.1	5.0	4.7	4.7
Males	2.0	2.3	2.6	2.9	2.7	3.0	3.1	3.2	2.8	2.2	1.8	1.7		1.9	1.8	2.1
Females	4.6	5.2	5.8	6.6	6.6	7.1	7.4	8.0	8.1	7.5	7.7	8.4		8.0	7.4	7.3
Divorced				-	-	0.1	0.1	0.1	0.3	0.4	0.9	2.0	4.2	5.2	4.6	6.4
Males				-	-	0.1	0.1	0.1	0.2	0.3	0.7	1.5		4.4	3.7	5.3
Females				-	-	0.1	0.1	0.2	0.4	0.4	1.1	2.4		6.0	5.5	7.4
Separated								0.9				2.3	2.4	2.7	2.5	2.7
Males								0.7				2.0		2.4	2.1	2.4
Females					0.1			1.0				2.5		3.0	2.8	3.0
Living common law														5.0	5.7	7.0
Males														5.1	5.9	7.2
Females														4.8	5.5	6.9

Source: See Table Notes and Data Sources.

For Southern Ontario, the absolute number of married persons rose throughout while the decline of the married share of population occurred later. The percentage married increased from 31.3% in 1871 to a peak of 49.3% in 1951, followed by three decades near that peak level. Between 1981 and 2021, while the total number of persons married continued to increase (for both males and females), the percentage married dropped, from 48.2% to 40.6%.

Another difference between Northern and Southern Ontario was that the proportion of females married relative to males married was more often higher in Northern Ontario than in Southern Ontario. In Northern Ontario, during the latter 1800s and 1900s, a higher proportion of women than men were married. That changed in the current century: in 2011, 40.5% of males were married compared to 39.2% of females. In Southern Ontario, during the latter 1800s and most of the 1900s, a higher proportion of women were married, similar to Northern Ontario. However, during the 1990s and until the present in Southern Ontario, a generally higher proportion of men than women were married.

Northern Ontario has also had generally increasing levels of widowhood. The total number of widowed persons in Northern Ontario rose in every census except 2011. In 1871, 4.3% of the population was widowed. This declined to a low of 1.8% in 1901, then increased to 6.4% in 2021. The earliest and more recent levels of widowhood have been higher than in Southern Ontario, although in most decades in between the levels of widowhood in Southern Ontario were higher. In Southern Ontario, the level of widowhood peaked at 5.6% in 1941 and declined thereafter to 4.7% in 2021—unlike the upward trend in Northern Ontario. In both Northern and Southern Ontario, the percentage of women widowed was much higher than that of men (as much as two to three times higher).

Official census counts of those divorced, separated, and living together unmarried ("common law") began in later decades, respectively, 1921, 1941, and 2001. "Married" has included same-sex partners since 2006 and same-sex partners living common-law since 2001. Northern Ontario has reported similar or higher levels of divorce and separation than Southern Ontario, although both have had historically increasing numbers, with the possible exception of 2011 in Northern Ontario. As well, both Northern Ontario and Southern Ontario have tended in most census years to have higher levels of divorce and separation among women than among men. However, in Northern Ontario before 1981 the levels of divorce and separation were higher among men than women; from 1981 on the pattern became higher levels among women than among men. More striking is the level of living common law, which is much higher in Northern Ontario for both men and women. In 2021, 11.2% of the Northern Ontario population were reported as living common law compared to 7.0% in Southern Ontario; in Northern Ontario, the male share approximated the female share (11.2%), while in Southern Ontario the male share was higher than the female share (7.2% versus 6.9%).

NATIONAL ORIGIN

In the sense used here, "national origin" indicates a family connection to a people or society with a common history, land, language, culture, and economic ties. In recent decades Statistics Canada has used the related terms "ethnic origin" or "cultural origin," although these latter terms diminish the political aspect of nation, not least in relation to the constitutional centrality of English–French relations and the recognition of First Nations as sovereign peoples by treaty.[17]

In approaching the data in Table 4.5, three points need note as background. First, the data have been reordered, beginning with the Indigenous national origins followed by others as grouped by size for Northern Ontario (British, French, Other European, African and Asian [non-European], Canadian, American).[18] Second, the data for total numbers from 1981 onward are affected by Statistics Canada's shift to allow both multiple-origin responses and tracing ancestry through the mother as well as the father. These changes led to a decline in single-origin responses and possibly more so for "long-established groups," according to Statistics Canada.[19] For consistency with pre-1981 censuses, this table uses single-origin data. Though long overdue, Statistics Canada's change in methodology is a factor in the peaking of the total numbers respondings in Northern Ontario in 1971, with decline thereafter. Similarly (though less dramatically), Southern Ontario had an increase in total numbers responding, though in 1981. Then, after a decline in 1991, the numbers responding climbed to another, higher total in 2021. As a result, comparisons of absolute changes before 1971 with those after are less useful than comparisons of relative shares of nationalities within the total responses. Third, Statistics Canada's change in 1991 to report "Canadian," then later "American," as ethnic origins also had a major impact, particularly in the dramatically increased "Canadian" share and reductions in several other shares after 1981.[20]

The Indigenous population in Northern Ontario remained and eventually grew despite the ravages of colonialism and relative decline until 1961 (as measured by national single-origins data). The Indigenous-origin totals in Table 4.5 include First Nations, Inuit, and Métis persons.[21] After 1961 there appears to be both an increase in absolute numbers and an increase in relative growth to the point that, in 2021, Indigenous origins was the largest single national origin at 19.5% apart from Canadian at 20.0%. By contrast, the Indigenous population in Southern Ontario was growing in absolute numbers but reached only 1% in 2021. It deserves comment too that Statistics Canada's observation about "long-established groups" tending to have more multiple origins needs to be considered in context. In particular, it should not be assumed that numbers of single origins necessarily decline for persons with long familial histories of residing in certain areas, especially if that involves an assumption that segregation or assimilation by ethnic or racial origin has occurred equally. For instance, between 1971 and 1991, before and after Statistics Canada's shift to allowing multiple origins, the Northern Ontario single-origin responses declined overall by about 39.7%. For British origins the decline was 53.1% and for Other European origins the decline was 67.4%, while for French origins it was much less, 28.5%. For Indigenous origins, responses actually increased generally from 1971 to 2021 *both* in absolute numbers of responses *and* as a share of the total.

Throughout the period until 1971 in Northern Ontario, Table 4.5 shows that populations with identified single paternal origins in the British Isles remained dominant. In terms of absolute numbers, the totals for English, Irish, Scottish, and Welsh grew until reaching 322,685 in 1971. As a proportion, however, British Isles origins reached a peak of 62.4% in 1881, then declined continuously to 41.6% in 1971 and 13.5% in 2021. The evidence for Southern Ontario shows an even greater dominance of British Isles origins. The total numbers also grew until 1971, to 4,253,325. However, the general British Isles–origins share was much higher, around 80% until 1921, and the relative decline in share that occurred was to 61.4% in 1971 (higher by 20 percentage points than in Northern Ontario) before a more rapid decline to 12.0% in 2021, approximate to the level in Northern Ontario. Again, these numbers must be interpreted in light of the shift in Statistics Canada methodology from 1981, particularly allowing multiple-origin responses in the census questions.

The numbers of persons indicating a French background in Northern Ontario grew continuously from 1871 to 1971, to 215,670. Their share of the population also generally increased, except for 1881, from 15.8% in 1871 to nearly 28% in the decades from 1951 to 1981. In 1991 the Northern Ontario population indicating French background by single origin reached a peak share of 32.9%, then declined sharply to 10.2% in 2021. In Southern Ontario, which includes Ottawa and eastern areas of Ontario, the number of those with French origin grew continuously to a peak number of 521,690 in 1971, about 2.4 times the 215,670 total in Northern Ontario. In 2021, using the single-origin

Table 4.5. Population by national origin in Northern Ontario and Southern Ontario, decennial census dates, 1871–2021.

	1871	1881	1901	1911	1921	1931	1941	1951	1961	1971	1981	1991	2001	2011	2021
Northern Ontario: persons															
Total population responding	7,866	20,320	100,401	214,759	266,900	360,108	456,012	536,394	722,174	776,505	683,300	468,105	380,070	314,645	389,870
Indigenous	3,935	4,678	12,213	11,359	14,262	16,384	18,618	20,134	25,943	30,550			48,330	43,705	76,215
British Isles	2,558	12,680	58,425	109,128	135,596	163,067	205,350	230,991	283,027	322,685	294,755	151,230	56,535	51,820	52,500
English	1,240	4,588	20,985	42,963	65,317	72,312	90,719						31,915	27,430	26,460
Irish	555	3,990	20,359	34,646	34,726	45,342	58,674						10,715	10,280	12,885
Scottish	738	4,062	16,790	30,773	34,277	43,266	54,164						12,530	11,370	12,300
Welsh, other	25	40	291	746	1,276	1,973	2,793						1,375	2,740	855
French	1,242	1,562	20,374	45,355	63,386	87,522	115,004	147,720	201,335	215,670	190,015	154,185	42,075	37,555	39,960
Other European (total)	94	958	9,038	43,497	51,657	91,205	115,181	132,438	202,235	150,630		49,180	63,085	51,915	77,975
Finnish					11,536	21,392	21,434	21,987	27,732						8,110
German	60	409	3,048	6,505	4,396	7,345	8,687	12,468	28,116	29,220		13,980	10,340	9,175	8,190
Italian	0	8	1,926	7,638	9,353	12,414	15,582	19,260	37,628	43,880		30,100	25,815	21,110	20,580
Jewish	0	12	186	1,289	1,237	1,684	2,078	1,443	1,007	1,390					
Netherland / Dutch	12	224	420	790	1,499	2,526	3,875	5,486	9,392	9,095		5,100	4,520	4,290	3,820
Polish				3,269	2,334	9,208	1,465	13,449	19,082	16,305			5,860	4,545	4,420
Russian	0	50	1,401	10,167	2,403	2,482	2,697	2,222	2,293	1,090			430	305	565
Scandinavian	22	244	1,458	5,497	7,033	11,253	14,244	15,270	19,116	15,815			2,520	1,965	1,765
Ukrainian					3,786	10,923	19,120	25,518	29,821	31,505			10,960	8,110	6,675

	1871	1881	1901	1911	1921	1931	1941	1951	1961	1971	1981	1991	2001	2011	2021
African	15	31	63	61	69	65	84		248						3,815
Chinese		0	45	394	692	843	821	729	1,478			1,980	1,815	2,085	2,650
Other Asian	0			3	811	893	824	1,569	1,623				1,670	2,300	12,810
Canadian												10,935	142,095	102,190	77,825
American													580	640	980
Not given	22	411	243	4,962	427	129	130	2,813	6,285	56,975	197,525	100,595	23,885	22,435	0
Northern Ontario: %															
Total population responding	100	100	100	100	100	100	100	100	100	100	100	100	100	100	100
Indigenous	50.0	23.0	12.2	5.3	5.3	4.5	4.1	3.8	3.6	3.9			12.7	13.9	19.5
British Isles	32.5	62.4	58.2	50.8	50.8	45.3	45.0	43.1	39.2	41.6	43.1	32.3	14.9	16.5	13.5
English	15.8	22.6	20.9	20.0	24.5	20.1	19.9						8.4	8.7	6.8
Irish	7.1	19.6	20.3	16.1	13.0	12.6	12.9						2.8	3.3	3.3
Scottish	9.4	20.0	16.7	14.3	12.8	12.0	11.9						3.3	3.6	3.2
Welsh, other	0.3	0.2	0.3	0.3	0.5	0.5	0.6						0.4	0.9	0.2
French	15.8	7.7	20.3	21.1	23.7	24.3	25.2	27.5	27.9	27.8	27.8	32.9	11.1	11.9	10.2
Other European (total)	1.2	4.7	9.0	20.3	19.4	25.3	25.3	24.7	28.0	19.4		10.5	16.6	16.5	20.0
Finnish					4.3	5.9	4.7	4.1	3.8						2.1
German	0.8	2.0	3.0	3.0	1.6	2.0	1.9	2.3	3.9	3.8		3.0	2.7	2.9	2.1
Italian	0.0	-	1.9	3.6	3.5	3.4	3.4	3.6	5.2	5.7		6.4	6.8	6.7	5.3
Jewish	0.0	0.1	0.2	0.6	0.5	0.5	0.5	0.3	0.1	0.2					
Netherland / Dutch	0.2	1.1	0.4	0.4	0.6	0.7	0.8	1.0	1.3	1.2		1.1	1.2	1.4	1.0
Polish				1.5	0.9	2.6	0.3	2.5	2.6	2.1			1.5	1.4	1.1

(cont)

Table 4.5. Population by national origin in Northern Ontario and Southern Ontario, decennial census dates, 1871–2021.

	1871	1881	1901	1911	1921	1931	1941	1951	1961	1971	1981	1991	2001	2011	2021
Russian	0.0	0.2	1.4	4.7	0.9	0.7	0.6	0.4	0.3	0.1			0.1	0.1	0.1
Scandinavian	0.3	1.2	1.5	2.6	2.6	3.1	3.1	2.8	2.6	2.0			0.7	0.6	0.5
Ukrainian					1.4	3.0	4.2	4.8	4.1	4.1			2.9	2.6	1.7
African	0.2	0.2	0.1	-	-	-	-		-						1.0
Chinese		0.0		0.2	0.3	0.2	0.2	0.1	0.2			0.4	0.5	0.7	0.7
Other Asian	0.0			-	0.3	0.2	0.2	0.3	0.2				0.4	0.7	3.3
Canadian												2.3	37.4	32.5	20.0
American													0.2	0.2	0.3
Not given	0.3	2.0	0.2	2.3	0.2	0.0	0.0	0.5	0.9	7.3	28.9	21.5	6.3	7.1	0.0
Southern Ontario: persons															
Total population responding	1,612,985	1,902,908	2,082,546	2,308,515	2,666,762	3,071,575	3,331,643	4,061,148	5,513,918	6,926,590	7,068,315	6,230,895	6,503,835	6,842,575	8,296,365
Indigenous	13,420	10,647	12,461	11,685	12,392	13,984	15,790	17,254	22,131	31,870			40,965	47,075	84,580
British Isles	1,330,484	1,535,350	1,673,719	1,817,971	2,146,419	2,376,704	2,524,480	2,850,928	3,428,509	4,253,325	4,193,045	2,385,285	1,203,075	1,099,505	992,685
English	438,189	531,247	680,428	841,469	1,146,343	1,247,300	1,366,249						667,785	579,455	488,785
Irish	558,887	623,272	603,973	573,491	555,767	602,489	606,665						222,885	211,605	245,860
Scottish	328,151	374,474	382,740	394,100	431,123	506,382	523,963						269,250	229,385	239,405
Welsh, other	5,257	6,357	6,578	8,911	13,186	20,707	26,603						43,115	79,060	18,635
French	74,141	101,181	138,297	157,087	184,889	212,210	258,986	329,957	446,606	521,690	462,885	373,400	146,645	135,230	142,275

	1871	1881	1901	1911	1921	1931	1941	1951	1961	1971	1981	1991	2001	2011	2021
Other European (total)	181,106	215,572	239,450	280,706	300,992	446,532	511,460	752,948	1,447,855	1,572,400		906,760	1,373,240	1,377,240	1,956,720
Finnish					1,299	5,745	5,393	7,340	12,174						7,355
German	158,548	187,985	200,271	185,815	126,149	166,661	158,415	209,560	372,601	446,095		275,440	215,880	189,740	158,500
Italian	304	679	3,307	13,627	24,602	38,122	44,503	68,362	236,236	419,215		456,665	455,925	435,685	412,745
Jewish	48	242	5,151	25,726	46,561	60,699	67,797	73,477	64,273	133,800					
Netherland / Dutch	19,980	21,939	22,860	34,222	49,013	57,715	69,126	92,887	181,265	197,845		174,655	164,615	156,195	147,840
Polish				7,333	13,453	33,176	43,663	76,376	130,442	127,810			156,070	218,240	143,525
Russian	392	737	3,174	2,451	6,202	7,568	8,521	14,663	26,034	11,490			28,395	45,145	49,985
Scandinavian	664	1,334	2,396	2,753	5,683	9,507	12,981	22,160	44,537	44,410			7,205	7,250	6,805
Ukrainian					4,521	13,503	29,038	68,077	98,090	128,375			79,100	69,805	70,885
African	13,420	12,066	8,872	6,686	7,151	6,821	7,411		10,814						333,170
Chinese		22	716	2,372	5,094	6,076	5,322	6,268	13,677			271,890	441,875	579,470	663,915
Other Asian	8			49	2,574	4,485	5,053	13,572	22,499				463,055	741,610	2,114,655
Canadian												514,305	1,455,960	1,155,150	928,620
American													8,200	10,760	16,785
Not given	4,781	28,070	9,031	31,959	7,251	4,763	3,141	90,221	121,827	547,305	2,413,390	1,779,255	1,370,820	1,696,535	1,430
Southern Ontario: %															
total population responding	100	100	100	100	100	100	100	100	100	100	100	100	100	100	100
Indigenous	0.8	0.6	0.6	0.5	0.5	0.5	0.5	0.4	0.4	0.5			0.6	0.7	1.0
British Isles	82.5	80.7	80.4	78.8	80.5	77.4	75.8	70.2	62.2	61.4	59.3	38.3	18.5	16.1	12.0
English	27.2	27.9	32.7	36.5	43.0	40.6	41.0						10.3	8.5	5.9
Irish	34.6	32.8	29.0	24.8	20.8	19.6	18.2						3.4	3.1	3.0

(cont)

Table 4.5. Population by national origin in Northern Ontario and Southern Ontario, decennial census dates, 1871–2021.

	1871	1881	1901	1911	1921	1931	1941	1951	1961	1971	1981	1991	2001	2011	2021
Scottish	20.3	19.7	18.4	17.1	16.2	16.5	15.7						4.1	3.4	2.9
Welsh, other	0.3	0.3	0.3	0.4	0.5	0.7	0.8						0.7	1.2	0.2
French	4.6	5.3	6.6	6.8	6.9	6.9	7.8	8.1	8.1	7.5	6.5	6.0	2.3	2.0	1.7
Other European (total)	11.2	11.3	11.5	12.2	11.3	14.5	15.4	18.5	26.3	22.7		14.6	21.1	20.1	23.6
Finnish					-	0.2	0.2	0.2	0.2						0.1
German	9.8	9.9	9.6	8.0	4.7	5.4	4.8	5.2	6.8	6.4		4.4	3.3	2.8	1.9
Italian	-	-	0.2	0.6	0.9	1.2	1.3	1.7	4.3	6.1		7.3	7.0	6.4	5.0
Jewish	-	-	0.2	1.1	1.7	2.0	2.0	1.8	1.2	1.9					
Netherland / Dutch	1.2	1.2	1.1	1.5	1.8	1.9	2.1	2.3	3.3	2.9		2.8	2.5	2.3	1.8
Polish				0.3	0.5	1.1	1.3	1.9	2.4	1.8			2.4	3.2	1.7
Russian	-		0.2	0.1	0.2	0.2	0.3	0.4	0.5	0.2			0.4	0.7	0.6
Scandinavian	-	0.1	0.1	0.1	0.2	0.3	0.4	0.5	0.8	0.6			0.1	0.1	0.1
Ukrainian					0.2	0.4	0.9	1.7	1.8	1.9			1.2	1.0	0.9
African	0.8	0.6	0.4	0.3	0.3	0.2	0.2		0.2						4.0
Chinese		-	-	0.1	0.2	0.2	0.2	0.2	0.2			4.4	6.8	8.5	8.0
Other Asian					0.1	0.1	0.2	0.3	0.4				7.1	10.8	25.5
Canadian												8.3	22.4	16.9	11.2
American													0.1	0.2	0.2
Not given	0.3	1.5	0.4	1.4	0.3	0.2	0.1	2.2	2.2	7.9	34.1	28.6	21.1	24.8	0.0

Source: See Table Notes and Data Sources

measure, the French-origin count in Southern Ontario was 142,275, or 3.6 times larger than the 39,960 total in Northern Ontario. However, the Southern Ontario share, which was 4.6% in 1871, reached a peak (around 8.1%) earlier, in 1951 and 1961, then declined thereafter, to 7.5% in 1971, and down to 1.7% in 2021, or less than one-fifth the level in Northern Ontario.

For those with Other European (neither British Isles nor French) origins, the numbers in Northern Ontario reached a peak of 202,235 in 1961. Relative to the Northern population their peak share also occurred in 1961, at 28.0%. The numbers for individual European origins varied considerably over the decades, but in 1961 the larger origins (over 2%) included Finnish (3.8%), German (3.9%), Italian (5.2%), Polish (2.6%), Scandinavian (2.6%), and Ukrainian (4.1%). In Southern Ontario, the Other European origins grew absolutely until 1971, to 1,572,400 or 22.7%, then dropped to 14.6% in 1991, followed by increases to 23.6% by single-origin share, or 3.6 percentage points higher than in Northern Ontario. The main Southern Ontario origins in 1961 were German (6.8%), Italian (4.3%), Netherlands (3.3%), and Polish (2.4%).

For persons with African (including African American) origins, both the numbers and share of population in Northern Ontario have been much lower than in Southern Ontario. Before the Second World War, the population numbers were likely under 100 for African origins and the population share likely 0.2% or less. In the postwar period the total numbers and share likely increased, though the data are not clear on when. In 2021 those indicating African by single origin numbered 3,815 or 1.0% of the Northern Ontario population.[22] The picture in Southern Ontario contrasts greatly, especially in recent decades. Southern Ontario had larger though declining numbers with African origins from 1871 (13,420) to lows of 6,686 in 1911 and 6,821 in 1931, and a share declining from 0.8% to 0.2% in 1931. By 1961 the numbers of those with African origins in Southern Ontario had risen to 10,814, though still at 0.2%. In later years, those identifying an African origin increased significantly, to 333,170 or 4.0% of the Southern Ontario population in 2021.

Before the Second World War in Northern Ontario, the numbers of those with Chinese origins were likely under 1,000 or 0.2% (1941). The population of "Other Asian" origins (includes South Asia) grew somewhat later, particularly after 1911, and reached a similar number and share in 1941. In the postwar decades both the numbers and share of those with Chinese and "Other Asian" origins did not grow a lot, though recently there has been an upsurge in those indicating an Other Asian single origin. In 2021, for Northern Ontario, the census reported 2,650 persons of Chinese origin (0.7%) and 12,810 persons of Other Asian origin (3.3%). Southern Ontario has seen much higher increases than Northern Ontario, which is related particularly to employment conditions. By 2021 the numbers of those indicating Chinese origin in that region had risen to 663,915 (8.0%) and for Other Asian origins to 2,114,655 (25.5%).

Statistics Canada's introduction of "Canadian" as an option for national origin had a major effect in Northern Ontario—from 2.3% initially in 1991 to 37.4% in 2001, 32.5% in 2011, and 20.0% in 2021. For Southern Ontario the comparable figures are 8.3% initially, then 22.4%, 16.9%, and 11.2% respectively. Further study with longitudinal data is needed to detail the source of the major shifts in responses for Canadian, although relative response declines of major origins suggest that in Northern Ontario the source was more from those with British Isles and Other European origins.[23]

LANGUAGES

While direct questions on speaking the official languages of English or French, as well as on mother tongue, began in the 1901 census, the latter was not then published. It was not until 1931 that the census authorities provided a more consistent form of reporting on official language and mother tongue. Hence, the discussion here for Northern Ontario is divided into two periods, the first from 1871 to 1931 to consider possible estimates of languages used, and the second from 1931 to 2021 to consider the results of more standardized questions on official languages and mother tongue. For present purposes, the terms "francophone" or "anglophone" refers to mother tongue unless otherwise noted.

Through out the 150-year period, language use and national minority language rights have had deeply political aspects, such as in education policy, languages in the court system, legislature, public services, and in cultural policy. Census language statistics, through their selection and framing of questions and reporting, have at times contributed to underestimates of the significance of minority language use, such as not providing counts for bilingualism or multilingualism. By implication this can be seen to reinforce oppressive power imbalances or to minimize the importance of national minority rights. At the same time, it is a vital to have realistic measures that can help address such concerns as assimilation and the lack or loss of language reproduction and rights.[24] As a whole, the Canadian censuses have been framed and reported in ways that have reinforced colonial and neocolonial state objectives, and this includes assimilation to speaking English, most obviously for Indigenous peoples but also for the francophone minority in Ontario. Census data does not address assimilation at the individual level, which requires historically linked or longitudinal data. But the census data here—with caution about their context—does provide social markers of trends in language use, especially in more recent censuses as the number of language-related questions has expanded, such as including language use in the workplace and at home.

To begin, the estimates in Table 4.6 are based on census counts for national origins together with counts for official languages in 1891 (French only), 1901, and 1931. For these early decades, the counts for national origin are taken generally as minimum counts for mother tongue as well as language spoken. This is plausible for the settler-population languages, particularly English and French, given the dominance of English and to a lesser degree French in leading colonial settlement. It does not apply to Indigenous languages especially in later decades due to the loss and prohibition of Indigenous language use from colonial displacement and cultural oppression in such actions as the Gradual Civilization Act (1857), the Indian Act (1876), and residential schools (Royal Commission on Aboriginal Peoples 1996, vol. 1, part two). Another problem with national origin and mother-tongue counts is that they do not provide clear or consistent measures of second- or multiple-language knowledge or use, although bilingualism and multilingualism existed, including among Indigenous peoples.

For settler-population languages, taking national origin as minimum language counts is also plausible in these earlier decades, given the extent then of community separation in communication and transportation and, in larger communities, segregation among neighbourhoods. As well, the heavier gender segregation in work and home would likely have mitigated the dominance and assimilative tendencies towards English in non-anglophone households. Further, using national origin in the more male-dominated decades of early colonization could lead to undercounting mother tongue and language spoken due to the census method of counting national origin through the father. For instance, families with British Isles–origin fathers but French mothers and French as mother tongue would be counted as anglophone despite being francophone or bilingual.

In general, the dominance of English in most workplaces, communications, schooling, and government institutions led to assimilation of non-anglophones, including francophones, to a greater degree than indicated by nation origin and more so in later decades. Hence, direct measures for speaking English tended to be higher than the national-origin counts for those from the British Isles alone. This is evident in data from the early period showing that francophones were bilingual to a much higher degree than anglophones. As illustrated in table 4.6 under the 1901 census data on language spoken, those with national origins in the British Isles were 58.2% of the population of Northern Ontario, while the portion of the population who could speak English was much higher at 85.3%. In terms of French, those of French origin were counted at about 20.3% while 23.7% of the population could speak French. The latter changed in later decades with greater francophone assimilation to English, whether through direct repression of French-language education such as with Ontario's Regulation 17 (1912), denial of public services, or certain approaches to bilingualism.[25] Even clearer is that of the 85.3% of the population in Northern Ontario who spoke English, only about 3% (2.5 percentage points) could speak French or were bilingual, while about 56% (13.2 percentage points) of those who spoke French could speak English. Francophone bilingualism would rise to even higher levels in later decades.

We can now summarize key trends indicated by Table 4.6. In Northern Ontario at the time of the 1871 census, Indigenous languages were likely the most used. English might have been primary for a third of the population (insofar as those not only of English, but also of Irish, Scottish, and Welsh national backgrounds used English), and French for a sixth of the population. Many Indigenous peoples could speak French through the history of the fur trade, but as noted the early census enumerations did not provide any clear indications of bilingualism or multilingualism. The share of anglophones increased more rapidly with the first decade of rapid colonization, English becoming the dominant language by 1881. The total number of French speakers increased, especially from the 1880s to the First World War; also the percentage share likely rose from a low of around 8% in 1881 to 14% in 1891 to more than 20% in 1901, and continued at that level until 1931, a rising trend reflecting the then increasing migration from Quebec.

The major increase in continental European immigration that occurred from 1901 to 1931, becoming about a third of the Northern Ontario population, had much less impact on the dominance of the

Table 4.6. Estimates of official languages spoken in Northern Ontario and Ontario, decennial census dates, 1871–1931.

	1871 reported	1871 percent	1881 reported	1881 percent	1891 reported	1891 percent	1901 reported	1901 percent	1911 reported	1911 percent	1921 reported	1921 percent	1931 reported	1931 percent
Northern Ontario														
Total Northern Ontario population	7,866	100	20,320	100	54,876		100,401		214,759		266,903		360,108	
1891 Census														
French-Canadians					7,733	14.1								
1901 Census (age 5 and over)							87,288	100						
Can speak English							74,450	85.3						
Can speak French							20,702	23.7						
English, can speak French							2,223	2.5						
French, can speak English							11,500	13.2						
Cannot speak English							12,838	14.7						
Cannot speak French							66,586	76.3						
1931 Census														
Population by language spoken													360,072	100.0
English only													251,629	69.9
French only													24,584	6.8
English and French													62,468	17.3
Neither English nor French													21,327	5.9
Censuses 1871–1931														
Population by national origin	7,866	100	20,320	100	n/a		100,401	100	214,759	100	266,900	100	360,108	100

	1871 reported	1871 percent	1881 reported	1881 percent	1891 reported	1891 percent	1901 reported	1901 percent	1911 reported	1911 percent	1921 reported	1921 percent	1931 reported	1931 percent
British Isles	2,558	32.5	12,680	62.4			58,425	58.2	109,128	50.8	135,596	50.8	162,880	45.2
English	1,240	15.8	4,588	22.6			20,985	20.9	42,963	20.0	65,317	24.5	72,312	20.1
Irish	555	7.1	3,990	19.6			20,359	20.3	34,646	16.1	34,726	13.0	45,329	12.6
Scottish	738	9.4	4,062	20.0			16,790	16.7	30,773	14.3	34,277	12.8	43,266	12.0
Welsh	25	0.3	40	0.2			291	0.3	746	0.3	1,276	0.5	1,973	0.5
French	1,242	15.8	1,562	7.7			20,374	20.3	45,355	21.1	63,386	23.7	63,386	17.6
Indigenous	3,934	50.0	4,678	23.0			8,599	8.6	11,359	5.3	14,262	5.3	14,262	4.0
Other	132	1.7	1,400	6.9			13,003	13.0	48,917	22.8	53,656	20.1	119,580	33.2
English-speaking (est. minimum)	2,558	32.5	12,680	62.4	n/a		58,425	58.2–85.3	109,128	50.8	135,596	50.8	162,889	45.2–87.2
French-speaking (est. minimum)	1,242	15.8	1,562	7.7	7,733	14.1	20,374	20.3–23.7	45,355	21.1	63,386	23.7	63,386	17.6–24.1
Ontario														
Total Ontario population	1,612,985		1,902,908		2,114,321		2,082,546		2,308,515		2,933,662		3,431,683	
1891 Census														
French-Canadian					101,123	4.8								
1901 Census (age 5 and over)							1,871,347	100						
Can speak English							1,823,503	97.4						
Can speak French							120,075	6.4						
English, can speak French							25,355	1.4						
French, can speak English							58,708	3.1						
Cannot speak English							47,844	2.6						
Cannot speak French							1,751,272	93.6						

(cont)

Table 4.6. Estimates of official languages spoken in Northern Ontario and Ontario, decennial census dates, 1871–1931.

	1871		1881		1891		1901		1911		1921		1931	
	reported	percent	reported	percent	reported	percent	reported	percent	reported	percent	reported	percent	reported	percent
1921 Census (age 10 and over)											2,324,464	100		
English only											1,910,414	82.2		
English and French only											194,813	8.4		
French only											22,917	1.0		
Mother tongue and English											168,355	7.2		
Mother tongue and French											221	-		
Mother tongue and English and French											6,606	0.3		
Mother tongue only, no English or French											21,138	0.9		
Mother tongues excluding Indigenous persons											2,305,027	100		
English											1,956,298	84.9		
French											170,197	7.4		
Other mother tongue											178,532	7.7		
1931 Census													3,431,683	100
English only													3,096,682	90.2
French only													64,534	1.9
English and French													219,532	6.4
Neither English nor French													50,935	1.5

	1871 reported	1871 percent	1881 reported	1881 percent	1891 reported	1891 percent	1901 reported	1901 percent	1911 reported	1911 percent	1921 reported	1921 percent	1931 reported	1931 percent
Mother tongue excluding Indigenous persons													3,431,683	100.0
English													2,796,821	81.5
French													235,396	6.9
Other mother tongues													399,466	11.6
Censuses 1871–1931														
Population by national origin	1,620,851	100	1,923,228	100	n/a		2,182,947	100	2,523,274	100	2,933,662	100	3,431,683	100
British Isles	1,333,042	82.2	1,548,030	80.5			1,732,144	79.3	1,927,099	76.4	2,282,015	77.8	2,539,771	74.0
English	439,429	27.1	535,835	27.9			701,413	32.1	884,432	35.1	1,211,660	41.3	1,319,612	38.5
Irish	559,442	34.5	627,262	32.6			624,332	28.6	608,137	24.1	590,493	20.1	647,831	18.9
Scottish	328,889	20.3	378,536	19.7			399,530	18.3	424,873	16.8	465,400	15.9	549,648	16.0
Welsh	5,282	0.3	6,397	0.3			6,869	0.3	9,657	0.4	14,462	0.5	22,680	0.7
French	75,383	4.7	102,743	5.3			158,671	7.3	202,442	8.0	248,275	8.5	299,732	8.7
Indigenous	12,978	0.8	15,325	0.8			8,599	0.4	23,044	0.9	26,654	0.9	30,368	0.9
Other	199,448	12.3	257,130	13.4			283,533	13.0	370,689	14.7	376,718	12.8	561,812	16.4
English-speaking (est. minimum)	1,333,042	82.2	1,548,030	80.5			1,732,144	79.3-97.4	1,927,099	76.4	2,282,015	77.8-90.6	2,539,771	74.0-96.6
French-speaking (est. minimum)	75,383	4.7	102,743	5.3	101,123	4.8	158,671	6.4-7.3	202,442	6.4-7.3	248,275	8.5-9.4	299,732	8.3-8.7

Notes: The estimated minimum counts are from national origin for British Isles and for French. The 1891 census did not do a count for national origin but did for "French-Canadians." For 1901, 1921, and 1931, the range of percentages is comprised of the percentage for national origin and the percentage for language spoken, including bilingual responses with French. The 1921 census data for official languages spoken and mother tongue were not available at the district level. The 1931 Census subtotals did not always add precisely.

Source: See Table Notes and Data Sources.

English language. The 1931 census counted nearly 70% of the population as speaking English. If one considers that most of those who spoke both English and French were likely francophone, then it is also likely that another at least 20% of the population were francophones. This suggests that fewer than 10% of the enumerated Northern Ontario population then spoke neither the dominant English nor French.

Due to the limits of subprovincial data in some censuses, and for consistency, the second page of Table 4.6 provides data for Ontario as a whole. Here we can see that Ontario (including Northern Ontario) was ever more dominated by English throughout the period. In 1871 anglophones likely numbered at least 80%, while francophones were about 5%, Indigenous persons 1%, and others 13%. In 1931 the Indigenous population count, and likely Indigenous languages, were still under 1%. Further, the Indigenous population was excluded from reported counts for official languages. At the same time, the census reported that 90% of the non-Indigenous population spoke English only, and another 6.4% could speak both English and French, meaning a total of over 96% could speak English. The francophone percentage increased to between 8 and 9% from 1911 to 1931, using the census count by national origin. Using the more direct language measures, the 1931 census data suggests a similar level for French spoken (8.3%, adding French spoken to English and French spoken) and somewhat less for mother tongue (7.9%). In 1931 the percentage of those from other national origins (than British, French, and Indigenous) was 16.4%, or half that of Northern Ontario alone, while 11.6% had a maternal language other than English or French. The census counted only 1.5% of the non-Indigenous Ontario population as speaking neither English nor French.

For the decades from 1931 on, the censuses provided more consistent measures of language, particularly through counts of official languages spoken and of mother tongue. Using both these measures, Table 4.7 shows the overwhelming dominance of English throughout the period 1931–2021. In terms of official languages, for the numbers of those speaking English, Northern Ontario had an increase in absolute numbers to a peak in 1981, followed by decline. Relative to the population, though, from 1941 for the entire period, the percentage of English-only speakers was high, around 70% or over. During the 50 years from 1951 to 2001, the English-only share hovered around 71–72%, then increased to 75.4% in 2021. By contrast, and indicative of the asymmetry in power, the smaller numbers of those speaking French only reached a peak in 1961, but relative to the population their share declined throughout, from 6.8% in 1931 to 0.9% in 2021. This pattern is similar but at an even lower level for those speaking neither English nor French: their numbers peaked absolutely in 1961, but relative to the population, their percentage declined, from 5.9% in 1931 to 0.3% in 2021. By contrast, the numbers speaking both English and French tended to grow until 1991, and rose relative to the population, from 17.3% in 1931 to a peak of 26.4% in 2001. Given higher francophone than anglophone bilingualism, the combined French-only and English-and-French categories indicate the francophone share at about 24.1% in 1931 increasing to about 27.0% in 1971, to a peak of 27.9% in 2001, then declining to 24.4% in 2021.

Southern Ontario data in Table 4.7 show an even greater dominance of English throughout the nine decades. Until 1961 English only was above 90%, about 20 percentage points higher than in Northern Ontario. Thereafter, the English-only share declined to about 87.1% in 2021, though it was still about 12 percentage points higher than in Northern Ontario. The small decline of the English-only percentage was mainly a result of the doubling of the bilingual English-and-French numbers, from 5.1% in 1931 to 10.1% in 2021. The French-only population declined absolutely after 1961, the only official language category to have such a decline in recent decades; relatively, it declined throughout, from 1.3% in 1931 to 0.2% in 2021. The number of those speaking neither English nor French was small in relative terms throughout, at or below 1% in the early decades and rising to 2.6% in 2021.

Table 4.7 also includes counts by mother tongue for English and French as well as Indigenous and other languages. The loss of mother-tongue numbers and shares among subordinate languages

Table 4.7. Official languages spoken in Northern Ontario and Southern Ontario, decennial census dates, 1931–2021.

	1931	1941	1951	1961	1971	1981	1991	2001	2011	2021
Northern Ontario										
Official language spoken: population	360,108	456,011	536,394	722,174	776,500	779,155	776,090	738,470	724,465	734,385
English only	251,729	332,328	384,229	521,874	552,545	561,790	557,040	528,200	533,535	553,380
French only	24,584	25,963	32,682	40,610	38,810	23,875	18,130	11,285	8,910	6,430
English and French	62,468	87,006	107,071	141,418	171,075	186,035	195,710	194,740	180,020	172,595
Neither English nor French	21,327	10,714	12,412	18,272	14,065	7,455	5,175	3,230	1,995	1,975
Official language spoken: % of population	100	100	100	100	100	100	100	100	100	100
English only	69.9	72.9	71.6	72.3	71.2	72.1	71.8	71.5	73.6	75.4
French only	6.8	5.7	6.1	5.6	5.0	3.1	2.3	1.5	1.2	0.9
English and French	17.3	19.1	20.0	19.6	22.0	23.9	25.2	26.4	24.8	23.5
Neither English nor French	5.9	2.3	2.3	2.5	1.8	1.0	0.7	0.4	0.3	0.3
Mother tongue: population	n/a	456,011	536,394	722,174	776,510	786,015	756,060	727,325	713,860	711,215
English		243,908	306,188	420,133	486,375	526,335	538,315	520,975	532,650	551,990
French		103,983	124,841	160,887	171,785	160,905	143,790	137,760	125,680	106,955
Indigenous languages		16,591	17,842	20,906	21,435	n/a	4,045	12,305	13,405	12,170
Other		91,529	87,523	120,248	96,915	n/a	73,965	56,285	42,125	40,100
Mother tongue: % of population		100	100	100	100	100	100	100	100	100
English		53.5	57.1	58.2	62.6	67.0	71.2	71.6	74.6	77.6
French		22.8	23.3	22.3	22.1	20.5	19.0	18.9	17.6	15.0
Indigenous languages		3.6	3.3	2.9	2.8	n/a	0.5	1.7	1.9	1.7
Other		20.1	16.3	16.7	12.5	n/a	9.8	7.7	5.9	5.6

	1931	1941	1951	1961	1971	1981	1991	2001	2011	2021
Southern Ontario										
Official language spoken: population	3,071,575	3,331,644	4,061,148	5,513,918	6,926,605	7,755,105	9,200,960	10,547,080	11,997,595	13,365,405
English only	2,844,953	3,092,938	3,731,355	5,026,892	6,171,555	6,839,275	8,036,595	9,162,545	10,450,825	11,643,195
French only	39,950	35,570	46,292	54,626	54,035	36,655	36,115	31,020	34,070	32,880
English and French	157,064	196,189	252,894	351,852	544,990	738,445	940,530	1,124,975	1,215,785	1,346,770
Neither English nor French	29,608	6,947	30,607	80,548	156,025	140,730	187,755	229,545	296,925	342,570
Official language spoken: % of population	100	100	100	100	100	100	100	100	100	100
English only	92.6	92.8	91.9	91.2	89.1	88.2	87.3	86.9	87.1	87.1
French only	1.3	1.1	1.1	1.0	0.8	0.5	0.4	0.3	0.3	0.2
English and French	5.1	5.9	6.2	6.4	7.9	9.5	10.2	10.7	10.1	10.1
Neither English nor French	1.0	0.2	0.8	1.5	2.3	1.8	2.0	2.2	2.5	2.6
Mother tongue: population		3,331,644	4,061,148	5,513,918	6,926,595	7,839,095	9,019,655	10,395,615	11,720,910	12,719,390
English		2,829,412	3,449,254	4,414,490	5,485,195	6,152,435	7,040,375	7,444,250	8,144,390	8,627,665
French		185,163	216,661	264,415	310,260	314,700	320,250	347,875	367,620	356,165
Indigenous languages		8,919	6,969	5,848	7,150	n/a	485	1,965	2,110	2,305
Other		308,150	388,264	829,165	1,123,990	n/a	1,659,020	2,601,525	3,206,790	3,733,255
Mother tongue: % of population		100	100	100	100	100	100	100	100	100
English		84.9	84.9	80.1	79.2	78.5	78.1	71.6	69.5	67.8
French		5.6	5.3	4.8	4.5	4.0	3.6	3.3	3.1	2.8
Indigenous languages		0.3	0.2	0.1	0.1	n/a	-	-	-	-
Other		9.2	9.6	15.0	16.2	n/a	18.4	25.0	27.4	29.4

Source: See Table Notes and Data Sources.

asymmetrically to the growth of English mother-tongue numbers can be seen as a long-term indicator of assimilation into English in Ontario. Given the history of settler colonialism in Ontario, the table includes under mother tongue some official counts of Indigenous languages. As with the population counts, language counts of Indigenous peoples are likely undercounts to some degree. More important, however, these overall low numbers show the destructive consequences of colonization for Indigenous languages and cultures.

In Northern Ontario, even with the greater presence of First Nations and the Franco-Ontarian national minority, it is not surprising after decades of assimilation to see a growing portion of the population with English as mother tongue, 53.5% in 1941 rising to 77.6% in 2021. Though this is nearly three-quarters of the Northern Ontario population, we will see that there exist important sub-regional differences. As well, for 1991 to 2011 data there are possible indications, for Indigenous languages particularly, that some absolute and relative growth was occurring. For francophones, the general trend appears as continuing decline. Francophone numbers rose to a peak in 1971 and have been declining in absolute terms in each decade since then, as has the relative share. Indeed, from 1951 (at 23.3%) the francophone share fell to 15.0% in 2021, which reflects both assimilation as well as out-migration among francophones. This said, the relative and absolute decline of "other" mother tongues was more rapid, and accounted even more than that for francophones for the rise of English as a mother tongue. The "other" mother-tongue numbers rose to an absolute peak in 1961, and have been declining ever since, while their share declined from 20.1% in 1941 to 5.6% in 2021.

The picture in Southern Ontario shows absolute growth by mother tongue not only for English but also for other mother tongues. The number of those reporting a French mother tongue rose absolutely until 2011 but declined in 2021. There may be stability in the numbers for Indigenous languages as mother tongues in 2001–2021, though the numbers are much smaller than those in Northern Ontario and more subject to small errors in measurement. While the percentage of those capable of speaking English has been over 95% throughout the period,[26] the percentage of those reporting English as mother tongue declined, from a high during the period of 84.9% in 1941 and 1951 to 67.8% in 2021. The percentage reporting French as their mother tongue also declined, but less, from 5.6% in 1941 to 2.8% in 2021, while their absolute numbers continued to grow until 2011, then declined in 2021, as in Northern Ontario. Most of the decline in English reported as a mother tongue is accounted for by the rapid increase in the numbers of persons with other mother tongues, likely from new patterns in immigration in Southern Ontario.

Although the pattern of colonial settlement in Northern Ontario led to the general dominance of English, there exist major differences within Northern Ontario by district and community. Table 4.8 on the district distribution of languages by English, French, and Indigenous mother tongues and national origins indicates for 2016 that those reporting British Isles single-ethnic origins were about 42.2%, while three-quarters of the population reported English as their mother tongue. Across Northern Ontario districts or census divisions, those with British Isles origins had their largest numbers in Thunder Bay (21.6% of British Isles origins in Northern Ontario), Greater Sudbury (20.9%), Algoma (17.9%), Nipissing (12.2%), and Cochrane (8.0%). Numbers by mother tongue follow at similar levels for Thunder Bay (22.8% of British Isles mother tongue in Northern Ontario), Greater Sudbury (19.6%), Algoma (17.8%), and Nipissing (11.0%), but the Kenora District (at 9.0%) has somewhat higher numbers than Cochrane (7.3%).

For the Indigenous languages in 2016, about 18.8% of Northern Ontario reported Indigenous ancestry, while under 1% counted by Statistics Canada reported an Indigenous mother tongue, mostly Algonquian languages, particularly Ojibway, Oji-Cree, and Cree.[27] Across Northern Ontario, the largest number of persons reporting Indigenous origins (which include First Nations, rural, and small-town areas) were in the census divisions of Kenora (23.3% of Indigenous

Table 4.8. District distribution of Northern Ontario population by mother tongue and national origin, 2016.

	Algoma	Cochrane	Kenora	Manitoulin	Nipissing	Rainy River	Sudbury	Greater Sudbury	Thunder Bay	Timis-kaming	Northern Ontario	As % of population
Total population	114,094	79,682	65,533	13,255	83,150	20,110	21,546	161,647	146,048	32,251	737,316	100
Mother tongues												
Non-institutional pop. single responses	111,370	76,890	64,010	12,880	80,485	19,705	21,085	156,180	142,290	31,340	716,235	100
- % of Northern Ontario	15.5	10.7	8.9	1.8	11.2	2.8	2.9	21.8	19.9	4.4	100	
Indigenous languages	520	165	1,095	365	265	565	75	230	1,895	20	5,195	0.7
- % of Northern Ontario	10.0	3.2	21.1	7.0	5.1	10.9	1.4	4.4	36.5	0.4	100	
English	95,835	39,110	48,490	10,550	58,890	18,175	15,025	105,355	122,595	23,025	537,050	75.0
- % of Northern Ontario	17.8	7.3	9.0	2.0	11.0	3.4	2.8	19.6	22.8	4.3	100	
French	6,830	33,895	1,095	365	18,635	275	5,280	40,955	4,880	7,280	119,490	16.7
- % of Northern Ontario	5.7	28.4	0.9	0.3	15.6	0.2	4.4	34.3	4.1	6.1	100	
National origins												
Population in private households	112,055	78,510	64,615	12,955	81,285	19,755	21,245	158,780	143,085	31,675	723,960	100
- % of Northern Ontario	15.5	10.8	8.9	1.8	11.2	2.7	2.9	21.9	19.8	4.4	100	
North American Indigenous origins	17,030	14,470	31,715	5,315	12,550	5,325	4,135	19,880	22,470	3,430	136,320	18.8
- % of Northern Ontario	12.5	10.6	23.3	3.9	9.2	3.9	3.0	14.6	16.5	2.5	100	

First Nations	11,970	10,230	28,425	5,015	8,315	4,165	2,435	11,085	18,395	1,965	102,000	14.1
- % of Northern Ontario	11.7	10.0	27.9	4.9	8.2	4.1	2.4	10.9	18.0	1.9	100	
Inuit	80	205	90	10	120	0	35	170	130	10	850	0.1
- % of Northern Ontario	9.4	24.1	10.6	1.2	14.1	0.0	4.1	20.0	15.3	1.2	100	
Métis	5,480	4,440	3,520	300	4,525	1,390	1,810	9,000	4,375	1,545	36,385	5.0
- % of Northern Ontario	15.1	12.2	9.7	0.8	12.4	3.8	5.0	24.7	12.0	4.2	100	
British Isles origins	54,605	24,560	21,570	5,630	37,340	9,340	8,000	63,850	65,905	14,580	305,380	42.2
- % of Northern Ontario	17.9	8.0	7.1	1.8	12.2	3.1	2.6	20.9	21.6	4.8	100	
English	30,915	13,235	12,240	3,365	20,665	5,510	4,230	31,805	38,070	8,550	168,585	23.3
- % of Northern Ontario	18.3	7.9	7.3	2.0	12.3	3.3	2.5	18.9	22.6	5.1	100	
Irish	24,080	10,095	8,220	2,505	16,480	3,910	3,645	30,355	26,060	6,010	131,360	18.1
- % of Northern Ontario	18.3	7.7	6.3	1.9	12.5	3.0	2.8	23.1	19.8	4.6	100	
Scottish	23,850	8,905	9,960	2,710	14,655	4,180	3,305	24,990	29,495	5,775	127,825	17.7
- % of Northern Ontario	18.7	7.0	7.8	2.1	11.5	3.3	2.6	19.6	23.1	4.5	100	
French origins	27,075	29,045	8,520	1,575	26,715	3,415	7,945	60,485	25,890	9,465	187,300	25.9
- % of Northern Ontario	14.5	15.5	4.5	0.8	14.3	1.8	4.2	32.3	13.8	5.1	100	

Notes: Other British Isles origins (Cornish, Channel Islander, Manx, Welsh, other) not included here. French origins includes French European as well as Acadian and Québécois origins.

Source: See Table Notes and Data Sources Table 4.7 for 1911. Mother tongues are from 100% data. National (ethnic) origins are from 25% sample data.

origins in Northern Ontario), Thunder Bay (16.5%), Greater Sudbury (14.6%), Algoma (12.5%), and Cochrane (10.6%). In terms of mother tongue, those reporting an Indigenous mother tongue were concentrated in the census divisions of Thunder Bay (36.5% of Indigenous mother tongues in Northern Ontario), Kenora (21.1%), Rainy River (10.9%), Algoma (10.0%), and Manitoulin (7.0%).

For francophones, there was evidence of assimilation to English over the census periods, though not as dramatic as that for Indigenous persons: about 25.9% reported French as their ethnic origin, but about 16.7% reported French as their mother tongue. Across Northern Ontario census divisions, the largest numbers of those with French origin were counted in Greater Sudbury (32.3%), Cochrane (15.5%), Algoma (14.5%), Nipissing (14.3%), and Thunder Bay (13.8%). By mother tongue, the numbers across Northern Ontario were more concentrated for the census divisions of Greater Sudbury (34.3%), Cochrane (28.4%), and Nipissing (15.6%), while Algoma (at 5.7%) and Thunder Bay (at 4.1%) had lower numbers by mother tongue, suggesting even higher levels of assimilation in the latter.

Differences in language use in Northern Ontario are even more evident at lower levels of aggregation, such as the municipality or rural township. The historical concentration of populations and their local economic and social conditions at these levels gave rise to differences in language use and attachments that are not evident in provincial or larger aggregate measures. Further, census authorities in recent decades have introduced important new measures of language use, particularly for work language and home language, so it is useful to take these into account in relation to the earlier measures on national origin and mother tongue. Appendix Table A shows the results of counts in the 2016 census for the six measures related to language across different levels of geography for Northern Ontario. The six measures for Ontario in aggregate are compared with those for the two largest francophone census divisions, Greater Sudbury and Cochrane (District), as well as for three communities

within the District of Cochrane: the City of Timmins and two majority francophone communities, the town of Hearst and the township
of Moonbeam. Both the municipality of Greater Sudbury and the
Cochrane District are "designated areas" under Ontario's French
Language Services Act (*Loi sur les services en français*).[28]

These district-level and other more local-level analyses can show
generally the role of geographical concentrations of population by
national background and language, but they also point particularly to
the dual role of workplaces in leading language use. Institutions and
businesses where work is conducted in minority languages have played
a role in reproducing the language, not simply as workplaces but often
also in the services they provide, such as in education, health, media,
religion, cultural expression, and public administration. In this way,
higher local counts of workplace use of language can also indicate
higher local levels of minority-language services.

For Northern Ontario it is useful to conclude the discussion of the
importance of local-level variation and workplace measures by comparing the hierarchical pattern of language use in Ontario with those
for certain regional and local areas with larger minority-language
populations. Here we use four different language counts from the 2016
census data for English and French, and for Indigenous languages in a
case where the minority numbers are larger.[29] For Ontario as a whole,
the highest level of use of English is as a work language (97.2%), followed by home language (82.5%), mother tongue (68.8%), and national
(ethnic) origin (37.0%). By contrast, the hierarchy for French is reversed
and the range is much more compressed, the lowest being French at
the workplace (1.3%), as home language (2.2%), as mother tongue (3.8%),
and as origin (10.4%). But if one considers Northern Ontario areas
with larger francophone populations, the picture shifts, especially
for majority-francophone communities. In general, the English level
for workplace use is lower and the French level for workplace use is
correspondingly higher, while the gaps between workplace language

and mother tongue diminish. The latter is especially evident in such majority-francophone communities as Hearst and Moonbeam.

In contrast to Ontario, for the Cochrane District, which has the highest percentage of francophones (by mother tongue) of the Northern Ontario districts, for English measures the hierarchy is compressed, with the workplace at 81.2 %, home language at 66.7%, mother tongue at 50.9%, and national origin at 31.3 %. On the other hand, for French measures the subordinate language hierarchy remains but the percentage-point range is less compressed, from workplace use at 18.5%, to home language at 31.5%, to mother tongue at 44.1%, to national origin at 37.0%.[30] The Cochrane District also has a larger Indigenous population and measured use of Indigenous languages. Here one can see a similar type of subordinate language hierarchy to that for French, though more extreme. Grouping identified Indigenous languages in 2016, the census authorities counted only a 0.2% level in workplaces, 0.8% in home use, and 2.1% by mother tongue, though 18.4% by national origin.

Finally, in the majority-francophone town of Hearst, the English- and French-language conditions are somewhat reversed. The level of English workplace use was at 20.3%, home use at 12.4%, mother tongue at 9.9%, and national origin at 9.5%. For French, workplace use was much higher at 79.7%, home use at 86.7%, mother tongue at 88.5%, and national origin at 35.2%.[31] These striking differences at the local level suggest not simply a much reduced level of assimilation but also the possibility of higher levels of reproduction for minority languages even within an Ontario dominated by English.

NOTES

1. See Hobsbawm (1990) and Fisch (2015, Chapters 7–8).
2. Census of 1871, Vol. I, Table II. Catholics numbered about 274,000, Methodists from 287,000 to 462,000 (depending on grouping of sub-denominations), Presbyterians from 230,000 to 256,000, and the "Church of England" (Anglicans) about 331,000 out of the total population count of about 1,621,000.

3. Indicative of other Northern Ontario mining towns, a significant portion (about 20%) of the population of Bruce Mines was counted as having a French background, while a majority were counted as being of English, Irish, and Scottish origins. The census counted only 40 "Indians," about 3% of the population. The census did not count any persons as Welsh, though it is likely that some mineworkers were of Welsh origin. The religions were more varied and reflective of the changing class character of settlement brought by corporate mining: the largest denominations were Wesleyan Methodists, followed by Catholics, Church of England, and Presbyterians. Many Wesleyan Methodists were likely skilled Cornish miners. One historian has called Bruce Mines "the Cornwall of Canada" (Schwartz 2022).

4. Census of 1871, Vol. I, Table II. It is likely in this period that the characterization "pagans" was applied mostly to Indigenous peoples, insofar as they were counted.

5. In 1891 the census added questions about the birthplaces of parents, though this was not carried on consistently in later censuses. From this data the census authorities held "we procure important facts respecting intermarriages of persons born in different provinces, intermarriages of foreigners and natives, of French-speaking Canadians with English-speaking, etc., tending to show the extent to which assimilation has been carried on by the free volition of the people moving over a large area of country" (Census of Canada, 1891, Bulletin No. 11).

6. The 1871 Census (Vol. I, xxii) did not define or discuss in any depth this "new feature" but commented simply that "None of the former censuses of the various Provinces had it, except insofar as the French origin was concerned, in the former Province of Canada. What is given in previous returns under the head origin, was simply the enumeration of people by their place of birth. ... The two tables of *origins* and *birth* places of the people taken in connection with the others, afford invaluable means of statistical comparisons and deductions."

7. See, for example, on related census history and issues, Filippova and Guérin-Pace (2013), Potvin (2005), Goldscheider (2004, 79-83), Boyd, Goldmann, and White (2000), Wargon (2000), Howard-Hassmann (1999), Simon (1997), Beaud and Prévost (1993), Boyd (1993), White, Badets, and Renaud (1993), and Herberg (1990).

8. The 1891 Census had reported on numbers of French-speaking Canadians alone, as part of data on sex and conjugal condition (Vol. I, Table III, "Civil Condition"). The 1901 Census reported on those speaking English, French, both, and neither, but not on mother tongue, in the context of reporting on literacy (Vol. IV, Table XIII).

9. Both of these were under a supra-head which made clear that these counts were for distinct populations even if their numbers were already included in other columns (such as under Natives, Not of French Origin) presumably to avoid double counting (Census of 1851, Vol. I, Table 1; Census of 1861, Vol. I, Table 2).

10. The introduction to the 1901 Census (Vol. I, xviii) noted "the expression 'new nationality' was in this sense introduced in the speech with which the Governor General opened the first Canadian Parliament—it is proper to use Canadian ... as descriptive of every person whose home is in the country and has acquired rights of citizenship in it." This then included "a person born in the United Kingdom or any of its colonies, whose residence in Canada is not merely temporary."

11. Census of 1921, "Origins, Birthplace, Nationality and Language of the Canadian People," Census Study; Census of 1931, Vol. XIII, Monographs, "Racial Origins and Nativity of the Canadian People."

12. Such changes are described in the 1981 Census publication No. 95-942 (xxviii-xxx). Multiple responses for English, Irish, Scottish, Welsh, and other British were reported as a single British response; while multiple responses for Franco-Ontarian and another francophone origin such as Québécois were deemed to be a French multiple origin.

13. Statistics Canada 2020a, 4. "Responses ... reflect respondents' perceptions of their background. As such, many factors can influence changes in responses over time, including the contemporary social environment, the respondent's knowledge of their family history, and their understanding of and views on the topic. ... Over time, there have been differences in wording, format, examples and instructions of the ethnic-origin question used in the census. As a result, the historical comparability of ethnic-origin data has been affected by these factors, as well as by changes in data processing, proxy responses and the social environment at the time of the census."

14. Statistics Canada (2021, "Gender"): "Beginning in 2021, the variable 'gender' is expected to be used by default in most social statistics programs at Statistics Canada." See also Statistics Canada (2020b). In the 2016 census, respondents who could not respond for the sex question to either of the binary options of male or female were asked "to leave their answer blank and provide a comment at the end of the questionnaire" (Statistics Canada 2023, 20). Statistics Canada has noted that it has "a variant classification of sex at birth, which includes an additional category for intersex," but it has not collected such data (Statistics Canada 2022b, 2). The availability of gender data in 2021 also increases the number of marital status categories. This will enable deeper study of gender diversity in marriage and common-law relationships as well as more generally the greater variety of family structures, at least for large aggregations of population. See Statistics Canada (2021, "Gender diversity status of marriage or common-law union").

15. Gender data was collected for all ages of the population but reported for the population 15 years and over (Statistics Canada 2022a, 4). See, for example, Statistics Canada Table 98-10-0036-01, "Broad age groups and gender: Canada, provinces and territories", and Table 98-10-0037-01, "Broad age groups and gender: Canada and census metropolitan areas." For the two categories, men+

and women+, the male and female categories are combined and, as noted in these Statistics Canada tables, "individuals in the category 'non-binary persons' are distributed into the other two gender categories and are denoted by the '+' symbol." For Statistics Canada, non-binary includes "persons whose reported gender is both male and female, neither male nor female, or either male or female in addition to another gender. It includes persons whose reported gender is, for example, agender, pangender, genderqueer, genderfluid, or gender-nonconforming. It also includes persons whose reported gender is Two-Spirit, a term specific to some Indigenous peoples of North America" (2022a, 6). Statistics Canada emphasizes that sex at birth and gender (which relates to gender identity and gender expression) are separate concepts from sexual orientation, which relates to "sexual attraction, sexual behaviours and sexual identity (e.g., being asexual, bisexual, gay or lesbian, heterosexual or pansexual)" (Statistics Canada 2022b).

16. Statistics Canada (2022a, 8). The evidence given is: "According to the 2021 Census, 120,720 people in Canada were transgender or non-binary, over a total population of close to 37 million people." Statistics Canada also points to the small numbers of non-cisgendered persons (those whose gender as reported at the census date is the same as their assigned sex at birth) and confidentiality as the reason for not releasing data at geographies with smaller populations: only higher levels of geography allow data be disaggregated into the full five gender categories while maintaining confidentiality (2022a, 6). Statistics Canada reports for the population 15 and over that Ontario has 39,450 transgendered men, transgendered women, and non-binary persons, with shares of 0.10%, 0.11%, and 0.13%, respectively, or a total non-cisgendered share of 0.33% (from Statistics Canada Table 98-10-0037-01). The non-cisgendered shares for Toronto CMA, Ottawa CMA, Greater Sudbury CMA, and Thunder Bay CMA are 0.31%, 0.47%, 0.40%, and 0.41%, respectively (from Table 98-10-0036-01).

17. In early use, nation referred simply to a "territorial state," as Hobsbawm (1990, 24) noted about Adam Smith's use of it in his *Inquiry into the Nature and Causes of the Wealth of Nations* (1776). In this sense, nation is defined by a sovereign and the territory and population over which the sovereign rules, not necessarily by language(s) and other social features. In a later context, one reflecting a growing democratic impetus, the term "nation" came to carry the idea of "a people" with particular social characteristics, as distinct from the state. In one particular use, the term also became synonymous with "nation-state" and carried an implication that the recognition of a nation implied rights to self-determination and statehood, including a right of secession. Of course, Canada has had much debate around this, particularly over the recognition of Quebec as a nation, and what that entails. In recent years, debates have shifted beyond recognizing

Canada as "binational" to recognizing also the sovereign rights of Indigenous peoples and Canada as "multinational" or "plurinational."

18. For reasons of space some data on national origins have been omitted. The national origins in the table were selected by size and being available for most censuses. The grouping of British Isles origins was retained for lack of individual origin data from 1951 to 1991 and to facilitate comparisons with language data for English. As noted in the Table Notes and Data Sources in this volume, some origin names once used by the census authorities have been changed here.

19. According to Statistics Canada (2016a): "A high proportion of individuals from long-established groups in Canada reported more than one origin. North American Aboriginal origins and European origins were among the most commonly reported multiple origins in 2016."

20. The largest percentage-point drops in relative shares from 1971 to 2021 in Northern Ontario occurred for British Isles origins and French origins. Some Other European–origin shares also fell markedly (German, Polish, Scandinavian, and Ukrainian origins of those with data available). Such large relative declines suggest these single-origin responses and possibly others could have been more affected by introduction of the Canadian single-origin category.

21. See Table Notes and Data Sources for Table 4.5. Indigenous totals from 1981 to 2021 are based on single origins for Aboriginal identity. Before 1981 the Indigenous totals are based on "Indian" origin plus smaller numbers of "Half Breed" origin when separately counted or reported by the census; over these years, the censuses generally reported Inuit (or "Eskimo") persons with "Indians."

22. The data by single origins were not published at the census division level for African origins. The African- and Asian-origins total together did increase, including after 1971: the percentage share for both together was likely around 0.4% in 1941 to 1961 and, for Asian origins, increased perhaps to 1.4% in 2011 and 4.0% in 2021.

23. If one examines in Table 4.5 the "population responding" numbers, the total response decline for all national origins from 1971 to 1991 was -39.7%, while for British and Other European origins it was even higher, -53.1 and -67.4% respectively. By contrast French-origin responses declined less than the average, by -28.5% and the French-origin share increased. In Southern Ontario, the average response decline was -10.0%. The response decline for British Isles origins and Other European origins was -43.9% and -42.3% respectively, somewhat lower than in Northern Ontario but much higher than the average decline. For French origins, the response decline was similar to that in Northern Ontario (-28.4%), but much higher than the average decline in Southern Ontario.

24. UNDRIP, of which Canada is a signatory, provides: (Article 8.1) "Indigenous peoples and individuals have the right not to be subjected to forced assimilation or destruction of their culture." (Article 8.2) "States shall provide effective

mechanisms for prevention of, and redress for: (a) Any action which has the aim or effect of depriving them of their integrity as distinct peoples, or of their cultural values or ethnic identities" (United Nations 2008).

25. Many Franco-Ontarian struggles on language and national minority rights are chronicled in Sylvestre (2019). Some critics of Anglo (or Anglo-Celtic) elite domination have identified its roots in the settler-colonial character of the Canadian state and its continued consequences in official approaches to bilingualism and multiculturalism (see Haque 2012).

26. Combining English only and English and French.

27. It should be noted that Statistics Canada's counting of languages has some limitations as languages have regional variations and boundaries are not always well defined. Our thanks to the anonymous reviewer for this point of caution.

28. Northern Ontario has eight of Ontario's 26 designated areas. They include, besides Greater Sudbury and Cochrane District, all of Algoma District, Nipissing District, Sudbury District, and Timiskaming District, as well as part of Kenora District (Ignace Township) and part of Thunder Bay Township (Towns of Geraldton, Longlac and Marathon; Townships of Manitouwadge, Beardmore, Nakina and Terrace Bay) (https://www.ontario.ca/page/government-services-french).

29. Appendix Table A includes official counts for Indigenous languages for four of the language-use measures. The other measures, of official-language knowledge and first official language spoken, are included in the table and can be used to elaborate other dimensions of the discussion, such as on local variations in English–French bilingualism.

30. For the Greater Sudbury census division, with the largest absolute number of francophones in Northern Ontario but a somewhat lower francophone share, the English-language hierarchy is only somewhat compressed, with the workplace at 95.1%, home language at 84.6%, mother tongue at 50.9%, and national origin at 40.2%, while for French the reverse hierarchy begins with workplace use at 4.8%, home language at 13.3%, mother tongue at 26.2%, and national origin at 38.1%.

31. Another example, the smaller majority-francophone community of Moonbeam, is included in Appendix Table A. Here English in the workplace was counted at 53.0%, home use at 25.7%, mother tongue at 18.9%, and national origin at 15.6%. For French, one sees a similar pattern to that for Hearst though at a lower level: workplace use at 47.0%, home use at 74.3%, mother tongue at 79.8%, and national origin at 43.6%.

CHAPTER 5

THE EVOLUTION OF POPULATION AND EMPLOYMENT ACROSS DISTRICTS IN NORTHERN ONTARIO

In Northern Ontario the post-1945 shift from slowing population growth to absolute decline occurred at different rates and times in different districts (or census divisions), but by the 1990s the decline had become generalized to most districts. In this chapter we examine the population and employment peaks of these changes by district, the patterns of decline, and their relation to the employment–population ratio. This longer-term perspective is useful since analyses of Northern Ontario conditions for shorter periods are prone to conflate longer-term structural trends with shorter-term cyclical movements, especially those related to natural resource prices and production.

The district-level populations in Table 5.1 show different onsets to long-term decline. In the 1960s, three districts reached census population peaks: Timiskaming (1961), Rainy River (1961), and Cochrane

(1966), which includes Timmins. These were followed in the 1970s by Sudbury (District and City) (1971), and in the 1980s by Algoma (1981), which includes Sault Ste. Marie. By the 1990s it was evident that population decline in Northern Ontario was becoming generalized as two more districts reached census population peaks: Thunder Bay (1991) and Nipissing (1996), which includes North Bay. In aggregate, the census population of Northern Ontario had twin peaks, an initial peak in 1981 if 786,048 and a later, slightly higher peak in 1996 of 786,370.

For some districts, the decline has been persistent, such as for Timiskaming, where all twelve censuses following 1961 showed decline, or Algoma, where all eight censuses following 1981 showed decline. For other districts, decline was interspersed with stagnation or smaller upward movements. For instance, Cochrane has had declines since 1966 in eight of eleven censuses while Sudbury District and City has had declines in four of ten censuses since 1971, although the losses in declining years were larger than the gains in growth years. Only two Northern Ontario districts have had overall increases: Kenora and Manitoulin.[1]

Table 5.2 shows the rates of change in census populations by district as well as the growing numbers of census population declines in Northern Ontario. Not only did Northern Ontario as a whole see three census declines since the 1990s, but in every census in the decades between 1996 and 2021 at least half of all districts have had population declines.

The pattern of population decline or stagnation in most districts is also consistent with Statistics Canada's annual population estimates (Table 17-10-0039-01), though the specific peak years differ from the census dates and are limited by the coverage of the Annual Estimates to the period since 1986 only.[2]

Population decline in Northern Ontario is related to declining employment conditions both absolutely and relative to external employment conditions, especially the pulls of competing employment conditions and prospects in Southern Ontario and elsewhere. However, the exact relationship between population and employment

Table 5.1. Population by district in Northern Ontario, census dates, 1931–2021.

	1931	1941	1951	1956	1961	1966	1971	1976	1981	1986	1991	1996	2001	2006	2011	2016	2021
Northern Ontario	360,108	456,011	536,394	628,107	722,174	739,712	776,505	784,487	786,048	764,312	784,027	786,370	746,778	745,372	733,016	737,316	742,610
Algoma District	46,444	52,002	64,496	82,059	111,408	113,561	121,937	122,883	133,553	131,841	127,269	125,455	118,567	117,461	115,870	114,094	113,777
Cochrane District	58,033	80,730	83,850	86,768	95,666	97,334	95,836	96,825	96,875	93,712	93,917	93,240	85,247	82,503	81,122	79,682	77,963
Kenora District	25,919	33,372	39,212	47,156	51,474	53,995	53,230	57,980	59,421	52,834	58,748	63,335	61,802	64,419	57,607	65,533	66,000
Manitoulin District	10,734	10,841	11,214	11,060	11,176	10,544	10,931	10,893	11,001	9,823	11,192	11,413	12,679	13,090	13,048	13,255	13,935
Nipissing District	41,207	43,315	50,517	60,452	70,568	73,533	78,867	81,739	80,268	79,004	84,723	84,832	82,910	84,688	84,736	83,150	84,716
Rainy River District	17,359	19,132	22,132	25,483	26,531	25,816	25,750	24,768	22,798	22,871	22,997	23,163	22,109	21,564	20,370	20,110	19,437
Sudbury District	58,251	80,815	109,590	141,975	165,862	174,102	198,079	27,287	27,068	25,771	26,178	25,457	22,894	21,392	21,196	21,546	22,368
Sudbury District and City	58,251	80,815	109,590	141,975	165,862	174,102	198,079	194,992	186,847	178,247	187,388	189,506	178,162	179,301	181,572	183,193	188,496
Sudbury RM/Greater Sudbury	n/a	n/a	n/a	n/a	n/a	n/a	n/a	167,705	159,779	152,476	161,210	164,049	155,268	157,909	160,376	161,647	166,128
Thunder Bay District	65,118	85,200	105,367	122,890	138,518	143,673	145,390	150,647	153,997	155,673	158,810	157,619	150,860	149,063	146,057	146,048	146,862
Timiskaming District	37,043	50,604	50,016	50,264	50,971	47,154	46,485	43,760	41,288	40,307	38,983	37,807	34,442	33,283	32,634	32,251	31,424
Bordering districts																	
Muskoka District Municipality	20,985	21,835	24,713	25,134	26,705	27,691	31,938	36,691	38,370	40,235	48,005	50,463	53,106	57,563	58,017	60,599	66,674
Parry Sound District	25,900	30,083	27,371	28,095	29,632	28,355	30,240	32,654	33,528	33,828	38,423	39,906	39,665	40,918	42,162	42,824	46,909

Notes: Sudbury RM refers to the Regional Municipality of Sudbury.

Source: See Table Notes and Data Sources Table 2.2..

Table 5.2. Population change in Northern Ontario districts, % by census periods, 1931–2021.

	1931	1941	1951	1956	1961	1966	1971	1976	1981	1986	1991	1996	2001	2006	2011	2016	2021
Ontario	..	10.4	21.4	17.6	15.4	11.6	10.7	7.3	4.4	5.5	10.8	6.6	6.1	6.6	5.7	4.6	5.8
Southern Ontario	..	8.5	21.9	17.6	15.4	12.8	11.3	8.0	4.8	6.4	11.6	7.2	7.0	7.0	6.2	4.9	6.1
Northern Ontario	..	26.6	17.6	17.1	15.0	2.4	5.0	1.0	0.2	-2.8	2.6	0.3	-5.0	-0.2	-1.7	0.6	0.7
Algoma District	..	12.0	24.0	27.2	35.8	1.9	7.4	0.8	8.7	-1.3	-3.5	-1.4	-5.5	-0.9	-1.4	-1.5	-0.3
Cochrane District	..	39.1	3.9	3.5	10.3	1.7	-1.5	1.0	0.1	-3.3	0.2	-0.7	-8.6	-3.2	-1.7	-1.8	-2.2
Kenora District	..	28.8	17.5	20.3	9.2	4.9	-1.4	8.9	2.5	-11.1	11.2	7.8	-2.4	4.2	-10.6	13.8	0.7
Manitoulin District	..	1.0	3.4	-1.4	1.0	-5.7	3.7	-0.3	1.0	-10.7	13.9	2.0	11.1	3.2	-0.3	1.6	5.1
Nipissing District	..	5.1	16.6	19.7	16.7	4.2	7.3	3.6	-1.8	-1.6	7.2	0.1	-2.3	2.1	0.1	-1.9	1.9
Rainy River District	..	10.2	15.7	15.1	4.1	-2.7	-0.3	-3.8	-8.0	0.3	0.6	0.7	-4.6	-2.5	-5.5	-1.3	-3.3
Sudbury District and City	..	38.7	35.6	29.6	16.8	5.0	13.8	-1.6	-4.2	-4.6	5.1	1.1	-6.0	0.6	1.3	0.9	2.9
Sudbury RM / Greater Sudbury	..	n/a	n/a	n/a	n/a	n/a	n/a	n/a	-4.7	-4.6	5.7	1.8	-5.4	1.7	1.6	0.8	2.8
Sudbury District	..	38.7	35.6	29.6	16.8	5.0	13.8	-86.2	-0.8	-4.8	1.6	-2.8	-10.1	-6.6	-0.9	1.7	3.8
Thunder Bay District	..	30.8	23.7	16.6	12.7	3.7	1.2	3.6	2.2	1.1	2.0	-0.7	-4.3	-1.2	-2.0	0.0	0.6
Timiskaming District	..	36.6	-1.2	0.5	1.4	-7.5	-1.4	-5.9	-5.6	-2.4	-3.3	-3.0	-8.9	-3.4	-1.9	-1.2	-2.6
No. of districts / CDs		9	9	9	9	9	9	9	10	10	10	10	10	10	10	10	10
No. with increases		9	8	8	9	6	5	5	5	8	8	5	1	4	2	5	6
No. with decreases		0	1	1	0	3	4	4	5	2	2	5	9	6	8	5	4

Notes: For intercensal increases and decreases, only the Sudbury District and City total is counted. The 0.0% change in 2016 for Thunder Bay is counted as an increase.

Source: See Table Notes and Data Sources Table 2.2.

depends on a variety of factors within the region as well as extra-regional factors. Here we look more closely at the changes in employment in relation to population.

As shown in Table 5.3, total census-measured employment in Northern Ontario peaked around 1991 (at 352,120), the census preceding the 1996 peak census population. Male employment peaked earlier, around 1981 (at 211,280), and female employment peaked later, around 2006 (at 164,465). By contrast, total employment in Southern Ontario grew over all the census periods—both for male and female employment—including the periods that saw Northern employment plateau or decline after the 1990s.

The precipitous decline of male employment has been associated most visibly with closures and downsizing in the resource, primary manufacturing, and transportation industries, which have been male-dominated. In six of eight censuses since 1981, male employment has declined. Female employment was also affected directly and indirectly by declines in those industries, but it tended to increase through the decades with the growth of health, education, and other public sector services, and the growth of retail and other private sector services. However, employment in Northern Ontario service industries now appears to have slowed and turned to decline, so that female employment too has declined, since 2006, though overall less rapidly than male employment. In 2016 the female share of employment in Northern Ontario reached 49.5%, or nearly half of all employment, a somewhat higher share than in Southern Ontario. This situation may have changed between 2016 and 2021 as female employment fell more rapidly than male, reducing the female employment share to 48.0%.

As Table 5.4 reveals, employment peaks and subsequent declines varied by district but, by 2021, all districts (including Kenora and Manitoulin) were below their peak. Employment peaked in some districts within the past 15 years (Greater Sudbury and Kenora), in others a few decades previous, and in one (Timiskaming) by 1951. The table also indicates the male employment peaks for each district,

Table 5.3. Employment by sex in Northern Ontario and Southern Ontario, census dates, 1951–2021.

	1951	1961	1971	1976	1981	1986	1991	1996	2001	2006	2011	2016	2021
Northern Ontario	196,786	233,537	276,810	294,635	336,810	328,915	352,120	336,000	329,480	341,820	331,940	327,085	313,600
Males	167,064	181,951	193,225	193,650	211,280	194,925	196,410	182,065	172,880	177,355	168,350	165,330	163,035
Females	29,722	51,586	83,585	100,985	125,530	133,990	155,710	153,935	156,600	164,465	163,590	161,755	150,570
Females as % of total	15.1	22.1	30.2	34.3	37.3	40.7	44.2	45.8	47.5	48.1	49.3	49.5	48.0
Southern Ontario	1,654,045	2,091,092	2,900,095	3,321,915	3,878,170	4,224,115	4,689,820	4,741,670	5,384,425	5,822,425	5,965,065	6,285,065	6,179,295
Males	1,247,006	1,465,057	1,853,140	2,026,260	2,255,425	2,368,925	2,533,880	2,537,505	2,854,740	3,052,695	3,080,815	3,248,925	3,253,920
Females	407,039	626,035	1,046,955	1,295,655	1,622,745	1,855,190	2,155,940	2,204,165	2,529,685	2,769,730	2,884,250	3,036,140	2,925,370
Females as % of total	24.6	29.9	36.1	39.0	41.8	43.9	46.0	46.5	47.0	47.6	48.4	48.3	47.3
Ontario	1,850,831	2,324,629	3,176,905	3,616,550	4,214,980	4,553,030	5,041,940	5,077,670	5,713,905	6,164,245	6,297,005	6,612,150	6,492,895
Males	1,414,070	1,647,008	2,046,365	2,219,910	2,466,705	2,563,850	2,730,290	2,719,570	3,027,620	3,230,050	3,249,165	3,414,255	3,416,955
Females	436,761	677,621	1,130,540	1,396,640	1,748,275	1,989,180	2,311,650	2,358,100	2,686,285	2,934,195	3,047,840	3,197,895	3,075,940
Females as % of total	23.6	29.1	35.6	38.6	41.5	43.7	45.8	46.4	47.0	47.6	48.4	48.4	47.4
Northern Ontario as % of Ontario employment	10.6	10.0	8.7	8.1	8.0	7.2	7.0	6.6	5.8	5.5	5.3	4.9	4.8

Notes: 15 years and over by labour force activity (20% or 25% sample data). 2011 uses NHS Data. Southern Ontario employment totals are obtained by subtracting Northern Ontario totals from Ontario totals.

Source: See Table Notes and Data Sources Table 5.4.

given the importance of male-dominated resource industries, family structures, and greater male mobility, especially in earlier decades. In general, the peaking of male employment was followed within a decade by the peaking of population, beginning with Timiskaming and Cochrane, then for all districts except Manitoulin and Kenora. The peaking and decline of male and total employment occurred despite the absolute and relative growth of service industries and female employment in all districts. The growth of service industries was not sufficient to compensate for employment losses in other sectors because services growth has been limited by the generally declining or stagnating local and regional economic base conditions and by provincial and federal policies that reinforce hinterland-colonial structures, including austerity such as in cuts to education services.

In general, as population changes more slowly than employment, decreases in employment are expressed in lower *employment–population rates*. This refers to the number of employed people as a percentage of the whole population (or a part of the population such as those of working age); it is typically expressed as a percentage though it can sometimes be expressed as a ratio.[4] These rates, when relatively low or declining, are indicative of reduced employment opportunity, and can lead to net out-migration if employment conditions are more favourable elsewhere in the economy. Similarly, the rate tends to rise in times of employment growth and can lead to in-migration, also depending on conditions elsewhere. Lower employment–population rates can persist for extended periods of time, depending on external employment prospects and both monetary and non-monetary costs associated with out-migration. For hinterland-colonial Northern Ontario, its early phases of colonization were ones of employment growth, characterized generally by male employment–population rates that were higher than or comparable to those of established metropolitan areas in Southern Ontario. But in subsequent decades of employment and local decline, Northern Ontario has come to

Table 5.4. Employment by sex in Northern Ontario districts, with employment peaks, census dates, 1951–2021.

	1951	1961	1971	1976	1981	1986	1991	1996	2001	2006	2011	2016	2021
Algoma District	24,711	36,985	44,175	46,925	60,125	56,020	54,510	50,645	49,655	51,390	49,425	47,130	43,855
Males	20,878	28,913	31,020	31,100	38,430	33,515	30,415	27,220	25,845	26,260	24,600	23,695	22,600
Females	3,833	8,072	13,155	15,825	21,695	22,505	24,095	23,425	23,810	25,130	24,825	23,435	21,255
Females as % of total	15.5	21.8	29.8	33.7	36.1	40.2	44.2	46.3	48.0	48.9	50.2	49.7	48.5
Cochrane District	30,346	29,259	30,525	34,125	39,775	39,390	40,015	39,655	36,930	37,790	36,620	36,275	34,040
Males	26,152	23,478	21,670	22,965	25,680	24,290	22,910	21,955	19,950	20,420	18,895	18,685	18,010
Females	4,194	5,781	8,855	11,160	14,095	15,100	17,105	17,700	16,980	17,370	17,725	17,590	16,030
Females as % of total	13.8	19.8	29.0	32.7	35.4	38.3	42.7	44.6	46.0	46.0	48.4	48.5	47.1
Kenora District	13,214	16,569	18,415	21,485	24,800	23,850	26,385	26,720	27,085	28,590	25,055	26,935	26,715
Males	11,399	13,051	12,850	14,260	15,560	14,325	15,095	14,520	14,435	14,910	12,675	13,620	13,850
Females	1,815	3,518	5,565	7,225	9,240	9,525	11,290	12,200	12,650	13,680	12,380	13,315	12,865
Females as % of total	13.7	21.2	30.2	33.6	37.3	39.9	42.8	45.7	46.7	47.8	49.4	49.4	48.2
Manitoulin District	3,699	3,164	3,525	3,705	3,635	3,755	4,495	4,585	5,140	5,275	5,250	4,930	5,185
Males	3,063	2,403	2,315	2,310	2,280	2,270	2,490	2,420	2,575	2,760	2,475	2,400	2,610
Females	636	761	1,210	1,395	1,355	1,485	2,005	2,165	2,565	2,515	2,775	2,530	2,580
Females as % of total	17.2	24.1	34.3	37.7	37.3	39.5	44.6	47.2	49.9	47.7	52.9	51.3	49.8
Nipissing District	17,070	21,416	26,520	28,920	33,100	33,140	37,180	35,345	36,020	38,390	38,535	35,945	34,765
Males	14,074	16,234	17,760	18,450	20,275	19,615	20,405	18,640	18,790	19,795	19,380	17,770	17,885
Females	2,996	5,182	8,760	10,470	12,825	13,525	16,775	16,705	17,230	18,595	19,155	18,175	16,880
Females as % of total	17.6	24.2	33.0	36.2	38.7	40.8	45.1	47.3	47.8	48.4	49.7	50.6	48.6
Rainy River District	7,615	8,243	9,710	9,820	9,595	9,910	10,175	10,210	9,870	10,075	8,935	8,815	8,345
Males	6,554	6,427	6,700	6,325	5,915	5,875	5,730	5,445	5,265	5,315	4,455	4,355	4,260
Females	1,061	1,816	3,010	3,495	3,680	4,035	4,445	4,765	4,605	4,760	4,480	4,460	4,085
Females as % of total	13.9	22.0	31.0	35.6	38.4	40.7	43.7	46.7	46.7	47.2	50.1	50.6	49.0
Sudbury District	n/a	n/a	n/a	9,510	10,185	9,930	11,330	9,960	9,265	8,890	9,120	9,115	8,880

	1951	1961	1971	1976	1981	1986	1991	1996	2001	2006	2011	2016	2021
Males	n/a	n/a	n/a	6,525	6,765	6,290	6,695	5,780	5,200	4,925	4,790	4,685	4,725
Females	n/a	n/a	n/a	2,985	3,420	3,640	4,635	4,180	4,065	3,965	4,330	4,430	4,155
Females as % of total				31.4	33.6	36.7	40.9	42.0	43.9	44.6	47.5	48.6	46.8
Sudbury RM/Greater Sudbury	39,903	53,668	73,065	62,595	66,820	63,945	75,695	71,470	70,415	75,215	77,135	76,755	75,350
Males	34,461	42,559	53,200	41,940	41,640	36,600	41,495	38,670	36,145	38,790	39,465	38,940	39,345
Females	5,442	11,109	19,865	20,655	25,180	27,345	34,200	32,800	34,270	36,425	37,670	37,815	36,005
Females as % of total	13.6	20.7	27.2	33.0	37.7	42.8	45.2	45.9	48.7	48.4	48.8	49.3	47.8
Timiskaming District	17,749	15,832	15,295	15,565	16,455	16,485	16,350	15,265	14,525	14,765	13,885	14,070	13,230
Males	14,832	12,345	10,405	9,935	10,305	9,810	9,245	8,185	7,670	7,635	7,340	7,360	7,035
Females	2,917	3,487	4,890	5,630	6,150	6,675	7,105	7,080	6,855	7,130	6,545	6,710	6,200
Females as % of total	16.4	22.0	32.0	36.2	37.4	40.5	43.5	46.4	47.2	48.3	47.1	47.7	46.9
Thunder Bay District	42,479	48,401	55,580	61,985	72,320	72,490	75,985	72,145	70,575	71,440	67,980	67,115	63,235
Males	35,651	36,541	37,305	39,840	44,430	42,335	41,930	39,230	37,005	36,545	34,275	33,820	32,715
Females	6,828	11,860	18,275	22,145	27,890	30,155	34,055	32,915	33,570	34,895	33,705	33,295	30,515
Females as % of total	16.1	24.5	32.9	35.7	38.6	41.6	44.8	45.6	47.6	48.8	49.6	49.6	48.3
Employment peaks													
Algoma	M				M, T								
Cochrane							T				F		
Kenora										F, T			
Manitoulin	M				M					T	F		
Nipissing							M				F,T		
Rainy River								F, T					
Sudbury (district)			M				F, T						
Sudbury (RM)			M									F	
Thunder Bay					M		T			F	T		
Timiskaming	M, T									F			

T Total employment peak; M Male employment peak; F Female employment peak

Source: See Table Notes and Data Sources Table 2.2.

experience employment–population rates persistently lower than those in Southern Ontario.

In Table 5.5 we can see that, at the aggregate level for Northern Ontario, the employment–population rates increased from 35.6% in 1971 to an initial peak of 44.8% in 1991, reflecting peak total Northern employment, then to a higher peak of 45.8% in 2006 reflecting not only a -2.9% drop in employment, but also an even larger decline, -4.9%, in population. However, even including the census years with higher or peak employment–population rates, the Northern Ontario levels have been at least 4–5 percentage points below the Ontario average since 1971. Furthermore, there were major disparities within Northern Ontario. In 2016, for example, Northern Ontario's highest employment–population rates were in Greater Sudbury (CD) and Thunder Bay (District) at 47.5% and 46.0% respectively, though these were still below the Ontario average. By contrast, Manitoulin at 37.2%, Kenora at 41.1%, and Algoma at 41.3% had much lower levels than the already low Northern Ontario average of 44.3%. The overall employment to population disparities between Northern and Southern Ontario are of major magnitudes. For 2016 the employment–population ratio for Southern Ontario was 49.4% compared to 44.4% for Northern Ontario. This 5 percentage-point disparity would be equivalent to approximately 37,500 additional jobs or an 11.5% increase above existing employment in Northern Ontario. In the COVID-19 conditions of 2021 that disparity increased to around 6 percentage points.

In general, the loss of employment in a given area leads not only to a negative shift in employment–population rates and reduced employment opportunity, but also to increased unemployment, underemployment, and downward pressures on wages and labour market conditions. This builds push-pressures for out-migration. Insofar as external employment conditions are more favourable, workers, families, and students respond to the pull-pressures of exterior demand by out-migrating. In most cases, the out-migration comes after a workplace closure or other employment decline, although in some

Table 5.5. Employment–population rates (%) in Northern Ontario districts, census dates, 1971–2021.

	1971	1976	1981	1986	1991	1996	2001	2006	2011	2016	2021
Ontario	41.2	43.8	48.9	50.0	50.0	47.2	50.1	50.7	49.0	49.2	48.3
Northern Ontario	35.6	37.5	42.7	42.9	44.8	42.6	44.1	45.8	45.1	44.3	42.2
Algoma District	36.2	38.2	45.0	42.5	42.8	40.4	41.9	43.7	42.7	41.3	38.5
Cochrane District	31.9	35.2	41.1	42.0	42.6	42.5	43.3	45.8	45.1	45.5	43.7
Kenora District	34.6	37.0	41.7	45.1	44.9	42.2	43.8	44.4	43.5	41.1	40.5
Manitoulin District	32.3	34.0	33.0	38.2	40.2	40.2	40.5	40.3	40.2	37.2	37.2
Nipissing District	33.6	35.4	41.2	41.9	43.9	41.7	43.4	45.3	45.5	43.2	41.0
Rainy River District	37.7	39.6	42.1	43.3	44.2	44.1	44.6	46.7	43.9	43.8	42.9
Sudbury District and City	36.9	37.0	41.2	41.4	46.4	43.0	44.7	46.9	47.5	46.9	44.7
Sudbury RM/Greater Sudbury	n/a	37.3	41.8	41.9	47.0	43.6	45.3	47.6	48.1	47.5	45.4
Sudbury District	36.9	34.9	37.6	38.5	43.3	39.1	40.4	41.6	43.0	42.3	39.7
Thunder Bay District	38.2	41.1	47.0	46.6	47.8	45.8	46.8	47.9	46.5	46.0	43.1
Timiskaming District	32.9	35.6	39.8	40.9	41.9	40.4	42.2	44.4	42.5	43.6	42.1

Notes: Sudbury District and City comprises the Sudbury District/CD and, after 1971, the Sudbury Regional Municipality/Greater Sudbury CD.
Source: See Table Notes and Data Sources Tables 2.2 and 5.4.

cases out-migration starts earlier in anticipation of better opportunities elsewhere relative to anticipated employment losses or poorer opportunities locally. At the level of the whole economy, when macroeconomic conditions have higher average employment levels and lower unemployment levels, out-migration increases away from lower-prospect and poorer areas. But if average macroeconomic conditions in the whole economy have generally low employment and higher unemployment levels, then unemployment levels are typically even higher in already high-unemployment regions like Northern Ontario.

Table 5.6 presents the evolution in census-measured unemployment in Northern Ontario since 1951. In general, and especially in areas with higher levels of unemployment, official unemployment counts and rates are less reliable than employment counts and rates as indicators of labour market conditions.[5] Given the conditions of Northern Ontario, the unemployed-employed rate (or unemployed rate) is preferred here as a more direct indicator of the downward pressures that unemployment exerts on wages and labour conditions.[6]

As a whole for Northern Ontario, the numbers of unemployed and the unemployed rate tended to increase from 1951 to at least 1996. Further, the unemployed rate for Northern Ontario was above the average for Ontario for both males and females, and for all censuses except 2011 and 2021. It appears that as the female share of total employment increased, so did the female share of unemployment, and at a faster rate in the early census periods. In some census years, such as 1971 to 1986, the female unemployed–employed rate exceeded that for males. In 1981 not only the rate but the numbers of unemployed were higher for women in Northern Ontario, and particularly in the Algoma, Manitoulin, and Thunder Bay districts, and the Sudbury Regional Municipality. The numbers and rate of unemployed in Northern Ontario reached a peak in the 1996 census, then declined to 2006, but they both started to climb again until 2021, all the while at much higher levels than in the post-1945 boom decades.

In general, lower employment–population rates are also associated with higher levels of part-time work or underemployment. Table 5.7 provides data on full-time and part-time employment by sex from 1981 to 2021. The employment data in Table 5.7 are reported for the entire pre-census calendar year, and generally "full time" is defined as both full-year and full-time (30 hours per week or more).[7] This means that the employment totals, especially for part-time employment (fewer than 30 hours per week), will tend to be higher than counts based on a single week or similar shorter reference period at census dates. Hence, the employment totals in these data are not comparable with employment totals in earlier tables in this book. As well, the 1981 definition of full time is less consistent than those from 1986 to 2021. This means that the data are most useful for comparisons across different geographies in the same census or somewhat shorter period, such as from 1986 to 2021.

Overall, Northern Ontario has had a decline in full-time employment and increase in part-time employment over the period, particularly for males. This also appears as the general pattern for Ontario, though Northern Ontario had generally lower levels of full-time employment. The 2021 census reported that part-time employment was at 44.6% of all employment for Ontario compared to 45.9% for Northern Ontario; similarly, for Ontario, 40.3% of employed males had part-time jobs, compared to 44.0% in Northern Ontario. For females in Northern Ontario there likely were absolute increases in full-time employment during some decades such as in the 1980s, but in all census years except 2021 the percentage of full-time female employment was below the average for Ontario. However, in 2021, compared to the Ontario average, employed females in Northern Ontario had a slightly higher level of full-time employment (52.0% versus 50.9%) and slightly lower level of part-time employment (49.0% versus 49.1%).

As noted earlier, employment conditions or opportunities are most directly indicated by the employment–population rate. In Statistics Canada's labour force statistics this has come to be called

Table 5.6. Unemployment and unemployed rates by sex in Ontario, Northern Ontario, and Northern districts, census dates, 1951–2021.

	1951	1961	1971	1976	1981	1986	1991	1996	2001	2006	2011	2016	2021
Ontario	19,395	80,183	233,920	239,680	249,060	337,090	469,305	509,305	372,915	423,330	567,985	529,525	906,310
Males	14,282	60,384	131,635	120,860	119,040	163,025	257,120	258,150	187,375	207,620	292,865	275,370	430,365
Females	5,113	19,799	102,285	118,820	130,020	174,065	212,185	251,155	185,540	215,710	275,120	254,160	475,940
Female % of unemployed	26.4	24.7	43.7	49.6	52.2	51.6	45.2	49.3	49.8	51.0	48.4	48.0	52.5
Unemployed–employed rate (%)													
All	1.0	3.4	7.4	6.6	5.9	7.4	9.3	10.0	6.5	6.9	9.0	8.0	14.0
Males	1.0	3.7	6.4	5.4	4.8	6.4	9.4	9.5	6.2	6.4	9.0	8.1	12.6
Females	1.2	2.9	9.0	8.5	7.4	8.8	9.2	10.7	6.9	7.4	9.0	7.9	15.5
Northern Ontario	2,689	11,724	23,215	24,325	26,480	33,570	38,970	46,185	36,275	31,495	33,810	33,565	37,150
Males	2,134	9,694	14,365	13,615	12,830	18,935	22,525	25,875	21,495	17,520	19,450	20,615	19,125
Females	555	2,030	8,850	10,710	13,650	14,635	16,445	20,310	14,780	13,975	14,360	12,950	18,025
Female % of unemployed	20.6	17.3	38.1	44.0	51.5	43.6	42.2	44.0	40.7	44.4	42.5	38.6	48.5
Unemployed–employed rate (%)													
All	1.4	5.0	8.4	8.3	7.9	10.2	11.1	13.7	11.0	9.2	10.2	10.3	11.8
Males	1.3	5.3	7.4	7.0	6.1	9.7	11.5	14.2	12.4	9.9	11.6	12.5	11.7
Females	1.9	3.9	10.6	10.6	10.9	10.9	10.6	13.2	9.4	8.5	8.8	8.0	12.0
Algoma District	258	1,924	3,930	4,050	4,165	7,975	7,045	7,800	5,700	4,990	6,095	5,510	6,475
Males	178	1,573	2,385	2,145	1,560	4,720	3,995	4,225	3,160	2,730	3,570	3,355	3,370
Females	80	351	1,545	1,905	2,605	3,255	3,050	3,575	2,540	2,260	2,525	2,155	3,105
Female % of unemployed	31.0	18.2	39.3	47.0	62.5	40.8	43.3	45.8	44.6	45.3	41.4	39.1	48.0

	1951	1961	1971	1976	1981	1986	1991	1996	2001	2006	2011	2016	2021
Cochrane District	509	2,199	3,425	3,010	3,230	4,895	5,505	5,195	4,785	3,580	3,360	3,580	3,430
Males	418	1,896	2,255	1,800	1,730	2,745	3,365	3,125	3,070	2,025	2,100	2,320	1,740
Females	91	303	1,170	1,210	1,500	2,150	2,140	2,070	1,715	1,555	1,260	1,260	1,695
Female % of unemployed	17.9	13.8	34.2	40.2	46.4	43.9	38.9	39.8	35.8	43.4	37.5	35.2	49.4
Kenora District	125	576	1,215	1,505	1,300	2,510	2,415	3,630	3,365	2,740	2,860	3,550	2,530
Males	110	467	790	820	670	1,475	1,470	2,185	2,075	1,600	1,740	2,170	1,450
Females	15	109	425	685	630	1,035	945	1,445	1,290	1,140	1,120	1,380	1,080
Female % of unemployed	12.0	18.9	35.0	45.5	48.5	41.2	39.1	39.8	38.3	41.6	39.2	38.9	42.7
Manitoulin District	31	76	185	255	395	420	450	690	610	620	790	760	650
Males	26	60	125	155	185	200	265	410	335	305	480	490	355
Females	5	16	60	100	210	220	185	280	275	315	310	270	295
Female % of unemployed	16.1	21.1	32.4	39.2	53.2	52.4	41.1	40.6	45.1	50.8	39.2	35.5	45.4
Nipissing District	290	908	2,510	2,925	3,235	4,295	4,030	4,820	3,610	3,485	4,005	3,940	4,640
Males	209	757	1,525	1,655	1,670	2,180	2,200	2,675	2,010	1,785	2,240	2,430	2,355
Females	81	151	985	1,270	1,565	2,115	1,830	2,145	1,600	1,700	1,765	1,510	2,285
Female % of unemployed	27.9	16.6	39.2	43.4	48.4	49.2	45.4	44.5	44.3	48.8	44.1	38.3	49.2
Rainy River District	111	369	645	580	715	1,235	1,115	1,250	1,045	860	880	885	840
Males	92	314	380	365	380	745	660	755	600	500	510	545	480
Females	19	55	265	215	335	490	455	495	445	360	370	340	360
Female % of unemployed	17.1	14.9	41.1	37.1	46.9	39.7	40.8	39.6	42.6	41.9	42.0	38.4	42.9

(cont)

Table 5.6. Unemployment and unemployed rates by sex in Ontario, Northern Ontario, and Northern districts, census dates, 1951–2021.

	1951	1961	1971	1976	1981	1986	1991	1996	2001	2006	2011	2016	2021
Sudbury District	492	2,069	4,880	730	1,000	1,575	1,395	1,725	1,325	1,170	995	1,005	975
Males	400	1,613	2,705	425	565	825	860	980	820	635	555	615	500
Females	92	456	2,175	305	435	750	535	745	505	535	440	390	475
Female % of unemployed	18.7	22.0	44.6	41.8	43.5	47.6	38.4	43.2	38.1	45.7	44.2	38.8	48.7
Sudbury RM/Greater Sud.	n/a	n/a	n/a	4,960	5,965	660	7,115	9,840	7,090	6,400	6,545	6,990	8,710
Males	n/a	n/a	n/a	2,545	2,855	335	3,690	5,030	3,960	3,355	3,500	4,125	4,275
Females	n/a	n/a	n/a	2,415	3,110	325	3,425	4,810	3,130	3,045	3,045	2,865	4,435
Female % of unemployed	n/a	n/a	n/a	48.7	52.1	49.2	48.1	48.9	44.1	47.6	46.5	41.0	50.9
Thunder Bay District	686	2,772	4,885	4,545	5,195	8,105	7,935	8,980	7,145	6,335	6,635	6,020	7,695
Males	551	2,290	3,210	2,610	2,535	4,680	4,865	5,110	4,535	3,830	3,825	3,730	3,945
Females	135	482	1,675	1,935	2,660	3,425	3,070	3,870	2,610	2,505	2,810	2,290	3,750
Female % of unemployed	19.7	17.4	34.3	42.6	51.2	42.3	38.7	43.1	36.5	39.5	42.4	38.0	48.7
Timiskaming District	187	831	1,540	1,765	1,280	1,900	1,965	2,255	1,600	1,315	1,645	1,325	1,205
Males	150	724	990	1,095	680	1,030	1,155	1,380	930	755	930	835	655
Females	37	107	550	670	600	870	810	875	670	560	715	490	545
Female % of unemployed	19.8	12.9	35.7	38.0	46.9	45.8	41.2	38.8	41.9	42.6	43.5	37.0	45.2

Source: See Table Notes and Data Sources.

the *employment rate*.[8] This official approach takes as population the "working-age population," defined in recent decades as the population 15 years of age and over (including those 65 years of age and older). But there are at least three distinct ways to calculate employment rates depending on whether the population denominator is the total population, the working-age population (in Statistics Canada's terms), or a retirement-age-adjusted population such as 15–64 that excludes persons 65 years of age and over. These are compared in Table 5.8. From the table, it can be seen that the unemployment rate gap for the Northern economic regions is about two percentage points higher than the level for Ontario as a whole. However, for the official employment rates the Northern Ontario gaps are at least twice that for the unemployment measures.

It would go beyond the scope of the present volume to discuss in detail the various types of dependency ratios and their characteristics. But it is important to note that *economic* dependency ratios are a more realistic economic measure of the social burden of dependency than are demographic dependency measures. The crucial problem for policy with demographic dependency measures, especially in current conditions, is that they ignore productivity and employment conditions. Notably overlooked is the fact that higher employment can support larger numbers of persons than is claimed by demographic dependency ratios.[9] In fact, there is no special significance to a demographic dependency ratio of 1, as claimed by Cirtwill (2015); the situation depends on productivity and employment conditions.

The key element to note about demographic dependency ratios is that they are formulated as a ratio or fraction of the population considered dependent *by age*, usually older persons (65+) and children (0–14), while those aged 15–64 are deemed non-dependent or "(self-) supporting." In this case, the demographic dependency ratio is: [Pop (0–14) + Pop (65+)] / Pop (15–64). The signal problem with this ratio (or similar ones with variations in the age categories) is that it does not incorporate employment conditions, which for most of the population

Table 5.7. Full-time and part-time employment by sex in Northern Ontario and Ontario, 1981–2021.

	1981	1986	1991	1996	2001	2006	2011	2016	2021
Ontario total employment	4,676,635	4,941,970	5,548,265	5,497,945	6,165,120	6,529,845	6,478,095	7,342,210	6,977,855
full-time males	2,376,515	1,729,845	1,876,160	1,794,665	2,061,355	2,116,730	2,879,620	2,148,635	2,145,810
part-time males	295,675	1,009,150	1,110,315	1,131,880	1,180,590	1,274,490	476,030	1,632,645	1,451,440
full-time females	1,377,910	984,915	1,258,300	1,221,455	1,465,690	1,573,940	2,288,835	1,688,935	1,719,885
part-time females	626,535	1,218,060	1,303,490	1,349,945	1,457,485	1,564,685	833,610	1,871,995	1,660,720
All employment (%)									
full-time % of total	80.3	54.9	56.5	54.9	57.2	56.5	79.8	52.3	55.4
part-time % of total	19.7	45.1	43.5	45.1	42.8	43.5	20.2	47.7	44.6
male employment (%)									
full-time males	88.9	63.2	62.8	61.3	63.6	62.4	85.8	56.8	59.7
part-time males	11.1	36.8	37.2	38.7	36.4	37.6	14.2	43.2	40.3
female employment (%)									
full-time females	68.7	44.7	49.1	47.5	50.1	50.1	73.3	47.4	50.9
part-time females	31.3	55.3	50.9	52.5	49.9	49.9	26.7	52.6	49.1

	1981	1986	1991	1996	2001	2006	2011	2016	2021
Northern Ontario total	385,920	370,380	394,820	379,670	369,540	366,640	346,445	380,405	394,395
full-time males	210,355	121,360	120,635	115,545	110,050	113,255	151,685	103,625	113,935
part-time males	24,390	94,540	98,820	90,330	85,870	82,070	26,065	92,745	89,365
full-time females	95,040	54,440	70,120	70,355	75,515	84,005	118,570	84,600	99,280
part-time females	56,135	100,040	105,245	103,440	98,105	87,310	50,125	99,435	91,815
All employment (%)									
full-time % of total	79.1	47.5	48.3	49.0	50.2	53.8	78.0	49.5	54.1
part-time % of total	20.9	52.5	51.7	51.0	49.8	46.2	22.0	50.5	45.9
male employment (%)									
full-time males	89.6	56.2	55.0	56.1	56.2	58.0	85.3	52.8	56.0
part-time males	10.4	43.8	45.0	43.9	43.8	42.0	14.7	47.2	44.0
female employment (%)									
full-time females	62.9	35.2	40.0	40.5	43.5	49.0	70.3	46.0	52.0
part-time females	37.1	64.8	60.0	59.5	56.5	51.0	29.7	54.0	48.0

Notes: Data for 2011 are from the NHS and less consistent with that from other years.
Source: See Table Notes and Data Sources.

are the basis of being economically self-supporting or supporting of others—that is, being non-dependent. In economic dependency ratios, particularly based on employment, the ratios directly reflect employment (and unemployment) conditions in the population, in its simplest terms: Pop_{total}/Emp_{total}. Economic dependency ratios can be varied for purposes of comparison, such as with official labour force participation rates or employment rates, which are based on only the working-age population (15+). These latter together with the total population/employment dependency ratio are used in Table 5.8.[10]

This discussion is not to say that social dependency *per se* in Northern Ontario is not an issue to address. On the contrary, Table 5.8 shows that when employment is taken into consideration, the economic dependency ratios are higher in Northern Ontario relative to Ontario than are demographic dependency ratios. For total population, the Northeast and Northwest economic dependency ratios are 2.26 and 2.25, respectively, while Ontario as a whole is at 2.03.[11] By contrast, the working-age demographic dependency ratios are 1.56 and 1.54 compared to Ontario at 1.50. This emphasizes that the real root of dependency issues in Northern Ontario today (and since at least the 1970s) has been employment and labour conditions. The latter include not only wages but also such crucial conditions as health and safety, which have long been known to have major effects on economic dependency and the transfer payments system (Leadbeater 1999, 1997).

Table 5.8. Official labour force indicators and dependency ratios, Ontario and Northern Ontario, 2016.

	Ontario		Northeast Ontario		Northwest Ontario	
	popula-tion	% total	popula-tion	% total	popula-tion	% total
Total population	13,448,495	100	548,450	100	231,695	100
pop ages 0–14	2,207,970	16.4	82,355	15.0	39,820	17.2
pop ages 15–64	8,988,865	66.8	352,495	64.3	150,405	64.9
pop ages 15–19	811,670	6.0	30,070	5.5	13,990	6.0

	Ontario		Northeast Ontario		Northwest Ontario	
	popula-tion	% total	popula-tion	% total	popula-tion	% total
pop ages 20–64	8,177,195	60.8	322,425	58.8	136,415	58.9
pop ages 65+	2,251,655	16.7	113,600	20.7	41,465	17.9
pop ages 0–14 and 65+	4,459,625	33.2	195,955	35.7	81,285	35.1
pop ages 15+ ("working age")	11,038,440	82.1	456,165	83.2	187,740	81.0
average age	41.0		43.8		41.5	
median age	41.3		46.3		42.6	
Official labour force						
labour force (= E + U)	7,141,675	53.1	267,400	48.8	113,320	48.9
Employed	6,612,150	49.2	242,415	44.2	102,865	44.4
Unemployed	529,525	3.9	24,985	4.6	10,455	4.5
participation rate (LF% pop 15+)	64.7		58.6		60.4	
employment rate (E% pop 15+)	59.9		53.1		54.8	
unemployment rate (U% LF)	7.4		9.3		9.2	
Employment–population rates (%)						
E-pop ratio/total	49.2		44.2		44.4	
E-pop ratio/15+ ("working age")	59.9		53.1		54.8	
E-pop ratio/15–64	73.6		68.8		68.4	
E-pop ratio/20–64	80.9		75.2		75.4	
Dependency ratios						
demographic DRs						
pop total/pop 15–64	1.50		1.56		1.54	
pop total/pop 20–64	1.64		1.70		1.70	
economic DRs						
participation rate reciprocal	1.55		1.71		1.66	
employment rate reciprocal	1.67		1.88		1.83	
pop total/employed	2.03		2.26		2.25	

Notes: Northeast and Northwest are Statistics Canada's economic regions. The Northeast economic region includes the Parry Sound District. The numbers for the populations 15+ or of "working age" are those consistent with Statistics Canada's labour force definition, that is, the civilian, non-institutional, and non-Reserve population (as discussed earlier); hence, the working-age numbers are smaller than a full population count obtained by, say, subtracting the census population 0–14 from the total census population of all ages.

Source: See Table Notes and Data Sources Tables 2.2 and 5.4 for 2016.

NOTES

1. The southern-bordering districts of Muskoka and Parry Sound have also had long-term increases, though relatively less than for Southern Ontario and in different economic conditions.

2. The pattern of population decline or stagnation in most districts is also consistent with Statistics Canada's annual population estimates (Table 17-10-0039-01), though the specific peak years differ from the census dates and are limited by the coverage of the Annual Estimates to the period since 1986 only. For this period since 1986, district populations reached peaks during the 1980s in Algoma (1986), Cochrane (1986), and Timiskaming (1986), during the 1990s in Sudbury District (1992), Thunder Bay (1992), Regional Municipality of Sudbury (1993), Nipissing (1993), Kenora (1996), Rainy River (1995), and during the 2000s in Manitoulin (2007). The annual data indicate a peak District of Manitoulin population at 13,410 in 2007 while in 2018 it is 13,255. For more population data on Sudbury and District, see also Leadbeater (2008, table 1).

3. The employment data include full-time as well as part-time employment and self-employment.

4. The numbers of employed here include part-time as well as full-time employed though it is possible to formulate employment rates exclusively for full-time employment. Employment-to-population rates differ from labour force participation rates because the labour force includes both the employed as well as the unemployed.

5. As is well known, the official counts of the unemployed are affected by the job-search criterion, which itself is affected by employment conditions. Hence, there is generally less measured search effort in areas with already low employment rates and high unemployment rates. This phenomenon is recognized patronizingly as the "discouraged worker effect." As well, the social stigma of being unemployed leads to responses like "retired" though, if jobs were available, such non-labour force responses could evaporate into "employed." Another issue is that while the numerator of the unemployment rate represents fully unemployed persons, the denominator includes partially employed persons. Arguably, at least a portion of partially employed persons could be considered partially unemployed. Statistics Canada is aware of such issues and, in the past, has produced an "alternative" range of measures of unemployment that are much less publicized, though they can be helpful in illustrating the arbitrary character of the official or "headline" measure as the primary indicator of measured labour market conditions (Devereaux 1992). This is especially the case in areas like Northern Ontario, with its generally lower employment levels.

6. The official measure of unemployment uses the labour force as denominator (LF = E + U) so the unemployment percentage is lower than the unemployed–employed rate (unless U = 0) despite the nature of labour market competition, which relates to the numbers of unemployed relative to the numbers of jobs.

7. See Table Notes and Data Sources for Table 5.7. The Harper Conservative government's elimination of the 2011 Census's mandatory long form and its replacement by data from the National Household Survey (NHS) weakened the consistency of the 2011 census data, particularly for smaller geographies.

8. For this purpose, we take employment as including all levels of employment without adjusting for less than full-time or full-year employment. Such an adjustment would reduce employment–population rates and increase any corresponding economic-dependency rates.

9. From this perspective, GDP/pop = GDP/E × E/pop; hence, per capita GDP is a function of (labour) productivity (GDP/E) and the employment rate (E/pop), as discussed here. Patterns in agriculture illustrate the importance of productivity in assessing claims about demographic dependency. In 1881 nearly half the working population of Canada was in agriculture, by 1941 about one-quarter, and by 1971 about 6% (Statistics Canada 1983, series D1). Yet, the far larger population of Canada was generally fed, and wheat and other agricultural products were widely exported. Currently, agriculture accounts for less than 2% of the labour force.

10. Economic dependency ratios can also take other forms, such as transfer-dependency ratios, which when used with critical attention can be valuable in the analysis of hinterland-colonial conditions (Leadbeater 1999, 1997).

11. Demographic or age dependency ratios are typically expressed as ratios, such as used by the Northern Policy Institute (Cirtwill 2015). Such ratios can also be expressed as percentages. For example, a dependency ratio of 1.2:1 or simply 1.2 can be multiplied by 100 so that the dependency ratio is expressed as 120%. An alternative way of measuring dependency, particularly for economic dependency, takes into account that the non-dependent population itself also has to consume from total production or, in other terms, the non-dependent population supports both itself and the dependent population. In the example of the 1.2:1 ratio, the dependents are 54.5% of the population [1.2 /(1.2+1) *100] and the non-dependents are 45.5%. However, in the alternative approach the ratio is 2.2:1 or simply 2.2 or 220%. This alternative approach also has the advantage that the ratio can be obtained as the reciprocal of employment rates. In this example, if the employment rate is 45.5% then the economic dependency ratio is 1/.455 or 2.2.

CHAPTER 6

URBAN CONCENTRATION OF POPULATION AND EMPLOYMENT CONDITIONS

The overall decline of population and employment in Northern Ontario has affected communities of all sizes, their relationships with each other, and municipal government policy. Here we discuss key trends in urban population concentration and urban employment conditions. In mainstream economics, urbanization is often seen as indicating economic growth, with higher levels of urban concentration being associated with more efficiencies and higher levels of income. This idea has been deployed many times in Northern Ontario, not least in supporting the provincially forced urban amalgamation waves of the early 1970s and the late 1990s. It is also heard more recently in policy initiatives for hub cities, public services centralization, and urban clustering, such as in the provincial government's *Growth Plan for Northern Ontario* (2011) or work by Conteh (2017) for the Northern Policy Institute.

Urban concentration has reached a level today where over 80% of the population in Canada and 85% of people in Ontario live in urban areas (Statistics Canada 2012).[1] More than simply urbanization, the population shift from rural to urban areas, a process of *metropolitanization* has resulted in a few of the largest urban centres growing even more rapidly than the rural to urban shift. As of 2016 the Toronto census metropolitan area (CMA) alone has about 44% of the population of Ontario and three CMAs in Canada (Toronto, Montreal, and Vancouver) have over 35% of the country's population. Meanwhile, many rural and small urban areas decline in population. Northern Ontario has much less urban concentration of population than Southern Ontario. According to the 2016 census, urbanization in Northern Ontario is at 63.0%, compared to 87.6% in Southern Ontario (Statistics Canada 2017). In terms of metropolitanization, Northern Ontario has two CMAs (Greater Sudbury and Thunder Bay), making up 36.7% of the Northern Ontario population, while Southern Ontario has 14 CMAs, making up 84.2% of the Southern Ontario population.

At the outset we observe that most cities and towns in Northern Ontario have been facing population declines, like the region as a whole. This differs from the view sometimes heard that cities or large urban communities in Northern Ontario have not been affected by decline compared to rural and small-town areas, due mainly to people moving from rural and small-town areas into cities. As Table 6.1 shows, all nine cities in Northern Ontario have had overall declines in population during the period 1971 to 2021. Each city's population in the Table has been estimated to include preceding communities brought in by amalgamations (forced or otherwise), to be as consistent as much as possible with the 2021 definition of the city. From 1971 to 2021 the overall population decline for cities was about -2.2%, compared to -4.4% for the entire region of Northern Ontario. From the cities' collective population peak of 1996 to 2021, the cities' decline was -4.9% compared to -5.6% for Northern Ontario. The increase in the concentration of population in cities was only from about 63.7% in 1971 to a peak of 66.2% in the 2011, then back to 65.2% in 2021. What is not often appreciated is that the post-1996 declines in most cities (Sault Ste. Marie, Timmins, Kenora, Elliot Lake, Temiskaming Shores, and Dryden) were actually *larger* than the declines in Northern Ontario as a whole.

Table 6.2 considers employment and unemployment in Northern Ontario cities relative to Ontario as a whole, as reported in the 2016 census. Given the previous chapter's discussion, it is not surprising to see that Northern Ontario, relative to its working-age population, has a lower share of Ontario's jobs for both males and females. For males in Northern Ontario, employment was only 5.1% of Ontario employment relative to the male working-age population share, which was 5.9%; for females in Northern Ontario, it was 5.4% of Ontario employment relative to the female working-age population share of 5.7%. The disparity was expressed too in official measures of unemployment, particularly for male workers. Males in Northern Ontario have a much higher share of the province's unemployment (7.9% of the unemployed compared to 5.9% of the working-age population). For females in Northern Ontario, the unemployment share was only 5.4% of Ontario's unemployed compared to their 5.7% of the working-age population. This pattern, especially the lower share of employment, is also evident for Northern Ontario cities: relative to the size of their working-age population in Ontario (3.9% for males and females), the cities have only 3.5% of employment for males and only 3.7% for females. In terms of unemployment, the Northern cities' share of unemployment in Ontario is proportionately higher for men (4.8%) but lower for women (3.5%).

Table 6.1. Northern Ontario city populations and changes, census dates, 1971–2021.

Census dates	Greater Sudbury (CD)	Thunder Bay (CY/CSD)	Sault Ste. Marie (CY/CSD)	North Bay (CY/CSD)	Timmins (CY/CSD)	Kenora (CY/CSD)	Elliot Lake (CY/CSD)	Temiskaming Shores (CY/CSD)	Dryden (CY/CSD)	Cities total population	Northern Ontario population	Cities as % of Northern Ontario
2021	166,128	108,843	72,051	52,662	41,145	14,967	11,372	9,634	7,388	484,190	742,610	65.2
2016	161,647	107,909	73,368	51,553	41,788	15,096	10,741	9,920	7,749	479,771	737,316	65.1
2011	160,376	108,359	75,141	53,651	43,165	15,348	11,348	10,400	7,617	485,405	733,016	66.2
2006	157,909	109,140	74,948	53,966	42,997	15,177	11,549	10,732	8,185	484,603	745,372	65.0
2001	155,268	109,016	74,566	52,771	43,686	15,838	11,956	10,630	8,198	481,929	746,778	64.5
1996	164,049	113,662	80,054	54,332	47,499	16,365	13,588	11,257	8,289	509,095	786,370	64.9
1991	161,210	113,946	81,476	55,405	47,461	15,910	14,089	11,663	7,963	509,123	784,027	64.9
1986	152,476	112,272	80,905	50,623	46,657	15,292	17,984	11,281	7,775	495,265	764,312	64.8
1981	159,779	112,486	82,697	51,268	46,114	15,351	16,723	11,630	7,799	503,847	786,048	64.1
1976	167,705	111,476	81,048	51,639	44,747	15,936	8,849	11,583	7,934	500,917	784,487	63.9
1971	169,048	108,411	80,332	49,187	42,974	16,165	9,093	11,778	7,932	494,920	776,505	63.7
Change (persons)												
1971–2021	-2,920	432	-8,281	3,475	-1,829	-1,198	2,279	-2,144	-544	-10,730	-33,895	
1971–1996	-4,999	5,251	-278	5,145	4,525	200	4,495	-521	357	14,175	9,865	
1996–2021	-2,079	-4,819	-8,003	-1,670	-6,354	-1,398	-2,216	-1,623	-901	-24,905	-43,760	

Census dates	Greater Sudbury (CD)	Thunder Bay (CY/CSD)	Sault Ste. Marie (CY/CSD)	North Bay (CY/CSD)	Timmins (CY/CSD)	Kenora (CY/CSD)	Elliot Lake (CY/CSD)	Temiskaming Shores (CY/CSD)	Dryden (CY/CSD)	Cities total population	Northern Ontario population	Cities as % of Northern Ontario
Change (%)												
1971-2021	-1.7	0.4	-10.3	7.1	-4.3	-7.4	25.1	-18.2	-6.9	-2.2	-4.4	
1971-1996	-3.0	4.8	-0.3	10.5	10.5	1.2	49.4	-4.4	4.5	3.1	1.3	
1996-2021	1.3	-4.2	-10.0	-3.1	-13.4	-8.5	-16.3	-14.4	-10.9	-4.9	-5.6	
5-year change (%)												
2016-21	2.8	0.9	-1.8	2.2	-1.5	-0.9	5.9	-2.9	-4.7	0.9	0.7	
2011-16	0.8	-0.4	-2.4	-3.9	-3.2	-1.6	-5.3	-4.6	1.7	-1.2	0.6	
2006-11	1.6	-0.7	0.3	-0.6	0.4	1.1	-1.7	-3.1	-6.9	0.2	-1.7	
2001-06	1.7	0.1	0.5	2.3	-1.6	-4.2	-3.4	1.0	-0.2	0.6	-0.2	
1996-01	-5.4	-4.1	-6.9	-2.9	-8.0	-3.2	-12.0	-5.6	-1.1	-5.3	-5.0	
1991-96	-1.8	-0.2	-1.7	-1.9	0.1	2.9	-3.6	-3.5	4.1	0.0	0.3	
1986-91	5.7	1.5	0.7	9.4	1.7	4.0	-21.7	3.4	2.4	2.8	2.6	
1981-86	-4.6	-0.2	-2.2	-1.3	1.2	-0.4	7.5	-3.0	-0.3	-1.7	-2.8	
1976-81	-4.7	0.9	2.0	-0.7	3.1	-3.7	89.0	0.4	-1.7	0.6	0.2	
1971-76	-0.8	2.8	0.9	5.0	4.1	-1.4	-2.7	-1.7	0.0	1.2	1.0	

Sources: See Table Notes and Data Sources.

Table 6.2. City employment and unemployment by sex in Northern Ontario, 2016.

	Working-age population (15 years +)				Employed				Unemployed			
	Count		% in Ontario		Count		% in Ontario		Count		% in Ontario	
Ontario	M	F	M	F	M	F	M	F	M	F	M	F
Ontario	5,342,755	5,695,680	100	100	3,414,255	3,197,895	100	100	275,370	254,160	100	100
Toronto CMA	2,345,190	2,533,900	43.9	44.5	1,546,745	1,438,250	45.3	45.0	123,290	126,070	44.8	49.6
Toronto C	1,092,655	1,202,135	20.5	21.1	697,365	664,010	20.4	20.8	60,785	61,520	22.1	24.2
Ottawa CMA (ON)	390,260	417,360	7.3	7.3	257,430	249,565	7.5	7.8	20,530	18,115	7.5	7.1
Northern Ontario	316,590	327,320	5.9	5.7	174,805	170,475	5.1	5.3	21,740	13,700	7.9	5.4
Northeast ER	223,750	232,420	4.2	4.1	123,010	119,400	3.6	3.7	15,295	9,685	5.6	3.8
Northwest ER	92,840	94,900	1.7	1.7	51,795	51,075	1.5	1.6	6,445	4,015	2.3	1.6
Northern Ontario	Count		% in Northern Ontario		Count		% in Northern Ontario		Count		% in Northern Ontario	
Sudbury CMA	65,020	68,620	20.5	21.0	38,915	37,790	22.3	22.2	4,120	2,860	19.0	20.9
Thunder Bay CMA	49,450	51,690	15.6	15.8	28,585	28,365	16.4	16.6	2,905	1,840	13.4	13.4
Sault Ste. Marie CA	31,485	33,905	9.9	10.4	16,720	17,010	9.6	10.0	2,350	1,530	10.8	11.2

	Working-age population (15 years +)				Employed				Unemployed			
	M	F	M	F	M	F	M	F	M	F	M	F
North Bay CA	28,185	30,035	8.9	9.2	15,730	16,060	9.0	9.4	1,855	1,325	8.5	9.7
Timmins CA	16,810	17,295	5.3	5.3	10,570	9,955	6.0	5.8	1,070	660	4.9	4.8
Kenora CA	6,040	6,335	1.9	1.9	3,655	3,860	2.1	2.3	355	215	1.6	1.6
Elliot Lake CA	4,530	4,940	1.4	1.5	1,525	1,575	0.9	0.9	270	125	1.2	0.9
Temiskaming Shores CSD/C	3,845	4,325	1.2	1.3	2,230	2,285	1.3	1.3	225	155	1.0	1.1
Dryden CSD/C	3,075	3,345	1.0	1.0	1,890	1,775	1.1	1.0	180	130	0.8	0.9
Northern Ontario cities	208,440	220,490	65.8	67.4	119,820	118,675	68.5	69.6	13,330	8,840	61.3	64.5
% of Ontario	3.9	3.9			3.5	3.7			4.8	3.5		
Northern Ontario not cities	108,150	106,830	34.2	32.6	54,985	51,800	31.5	30.4	8,410	4,860	38.7	35.5
% of Ontario	2.0	1.9			1.6	1.6			3.1	1.9		

Source: See Table Notes and Data Sources Tables 2.2, 5.4, 5.6 and 6.1 for 2016.

Within Northern Ontario, the nine cities had about two-thirds of the working-age population, more than two-thirds of the jobs, and less than two-thirds of the unemployment. This too has a gendered aspect: the cities' share of employment within Northern Ontario was disproportionately higher for males (68.5% relative to the working-age population of 65.8) than for females (69.6% relative to 67.4%). As well, the cities' share of unemployment within Northern Ontario was disproportionately lower for males (61.3% relative to the working-age population of 65.8%) than for females (64.5% relative to 67.4%). While these averages are close to the situation for some individual cities, there also exist substantial differences in city conditions. Sudbury, Thunder Bay, Timmins, North Bay, and Kenora all had higher shares of employment relative to their working-age populations. However, Sault Ste. Marie and Elliot Lake both have lower shares of employment. Temiskaming Shores and Dryden were mixed, with slightly higher shares for males and proportionate shares for females. In terms of unemployment, most cities had lower shares of unemployment than the north as a whole for both males and females; the exceptions were Sault Ste. Marie, with higher unemployment shares for both males and females, and North Bay, with a higher unemployment share for females.

In examining city incomes and economic dependency, it becomes clearer that focusing on urban concentration or agglomeration is less than helpful in understanding the variety of urban conditions (Table 6.3). In general, the loss of full-year, full-time (FYFT) jobs, particularly in the higher-paid primary sector and related manufacturing jobs, leads to a decline in other FYFT jobs, an increase in unemployment, more part-time work, and increased transfer use. This can be seen in higher gaps between the median incomes for all earners (which includes part-year and part-time employment) and higher levels of transfers, as well as higher/lower transfers as a percentage of total income.

We turn now to *median* employment incomes and transfers by gender. Together with low-income (poverty) measures, the median helps give a clearer picture of income conditions, particularly for the lower half of the population.

To begin, we observe not only lower levels of employment in both Northeast and Northwest Ontario compared to Ontario as a whole, but also lower levels of FYFT employment as a portion of all employment. As Table 6.3 indicates, 48.0% of Ontario's employment was FYFT employment, while FYFT employment represented only 44.2% in Northeast Ontario and 43.8% in Northwest Ontario. This gap existed for both males and females. It is not surprising, then, that median employment income for all earners is lower in both Northeast and Northwest Ontario compared to the provincial median. When it comes to FYFT earners, median male FYFT employment income in Northern Ontario was somewhat higher than the Ontario level. However, median female employment income was much lower. The Ontario female-to-male FYFT income gap was 82.4%, while it was 73.5% for Northeast Ontario and 78.1% for Northwest Ontario. It is also not surprising that the median transfer incomes and transfer portion of total incomes are higher, for both males and females.

When examining Northern communities, all cities had male and overall FYFT employment levels lower than the average for Ontario. The gap was not as large for females, and three cities (Sudbury, North Bay, and Temiskaming Shores) had female FYFT levels higher than or equal to the Ontario average. In terms of employment incomes, most cities (Sudbury, Thunder Bay, Sault Ste. Marie, Timmins, Kenora, and Dryden) had median male FYFT incomes higher than or approximate to those of Ontario and of the Toronto CMA, though all except Timmins were below the level of Ottawa. By contrast, in all cities except Kenora, median female FYFT incomes were below the Ontario and Toronto CMA levels, and all including Kenora were much below the Ottawa level, demonstrating a much more significant gender income gap compared to much of the rest of the province.

Table 6.3. Income comparisons by sex for selected communities in Northern Ontario, for 2015.

	Median employment income ($)			Median for full-year full-time ($)			FYFT F as % of M	All income as % of FYFT	FYFT earners as % of all employment income earners			Median transfer income ($)			Transfers % of total income			Low income (LIM) after tax (%)			Median age (all)
	all	M	F	All	M	F			all	M	F	all	M	F	all	M	F	all	M	F	
Ontario	33,946	39,490	29,413	55,121	60,345	49,713	82.4	61.6	48.0	52.1	43.6	4,206	2,034	5,463	11.1	7.9	15.3	14.4	13.8	15.0	41.3
Toronto CMA	34,838	39,549	30,701	56,454	60,974	51,880	85.1	61.7	47.6	51.9	43.3	2,205	1,016	3,814	9.1	6.1	13.2	15.6	15.1	16.0	39.4
Toronto C	33,602	37,149	30,393	55,246	58,626	52,090	88.9	60.8	46.0	49.7	42.4	2,249	1,115	3,956	9.4	6.4	13.3	20.2	19.7	20.7	39.3
Ottawa CMA (ON)	41,100	46,359	36,799	65,140	70,402	60,342	85.7	63.1	51.4	55.2	47.6	3,349	1,499	4,437	8.6	6.2	11.7	12.2	11.9	12.5	40.2
Northeast ER	31,722	38,633	26,898	54,558	63,143	46,410	73.5	58.1	44.2	46.3	41.8	8,354	8,597	7,969	15.8	12.5	20.6	14.9	13.8	16.0	46.3
Northwest ER	32,240	37,371	28,319	53,793	60,751	47,462	78.1	59.9	43.8	45.9	41.5	7,590	7,339	7,692	15.2	12.0	19.5	13.2	12.4	14.0	42.6
Northern cities																					
Sudbury CMA	35,738	43,713	30,074	58,384	69,039	49,105	71.1	61.2	46.5	48.9	43.9	7,049	7,405	6,918	12.7	9.5	17.5	12.8	11.7	13.8	43.3
Thunder Bay CMA	34,572	40,488	30,326	54,751	60,922	48,753	80.0	63.1	44.4	47.4	41.3	7,518	7,601	7,468	14.2	11.4	17.9	13.8	13.0	14.5	45.0
Sault Ste. Marie CA	28,989	32,706	26,406	55,231	65,454	46,311	70.8	52.5	42.5	43.4	41.4	8,479	8,575	8,355	17.0	13.4	21.8	15.3	13.8	16.8	46.7
North Bay CA	31,457	36,509	27,770	51,541	56,676	47,337	83.5	61.0	46.1	48.6	43.6	7,969	8,074	7,891	15.3	12.2	19.4	15.7	14.7	16.5	45.1
Timmins CA	37,013	51,883	28,419	59,025	73,613	46,335	62.9	62.7	45.7	48.4	42.8	7,296	7,660	7,101	12.8	9.3	18.3	13.6	11.6	15.6	41.4
Kenora CA	35,864	41,495	31,706	57,774	63,024	51,357	81.5	62.1	47.5	51.1	43.8	7,726	8,128	7,448	13.2	10.4	16.9	10.9	9.6	12.1	44.9
Elliot Lake CA	22,736	24,845	21,472	48,282	56,435	43,602	77.3	47.1	33.4	34.3	32.5	13,340	14,229	12,259	31.0	27.3	35.6	23.2	22.9	23.4	58.8
Temiskaming Shores CSD/CY	33,036	42,697	26,517	50,148	57,311	45,224	78.9	65.9	47.4	50.3	44.3	9,125	10,280	8,695	16.6	12.5	21.9	13.9	12.4	15.5	46.5
Dryden CSD/CY	32,688	39,680	27,664	59,382	69,349	48,757	70.3	55.0	44.9	46.9	42.7	8,478	8,560	8,401	15.4	12.0	19.9	12.8	11.6	13.7	46.2

Selected communities	Median employment income ($)			Median for full-year full-time ($)			FYFT F as % of M	All income as % of FYFT	FYFT earners as % of all employment income earners			Median transfer income ($)			Transfers % of total income			Low income (LIM) after tax (%)			Median age (all)
	all	M	F	All	M	F			all	M	F	all	M	F	all	M	F	all	M	F	
Red Lake CSD/MU	49,536	74,581	35,104	66,039	94,430	52,519	55.6	75.0	47.8	47.8	48.2	3,936	2,568	4,792	7.5	5.1	12.3	6.2	5.8	6.6	38.0
Marathon CSD/T	38,144	66,560	22,400	74,246	93,903	48,483	51.6	51.4	47.1	50.9	43.2	7,094	8,376	6,544	12.3	9.2	18.5	11.3	9.3	13.2	44.9
Hearst CSD/T	39,680	52,693	29,440	58,613	61,875	51,541	83.3	67.7	45.4	49.0	41.5	9,432	12,032	8,091	16.0	13.2	20.2	13.4	10.8	15.6	47.9
Iroquois Falls CSD/T	30,992	40,283	24,205	61,052	69,392	48,419	69.8	50.8	36.6	38.3	34.5	9,560	11,152	8,432	17.1	13.1	23.5	12.8	12.2	13.3	49.6
Moosonee CSD/T	41,472	41,344	41,472	56,725	52,598	59,483	113.1	73.1	48.1	57.5	39.0	4,912	1,740	7,184	14.0	8.2	19.9	24.7	25.0	25.2	28.1
Schreiber CSD/TP	32,960	52,608	21,056	64,657	57.5	56,422	82.6	51.0	44.4	54.2	32.8	7,664	10,208	6,096	13.5	11.0	17.9	11.4	10.0	11.9	50.4
Hornepayne CSD/TP	49,280	69,888	29,888	88,480	94,377	46,766	49.6	55.7	37.3	43.7	30.2	4,560	4,480	4,624	8.7	6.2	15.1	6.7	4.9	6.7	42.6
Little Current pop centre	25,824	24,384	26,368	45,438	45,433	46,085	101.4	56.8	46.3	46.3	46.3	10,160	9,696	10,293	21.1	18.3	23.9	16.4	14.9	17.8	49.3
Wiikwemkoong FN	20,592	14,416	29,760	39,328	33,715	41,728	123.8	52.4	45.5	42.9	45.5	6,851	3,600	7,928	32.6	32.4	32.8	n.a.	n.a.	n.a.	33.7
Asubpeeschoseewagong FN	19,712	13,920	23,040	29,920	24,384	33,792	138.6	65.9	50.0	46.7	55.6	1,692	1,201	6,916	39.0	34.0	42.5	n.a.	n.a.	n.a.	27.3
Atikameksheng Anishnawbek	19,499	15,344	21,696	40,320	45,696	38,912	85.2	48.4	25.6	30.0	26.3	6,789	5,584	7,456	23.6	22.2	25.9	n.a.	n.a.	n.a.	37.9
Fort Severn FN	13,728	15,712	11,840	34,944	30,400	39,744	130.7	39.3	44.1	36.7	51.5	6,768	2,232	12,096	30.2	17.9	42.9	n.a.	n.a.	n.a.	24.9

Source: See Table Notes and Data Sources Table 6.1 for 2016.

Three cities—North Bay, Elliot Lake, and Temiskaming Shores—had median FYFT incomes below the levels not only for Ontario as a whole but also those of Northeast and Northwest Ontario. When looking at all incomes (again including part-year and part-time incomes), one can see, given the generally lower FYFT employment rates, that the level of all-income medians compared to FYFT medians was generally lower in Northern Ontario.

While there are general patterns in employment decline in Northern Ontario, the impacts of decline occur in different degrees depending on specific industry and labour conditions, particularly at the level of individual communities, whether cities, towns, or smaller communities. For instance, all Northern Ontario's cities have experienced employment loss but perhaps the most severe occurred at Elliot Lake—once touted as the world capital of uranium mining, but now struggling as a retirement centre. Elliot Lake has not only the lowest incomes for both males and females but also the largest gap between all incomes and FYFT incomes, the highest median transfer incomes, and the highest dependence on transfer income among cities. As further illustration of the wide range of employment conditions, Table 6.3 also includes data from selected smaller communities. Red Lake and Marathon are dependent mainly on mining, Hearst and Iroquois Falls on forest products, and Moosonee, Schreiber, and Hornepayne on rail transportation. Each community has different levels of activity in its primary industry, and also public sector employment, which has become the second basic sector in many Northern communities. Little Current has become a local centre for services and has grown more dependent on retirees, cottaging, and tourism.

Compared to most mining communities, Red Lake at the time of the 2016 census was a high-income boom town. Labour demand conditions within the male-dominated mining industry created an even wider gap with female FYFT wages; however, the generally higher level of labour demand helped lift the general conditions of all earners including non-FYFT females. Marathon, with less boom-town conditions than Red Lake, still had higher male FYFT wages but a larger gender wage gap and larger gap between FYFT and all incomes. Contrasting this, Iroquois Falls had suffered the closure of its paper mill, and conditions have been much more difficult: a major loss of employment and workers having to commute to outside jobs, which kept up the FYFT wages but caused an exceptionally large FYFT income gap with other incomes. One sees variants of these patterns for the rail/transport towns like Hornepayne and Schreiber as well as Moosonee, though the latter also has a more important public sector role that helps to stabilize employment conditions.

At the extreme of colonial and segregated conditions are First Nations reserves. There are particular differences in First Nation conditions that deserve individual study in their own right, but it is important to note general conditions (even in terms of official statistics), particularly to help dispel the colonial-racist myth of Indigenous privilege related to land, grants, taxes, and so on (Manuel and Derrickson 2017). Median incomes of First Nations residents are much below both Ontario and Northern Ontario levels. Further, most median transfer incomes are also below the levels of Northern Ontario and many of its non-Indigenous communities.

The multiple differences in employment conditions in Northern communities work their way into the pattern of economic dependency. In Table 6.4 one can see again that demographic dependency measures are misleading. Several areas have demographic dependency ratios at or even below the provincial average, but economic dependency ratios that are much higher. This pattern is observed in both larger communities like Thunder Bay and smaller communities like Hornepayne or First Nations communities. On the other hand, there are also communities with above-average demographic dependency ratios which have economic dependency ratios below the average for Ontario, such as Kenora and Hearst. This is not to suggest that the relation of population cohorts to employment and societal dependency is unimportant. Far from it: this is a central issue for community

Table 6.4. Demographic and economic dependency ratios for selected communities in Northern Ontario, 2016.

	Total	Population				Demographic dep. ratios		Statistics Canada labour force				Employment rates				Ec. dep. ratio
		Age 0–14 (%)	Age 15–64 (%)	Age 65+ (%)	Age 20–64 (%)	Pop total / pop 15–65	Pop total / pop 20–65	Working age (pop 15+) (%)	Labour force part. Rate (%)	Emp. Rate (%)	Unemp. Rate (%)	Emp. % Pop total	Emp. % Pop 15+	Emp. % Pop 15–64	Emp. % Pop 20–64	Pop total / emp.
Canada	35,115,730	16.6	66.6	16.9	60.8	1.50	1.64	81.6	65.2	60.2	7.7	49.1	60.2	73.7	80.7	2.04
Ontario	13,448,495	16.4	66.8	16.7	60.8	1.50	1.64	82.1	64.7	59.9	7.4	49.2	59.9	73.6	80.9	2.03
Toronto CMA	5,928,040	16.6	68.9	14.5	62.7	1.45	1.59	82.3	66.3	61.2	7.7	50.4	61.2	73.1	80.3	1.99
Ottawa CMA (ON)	991,730	16.7	67.9	15.4	61.7	1.47	1.62	81.4	67.6	62.8	7.1	51.1	62.8	75.3	82.8	1.96
Northeast ER	548,450	15.0	64.3	20.7	58.8	1.56	1.70	83.2	58.6	53.1	9.3	44.2	53.1	68.8	75.2	2.26
Northwest ER	231,695	17.2	64.9	17.9	58.9	1.54	1.70	81.0	60.4	54.8	9.2	44.4	54.8	68.4	75.4	2.25
Greater Sudbury CMA	164,690	15.5	66.2	18.3	60.4	1.51	1.66	82.7	62.5	57.3	8.4	47.4	57.3	71.7	78.5	2.11
Timmins CA	41,790	17.0	67.8	15.2	61.6	1.48	1.62	81.6	65.2	60.2	7.8	49.1	60.2	72.5	79.7	2.04
Thunder Bay District	146,050	15.0	65.7	19.4	60.2	1.52	1.66	83.0	60.3	55.3	8.2	46.0	55.3	70.0	76.4	2.18
Thunder Bay CMA	121,620	14.6	65.7	19.8	60.2	1.52	1.66	83.2	61.0	56.3	7.7	46.8	56.3	71.3	77.8	2.14
Thunder Bay D ex CMA	24,430	16.7	65.8	17.4	60.2	1.52	1.66	82.4	56.9	50.5	11.2	41.6	50.5	63.2	69.1	2.40
Algoma District	114,095	14.0	62.4	23.6	57.3	1.60	1.74	84.2	54.8	49.1	10.5	41.3	49.1	66.2	72.1	2.42
Sault St. Marie CA	78,160	14.5	63.5	22.0	58.3	1.57	1.72	83.7	57.5	51.6	10.3	43.1	51.6	67.9	74.1	2.32
Algoma D ex Sault St. Marie CA	35,935	13.1	59.8	27.1	55.3	1.67	1.81	85.3	49.0	43.7	10.8	37.3	43.7	62.3	67.5	2.68
Red Lake CSD/MU	4,105	17.9	68.9	13.0	63.0	1.45	1.59	80.8	72.9	69.1	5.2	55.8	69.1	80.9	88.6	1.79
Iroquois Falls CSD/T	4,535	13.9	62.8	23.3	57.9	1.59	1.73	83.9	49.8	44.3	11.1	37.2	44.3	59.1	64.2	2.69

	Population					Demographic dep. ratios		Statistics Canada labour force				Employment rates				Ec. dep. ratio
	Total	Age 0–14 (%)	Age 15–64 (%)	Age 65+ (%)	Age 20–64 (%)	Pop total / pop 15–65	Pop total / pop 20–65	Working age (pop 15+) (%)	Labour force part. Rate (%)	Emp. Rate (%)	Unemp. Rate (%)	Emp. % Pop total	Emp. % Pop 15+	Emp. % Pop 15–64	Emp. % Pop 20–64	Pop total / emp.
Moosonee CSD/T	1,480	30.1	64.9	5.4	57.4	1.54	1.74	71.6	65.6	60.4	8.6	43.2	60.4	66.7	75.3	2.31
Manitoulin District	13,255	16.0	59.3	24.8	53.5	1.69	1.87	81.8	52.5	45.5	13.4	37.2	45.5	62.8	69.6	2.69
Little Current pop centre	1,560	14.7	56.4	28.5	51.0	1.77	1.96	80.4	56.6	50.6	9.9	40.7	50.6	72.2	79.9	2.46
Kenora CSD/CY	15,095	16.0	64.6	19.4	59.2	1.55	1.69	82.0	65.3	60.7	7.1	49.8	60.7	77.0	84.1	2.01
Dryden CSD/CY	7,745	15.2	63.8	21.0	57.5	1.57	1.74	83.0	61.8	57.0	7.7	47.3	57.0	74.2	82.3	2.11
Kapuskasing CSD/T	8,290	15.6	63.0	21.5	57.7	1.59	1.73	82.3	56.3	51.3	8.9	42.2	51.3	67.0	73.2	2.37
Hearst CSD/T	5,070	14.5	62.5	23.0	56.9	1.60	1.76	83.6	61.6	58.4	5.2	48.8	58.4	78.1	85.8	2.05
Marathon CSD/T	3,270	15.6	70.6	13.8	65.3	1.42	1.53	82.7	64.7	59.9	6.9	49.5	59.9	70.1	75.9	2.02
Manitouwadge CSD/TP	1,940	12.9	65.7	21.1	59.3	1.52	1.69	87.6	49.7	45.0	10.1	39.4	45.0	60.0	66.5	2.54
Schreiber CSD/TP	1,055	12.3	68.2	19.9	62.6	1.47	1.60	90.0	60.5	54.7	9.6	49.3	54.7	72.2	78.8	2.03
Ignace CSD/TP	1,200	12.1	65.0	23.3	58.8	1.54	1.70	84.2	53.5	48.0	9.3	40.4	48.0	62.2	68.8	2.47
Hornepayne CSD/TP	980	16.3	70.9	13.3	63.3	1.41	1.58	81.6	70.6	56.9	18.6	46.4	56.9	65.5	73.4	2.15
Wiikwemkoong FN	2,500	25.6	64.2	10.2	7.6	1.56	1.77	74.4	50.3	37.4	26.7	27.8	37.4	43.3	49.1	3.60
Asubpeeschoseewagong FN	638	29.8	66.6	3.9	7.8	1.50	1.70	70.5	46.7	37.8	19.0	26.6	37.8	40.0	45.3	3.75
Atikameksheng Anishnawbek	386	18.1	68.7	11.7	11.7	1.46	1.75	81.6	57.1	44.4	19.4	36.3	44.4	52.8	63.6	2.76
Fort Severn FN	361	29.1	60.9	9.7	9.7	1.64	1.95	70.6	49.0	43.1	12.0	30.5	43.1	50.0	59.5	3.28

Source: See Table Notes and Data Sources Table 6.1 for 2016.

and regional development. However, to obscure the central role of employment and labour conditions in social dependency gives rise to inaccurate analysis and misleading policy.

The urban growth and concentration in Northern Ontario discussed contain several noteworthy observations. First, compared to Southern Ontario, urbanization in Northern Ontario is at a lower level (in 2016, 63.0% compared to 87.6%), and metropolitanization much lower still (36.7% compared to 84.2%). Population growth in Northern Ontario's nine cities reached a peak in the 1990s along with the Northern population as a whole. Most cities (except Sudbury) have declined since then. Overall, during the 50 years since 1971, there has been little change in the city share of Northern Ontario's population, an increase only from 63.7% to 66.2%.

Northern Ontario cities have a lower share of Ontario's jobs, for both males and females. Within Northern Ontario, for 2016, the nine cities had about two-thirds of the working-age population, more than two-thirds of employment, and less than two-thirds of unemployment, though there are considerable differences by city and by sex. Northern Ontario cities had FYFT employment levels lower than the average for Ontario (more so for males than for females). By contrast, for employment incomes, females had lower median incomes relative to the Ontario median for females than did males relative to the Ontario median for males. The median incomes for First Nations residents were much below the levels not only for Ontario but also for Northern Ontario, and so too were median transfer incomes.

The generally poorer employment conditions in Northern Ontario, including its urban areas, affects social dependency. Overall, economic dependency in Northern Ontario and its communities is higher than in Southern Ontario, and higher than as indicated by demographic dependency ratios. The hinterland-colonial conditions of Northern Ontario display such disparities not only relative to Southern Ontario but also among Northern Ontario communities.

NOTE

1. Since 1961, Statistics Canada has defined urban areas formally as areas with a population of at least 1,000 persons and a density of at least 400 persons per square kilometre. Rural populations and areas were all populations and areas outside urban areas. So urbanization in this context refers to an increasing percentage of a population residing in urban areas. (Hence, for a region x, $pop_{totalx} = pop_{urbanx} + pop_{ruralx}$ and the degree of urbanization is measured as $pop_{urbanx}/pop_{totalx} * 100$.) It can also be noted that, when referring to territory as opposed to population, urbanization might be taken to mean a larger number of square kilometres (or proportion of a given territory's area) with a population of at least 1,000 persons and density of at least 400 persons per square kilometre (that is, $terre_{totalx} = terre_{urbanx} + terre_{ruralx}$). In 2011, Statistics Canada took the dubious decision to rename "urban areas" as "population centres," while retaining the term "rural"; however, the present study retains the term "urban area" and, hence, its clearer connection with urbanization.

CHAPTER 7

ISSUES OF DISPARITY, DISTRIBUTION, AND ECONOMIC DEPENDENCY IN NORTHERN ONTARIO

This chapter discusses some key features of employment conditions and income distribution in Northern Ontario in light of the region's long-term decline in population and employment.

To begin, the colonial structure of Northern Ontario continues to be reproduced in the reserve system and in other colonial-racial disparities. As Table 7.1 indicates, the 2016 census counted about 125,000 persons with Aboriginal identity, or 17.3% of the Northern Ontario population. Even using flawed official labour force statistics, several measures show the colonial-racial gap between non-Indigenous persons and Indigenous persons, both on and off reserve. While Indigenous-identified persons made up 17.3% of the population and 15.2% of the working-age population (15 years of age and over), they comprised 13.6% of the employed population and 25.7% of unemployed persons. The gap between the Indigenous and average employment–population rates was nearly 10 percentage points (35.4% compared to 45.2%), while the gap for the employment rate was about 5.6 percentage points (between 48.2% and 53.8%). Unemployment levels were much higher for Indigenous persons, 16.3% compared to the 9.3% average in Northern Ontario, though both were unacceptably high, as was the 7.4% total rate for Ontario as a whole.

Statistics Canada's low-income measures, an official indicator of what many (but not Statistics Canada) have called "poverty" lines, shows much larger incidences of low income among Indigenous persons. The measure used here is after tax, that is, after taxes are paid and transfers received. The official low-income measure after tax (LIM-AT) has a cut-off income set at 50% of the median after-tax income of private households and is adjusted downward per person as household size increases. The incidence or percentage of low income in the population refers to the percentage of individuals in the population beneath the LIM-AT defined low-income (or poverty) line.[1] For Indigenous persons, even official measures indicate 26.3%, compared to the population average of 14.5%. The levels were high everywhere in Northern Ontario, with the highest such poverty levels being in the Thunder Bay district (35.9%).

The starkest evidence of colonial-racial disparities is seen in the data from the on-reserve population. Table 7.1 shows the disparities by historic treaty areas in Northern Ontario. The on-reserve Indigenous population has a far lower employment–population ratio than for Northern Ontario as a whole (27.8% compared to 45.2%) and there is a 13 percentage-point disparity in the employment rate (40.3% compared to 53.8%). Even recognizing its limitations, the official measure of unemployment is 22.4% for on-reserve Indigenous persons compared to an average of 9.3% for Northern Ontario in 2016. Statistics Canada did not publish low-income data for individual on-reserve populations, unlike for non-Indigenous communities.

Comprehending the importance of labour market conditions on distributional outcomes in Northern Ontario depends crucially on knowing the proportion of persons dependent on labour incomes (mainly wages and salaries) relative to profits or other property-based incomes, and relative to transfer payments. Using Statistics Canada's *class of worker* counts, Table 7.2 shows the size of the labour force and the percentage of employees relative to the self-employed for a wide variety of areas in Northern Ontario. In terms of the Statistics Canada definition, the "class of worker" category is based specifically on the *experienced* labour force, which includes persons employed at the time of the census as well as those who were unemployed but who had worked at a job since January 1, 2015.[2]

For those with at least some recent labour force experience, the class of worker count reports (in a somewhat simplified form) the number of employees relative to the number of self-employed persons. For Statistics Canada, employees are defined by the employee–employer relation (wage- and salary-earnership), including whether the pay is a wage, salary, commission, piece rate, tips, or in-kind goods and services.[3] The self-employment category is more varied, including employers with paid employees, persons working on their own account, and unpaid family workers; as well, the self-employed are differentiated by whether they are in a business that is incorporated or unincorporated. The self-employed category can include freelancers and independent contractors as well as dependent contractors who are one step removed from being in an employer–employee relation.

It is evident from Table 7.2 that the overall level of employee status was higher in Northern Ontario—90.8% in the Northeast and 92.1% in the Northwest—compared to Ontario as a whole at 88.2%. Further, this higher level than Ontario exists for both males and females, though it is larger for males. Historically, high levels of self-employment have been associated with farming regions with large numbers of male farm owners as well as small towns or urban centres with large numbers of independent businesses. The growth of the employee status

Table 7.1. Population and employment conditions by Indigenous identity for Northern Ontario Districts and historic treaty areas, 2016.

	Population			Working-age population (15+)			Employed (persons)			Unemployed (persons)			Employment–population rate (%)		Employment rate (%)		Unemployment rate (%)		Low-income (LIM-AT) (%)	
	Total	Indig.	%	Total	Indig.	%	Total	Indig.	%	Total	Indig.	%	Total	Indig.	Total	Indig.	Total	Indig.	Total	Indig.
Ontario (province)	13,242,160	374,395	2.8	11,038,440	284,845	2.6	6,612,145	153,735	2.3	529,525	22,410	4.2	49.9	41.1	59.9	54.0	7.4	12.7	14.4	23.7
Northern Ontario Districts																				
Algoma	112,050	15,455	13.8	96,055	11,910	12.4	47,135	5,590	11.9	5,510	1,080	19.6	42.1	36.2	49.1	46.9	10.5	16.2	16.2	27.8
Cochrane	78,515	12,835	16.3	64,990	9,420	14.5	36,275	4,755	13.1	3,580	840	23.5	46.2	37.0	55.8	50.5	9.0	15.0	14.2	25.1
Kenora	64,615	31,800	49.2	50,235	21,575	42.9	26,935	9,670	35.9	3,545	2,305	65.0	41.7	30.4	53.6	44.8	11.6	19.3	11.1	23.4
Manitoulin	12,955	5,260	40.6	10,845	3,940	36.3	4,935	1,690	34.2	760	465	61.2	38.1	32.1	45.5	42.9	13.4	21.6	14.7	19.9
Nipissing	81,280	11,540	14.2	68,990	9,140	13.2	35,945	4,405	12.3	3,940	810	20.6	44.2	38.2	52.1	48.2	9.9	15.5	17.2	24.7
Rainy River	19,755	5,400	27.3	16,240	3,875	23.9	8,815	2,010	22.8	885	325	36.7	44.6	37.2	54.3	51.9	9.1	13.9	13.7	18.9
Combined Sudbury & District	180,030	18,785	10.4	152,055	14,705	9.7	85,870	8,085	9.4	7,990	1,310	16.4	47.7	43.0	56.5	55.0	8.5	13.9	12.9	20.4
Greater Sudbury CD	158,785	15,060	9.5	133,730	11,685	8.7	76,750	6,565	8.6	6,985	1,030	14.7	48.3	43.6	57.4	56.2	8.3	13.6	12.8	21.3
Sudbury District	21,245	3,725	17.5	18,325	3,020	16.5	9,120	1,520	16.7	1,005	280	27.9	42.9	40.8	49.8	50.3	9.9	15.5	14.3	16.2
Thunder Bay	143,085	21,755	15.2	121,260	15,635	12.9	67,115	7,170	10.7	6,025	1,355	22.5	46.9	33.0	55.3	45.9	8.2	15.9	13.8	35.9

	Population			Working-age population (15+)			Employed (persons)			Unemployed (persons)			Employment–population rate (%)		Employment rate (%)		Unemployment rate (%)		Low-income (LIM-AT) (%)	
	Total	Indig.	%	Total	Indig.	%	Total	Indig.	%	Total	Indig.	%	Total	Indig.	Total	Indig.	Total	Indig.	Total	Indig.
Timiskaming	31,675	2,560	8.1	26,765	1,955	7.3	14,065	1,055	7.5	1,330	135	10.2	44.4	41.2	52.5	54.0	8.6	11.4	17.5	25.3
All Northern districts/CDs	723,960	125,390	17.3	607,435	92,155	15.2	327,090	44,430	13.6	33,565	8,625	25.7	45.2	35.4	53.8	48.2	9.3	16.3	14.5	26.3
Historic treaty areas: on reserve																				
Ontario (all treaty areas)	58,100	54,425	93.7	42,085	38,715	92.0	17,560	15,940	90.8	4,360	4,165	95.5	30.2	29.3	41.7	41.2	19.9	20.7	n/a	n/a
Northern Ontario treaty areas																				
Robinson-Huron [1850]	7,060	6,080	86.1	5,540	4,665	84.2	2,505	2,055	82.0	485	425	87.6	35.5	33.8	45.2	44.1	16.2	17.1	n/a	n/a
Robinson-Superior [1850]	3,345	3,075	91.9	2,475	2,230	90.1	950	845	88.9	330	305	92.4	28.4	27.5	38.4	37.9	25.9	26.5	n/a	n/a
Treaty 3 – Ontario [1873]	8,045	7,865	97.8	5,735	5,565	97.0	2,475	2,380	96.2	765	755	98.7	30.8	30.3	43.2	42.8	23.6	24.1	n/a	n/a
Treaty 5 – Ontario [1875]	4,075	4,045	99.3	2,585	2,555	98.8	940	920	97.9	380	380	100.0	23.1	22.7	36.4	36.0	28.7	29.2	n/a	n/a
Treaty 9 – Ontario [1905/06]	17,090	16,890	98.8	11,320	11,135	98.4	4,495	4,345	96.7	1,185	1,180	99.6	26.3	25.7	39.7	39.0	20.9	21.4	n/a	n/a
Est. Northern Ontario reserves	39,615	37,955	95.8	27,655	26,150	94.6	11,365	10,545	92.8	3,145	3,045	96.8	28.7	27.8	41.1	40.3	21.7	22.4	n/a	n/a

Notes: The low-income measure used is Statistics Canada's LIM-AT, that is, after taxes and transfers.

Source: Statistics Canada. 2018a.

has been associated with industrialization, particularly the growth of large industrial, financial, and commercial corporations, and, later, governmental operations. With the growth of corporate capitalism, wage and salary earners have become overwhelmingly the largest class in the economy. Employment and self-employment are also affected by cyclical factors. Depression and recession can be associated not only with less employment but, at times, increases in self-employment. In low-income countries and destitute regions, self-employment in marginal activities for survival is sometimes called the informal sector, and a portion of these activities that could be counted as self-employment. Higher levels of self-employment, then, are not necessarily indicative of a higher living standard or less precarity.

Table 7.2. Class of worker by sex, Ontario, Northern Ontario, and selected communities, 2016.

	Labour force experienced (persons)			Employee (%)			Self-employed (%)		
	all	males	females	all	males	females	all	males	females
Ontario	6,970,625	3,607,890	3,362,735	88.2	85.5	91.0	11.8	14.5	9.0
Toronto CMA	3,144,140	1,628,325	1,515,815	87.3	84.0	90.8	12.7	16.0	9.2
Toronto C	1,437,545	736,420	701,125	87.3	84.4	90.3	12.7	15.6	9.7
Ottawa CMA (ON)	532,695	271,510	261,185	89.7	87.9	91.6	10.3	12.1	8.4
Northeast ER	261,955	135,555	126,395	90.8	89.0	92.8	9.2	11.0	7.2
Northwest ER	110,620	56,665	53,955	92.1	90.5	93.7	7.9	9.5	6.3
Northern city total	256,975	131,270	125,710	92.0	90.4	93.7	8.0	9.6	6.3
Sudbury CMA	83,420	42,935	40,485	92.2	90.6	93.9	7.8	9.3	6.1
Thunder Bay CMA	60,640	30,865	29,775	92.1	90.3	93.8	7.9	9.7	6.2
Sault Ste. Marie CA	36,585	18,580	18,005	92.9	91.5	94.4	7.1	8.5	5.6
North Bay CA	34,205	17,205	16,995	90.3	88.1	92.6	9.7	11.9	7.4
Timmins CA	21,960	11,490	10,470	93.4	92.0	94.8	6.6	8.0	5.2
Kenora CA	8,005	3,975	4,035	91.2	89.1	93.2	8.8	10.8	6.8
Elliot Lake CA	3,405	1,745	1,660	89.3	88.5	90.1	10.9	11.5	9.9
Temiskaming Shores CY	4,855	2,445	2,415	89.5	88.3	90.3	10.6	11.5	9.5
Dryden CY	3,900	2,030	1,870	92.7	91.9	93.6	7.3	8.1	6.1

	Labour force experienced (persons)			Employee (%)			Self-employed (%)		
	all	males	females	all	males	females	all	males	females
First Nations									
Wiikwemkoong FN	815	390	425	96.9	96.2	97.6	3.7	5.1	2.4
Asubpeeschoseewagong FN	190	85	100	97.4	94.1	100.0	0.0	0.0	0.0
Atikameksheng Anishnawbek	165	75	85	90.9	100.0	88.2	9.1	0.0	11.8
Fort Severn FN	120	65	50	95.8	92.3	100.0	0.0	0.0	0.0
Farming									
Timiskaming District	15,215	8,105	7,110	88.8	87.6	90.2	11.2	12.4	9.8
Rainy River District	9,530	4,805	4,730	90.1	86.7	93.6	9.9	13.2	6.4
Manitoulin District	5,475	2,765	2,710	84.4	78.7	90.0	15.7	21.2	10.1
Algoma District	51,345	26,425	24,920	91.6	90.0	93.3	8.4	10.0	6.7
Forest									
Kapuskasing T	3,805	2,030	1,775	92.2	90.6	93.8	7.8	9.4	6.2
Sioux Lookout MU	2,945	1,475	1,465	94.2	92.9	95.9	5.8	7.1	4.4
Hearst T	2,585	1,350	1,230	89.0	87.8	91.1	10.6	12.6	8.9
Iroquois Falls T	1,865	960	905	93.6	93.2	93.9	6.7	6.8	6.6
Mining									
Kirkland Lake T	3,585	1,895	1,690	93.2	92.1	94.4	6.8	7.9	5.6
Red Lake MU	2,415	1,280	1,135	92.5	93.8	91.2	7.7	6.3	9.3
Marathon T	1,725	925	805	92.8	92.4	92.5	7.5	7.6	6.8
Cobalt T	470	250	220	95.7	96.0	95.5	4.3	6.0	0.0
Rail									
Capreol pop centre	1,285	670	615	96.9	96.3	97.6	3.1	3.0	2.4
Moosonee T	685	315	370	97.8	95.2	100.0	2.9	4.8	2.7
Schreiber TP	570	300	270	93.9	91.7	94.4	6.1	8.3	5.6
Hornepayne TP	565	310	255	93.8	91.9	98.0	5.3	6.5	3.9
Tourism/cottaging									
Atikokan T	1,285	645	635	91.8	90.7	92.9	7.8	8.5	7.1
Little Current pop centre	695	350	345	89.9	88.6	91.3	10.1	11.4	8.7
Nipigon TP	665	335	325	92.5	92.5	93.8	7.5	7.5	7.7
Temagami MU	345	215	130	88.4	86.0	92.3	11.6	11.6	7.7

Note: Some totals may not add due to rounding. This is especially the case for smaller communities. A percentage of 100.0 is typically the result of rounding; where rounding leads to a percentage greater than 100, the result is approximated as 100.0.

Source: See Table Notes and Data Sources Table 6.1 for 2016.

Table 7.2 also reports data on Northern Ontario cities and on selected smaller communities by leading industry. The employee status in 2016 for Northern Ontario cities was 92.0%, made up of 90.4% for males and 93.7% for females. Though the levels were somewhat lower for cities facing more decline (such as Elliot Lake and Temiskaming Shores), all cities were comparable to, if not higher in, employee status than the major metropolitan centres of Toronto and Ottawa. The selected First Nations, whether larger in population (such as Wiikwemkoong FN), near a large city (such as Atikameksheng Anishnawbek), or much further away (such as Fort Severn FN or Asubpeeschoseewagong FN), shared employee levels at least approximate to the Northern Ontario levels or much higher. Under "farming" are the four districts in Northern Ontario having the largest numbers of farms (Chapagain 2017: Table 1). Not surprisingly, one sees somewhat higher levels of self-employment for males in farming districts, particularly for Timiskaming, Rainy River, and Manitoulin Districts. Also not surprising are the higher-than-average employee status levels in selected single-industry communities dominated by corporate mines, mills, and rail operations, with the possible exception of the somewhat lower level in Hearst. One might expect higher levels of self-employment in communities dominated by tourism and cottaging industries, particularly in smaller-scale firm structure. But the selected communities vary, showing only slightly higher than average levels of self-employment in Temagami and Little Current, and for females in Nipigon, but lower for men at the latter, and lower than average for both men and women in Atikokan. Of course, the industry structure of all communities is mixed and generally not so clearly dominated by a single industry as they once were. Despite certain differences among Northern communities in degrees of self-employment, a very high overall level of the economically active population— around 90%—depends on wages and salary earnings. Hence, labour market conditions strongly influence their economic well-being.

As primary sector and related employment has declined in Northern Ontario, there has been an increased importance in public sector employment, especially in stabilizing employment or at least moderating decline. Without public sector employment many resource communities would decline to ghost towns (as commonly happened in the past) or be radically reduced in their public services, in particular public hospitals and publicly funded medical services, educational institutions (particularly local schools, colleges, and universities), and municipal and provincial government services. In many Northern communities, these public services are often among the largest employers. Table 7.3 presents data on the labour force and public sector employment. The public sector here is defined as including employment in health care and social services, educational services, and public administration (classes 61, 62, and 91 in the North American Industry Classification System or NAICS). Due to difficulties in obtaining accurate community-specific data, however, the table does not include important areas of transportation like the post office or Ontario Northland, nor public utilities like Ontario Hydro, Greater Sudbury Utilities, or Tbaytel, nor public broadcasting and cultural institutions like the CBC/Radio Canada.

To begin, even a relatively conservative count of total public sector employment in 2016 shows the levels for Northeast and Northwest Ontario at 30.4% and 35.7%, respectively, of the labour force, compared to the Ontario average of 24.4%. As well, relative to the population, public employment is substantially more important, especially for Northwest Ontario. The greatest impact is for female employment. No less than 45.8% and 50.3% of jobs held by females in Northeast and Northwest Ontario are in the public sector. For Northwest Ontario, this made the importance of public sector employment of females comparable to that of Ottawa. Table 7.3 shows also that there was considerable range in total public sector employment among the districts, from low levels in Cochrane District (28.6%), Sudbury District (26.0%), and Timiskaming District (28.0%) to the highest level in Kenora District (39.4%).

Table 7.3. Labour force-population rates and public sector employment in Ontario, Northern Ontario, districts, and selected communities, 2016.

	Labour force (persons)	LF-pop rate (%)	Public sector (persons)	% of LF	% of pop
Ontario	6,970,625	51.8	1,698,660	24.4	12.6
males	3,607,890	55.0	514,200	14.3	7.8
females	3,362,735	48.8	1,184,455	35.2	17.2
Toronto CMA	3,144,140	53.0	636,675	20.2	10.7
males	1,628,320	56.6	187,185	11.5	6.5
females	1,515,815	49.7	449,480	29.7	14.7
Ottawa CMA (ON)	532,695	53.7	212,345	39.9	21.4
males	271,515	56.3	82,010	30.2	17.0
females	261,180	51.3	130,330	49.9	25.6
Northeast ER	261,955	47.8	79,685	30.4	14.5
males	135,555	50.2	21,825	16.1	8.1
females	126,395	45.4	57,855	45.8	20.8
Northwest ER	110,625	47.7	39,530	35.7	17.1
males	56,670	49.2	12,380	21.8	10.8
females	53,955	46.3	27,145	50.3	23.3
Algoma District	51,345	45.0	15,845	30.9	13.9
males	26,425	47.3	4,565	17.3	8.2
females	24,920	42.8	11,280	45.3	19.4
Sault Ste. Marie CA	36,580	46.8	11,355	31	14.5
males	18,580	49.0	3,325	17.9	8.8
females	18,005	44.7	8,030	44.6	19.9
Elliot Lake CA	10,740	31.8	1,255	36.8	11.7
males	5,140	34.0	415	23.7	8.1
females	5,600	29.6	845	50.9	15.1
Hornepayne TP	980	57.7	155	27.4	15.8
males	525	59.0	20	6.5	3.8
females	455	57.1	135	51.9	29.7
Cochrane District	39,285	49.3	11,230	28.6	14.1
males	20,700	52.3	2,915	14.1	7.4
females	18,575	46.3	8,310	44.7	20.7
Timmins CA	21,960	52.5	5,915	26.9	14.2
males	11,490	55.6	1,465	12.8	7.1
females	10,475	49.6	4,455	42.5	21.1
Cochrane T	2,695	50.7	615	22.8	11.6
males	1,440	54.8	175	12.2	6.7
females	1,255	46.7	435	34.7	16.2
Iroquois Falls T	1,865	41.1	675	36.2	14.9
males	960	43.0	170	17.7	7.6
females	910	39.5	500	54.9	21.7

	Labour force (persons)	LF-pop rate (%)	Public sector (persons)	% of LF	% of pop
Moosonee T	685	46.3	360	52.6	24.3
males	315	43.4	115	36.5	15.9
females	375	50.0	250	66.7	33.3
Kenora District	29,245	44.6	11,530	39.4	17.6
males	15,100	45.9	3,960	26.2	12.0
females	14,145	43.3	7,570	53.5	23.2
Kenora CA	8,005	53.0	3,000	37.5	19.9
males	3,970	53.8	915	23.0	12.4
females	4,035	52.3	2,085	51.7	27.0
Dryden CY	3,900	50.4	1,235	31.7	15.9
males	2,030	54.7	375	18.5	10.1
females	1,865	46.2	855	45.8	21.2
Red Lake MU	2,420	59.0	585	24.2	14.3
males	1,275	60.9	135	10.6	6.4
females	1,135	56.3	450	39.6	22.3
Asubpeeschoseewagong FN	190	29.9	145	76.3	22.8
males	85	26.2	60	70.6	18.5
females	100	31.7	85	85.0	27.0
Fort Severn FN	115	31.5	75	65.2	20.5
males	65	35.1	25	38.5	13.5
females	55	31.4	35	63.6	20.0
Manitoulin District	5,475	41.3	1,875	34.2	14.1
males	2,765	41.9	505	18.3	7.7
females	2,710	40.8	1,370	50.6	20.6
Little Current pop cntr	695	44.6	235	33.8	15.1
males	350	47.0	50	14.3	6.7
females	350	43.2	185	52.9	22.8
Wiikwemkoong	820	32.8	430	52.4	17.2
males	395	32.5	135	34.2	11.1
females	425	33.1	295	69.4	23.0
Gore Bay T	370	42.8	65	17.6	7.5
males	180	41.9	10	5.6	2.3
females	190	44.2	65	34.2	15.1
Nipissing District	38,965	46.9	12,990	33.3	15.6
males	19,730	48.7	4,120	20.9	10.2
females	19,235	45.1	8,870	46.1	20.8
North Bay CA	34,200	48.6	11,345	33.2	16.1
males	17,205	50.2	3,725	21.7	10.9
females	17,000	47.1	7,620	44.8	21.1
Rainy River District	9,530	47.4	3,310	34.7	16.5
males	4,805	48.3	925	19.3	9.3

Table 7.3. Labour force-population rates and public sector employment in Ontario, Northern Ontario, districts, and selected communities, 2016.

	Labour force (persons)	LF-pop rate (%)	Public sector (persons)	% of LF	% of pop
females	4,730	46.5	2,395	50.6	23.6
Fort Frances T	3,820	49.4	1,450	38.0	18.7
males	1,805	48.5	410	22.7	11.0
females	2,015	50.2	1,040	51.6	25.9
Sudbury District	9,965	46.2	2,595	26.0	12.0
males	5,215	47.5	620	41.6	5.6
females	4,750	44.9	1,975	11.9	18.7
Greater Sudbury CMA	83,420	50.7	25,885	31.0	15.7
males	42,935	53.3	6,665	15.5	8.3
females	40,485	48.1	19,225	47.5	22.9
Atikameksheng Anishnawbek	165	42.9	70	42.4	18.2
males	75	40.5	15	20.0	8.1
females	85	42.5	55	64.7	27.5
Thunder Bay District	71,850	49.2	24,675	34.3	16.9
males	36,765	50.8	7,500	20.4	10.4
females	35,080	47.6	17,175	49.0	23.3
Thunder Bay CMA	60,640	49.9	21,035	34.7	17.3
males	30,865	51.7	6,475	21.0	10.8
females	29,775	48.1	14,555	48.9	23.5
Marathon T	1,725	52.8	480	27.8	14.7
males	920	54.9	120	13.0	7.2
females	800	50.0	360	45.0	22.5
Schreiber TP	570	54.0	145	25.4	13.7
males	300	54.1	35	11.7	6.3
females	270	53.5	120	44.4	23.8
Timiskaming District	15,210	47.2	4,265	28.0	13.2
males	8,105	50.7	1,030	12.7	6.4
females	7,105	43.7	3,225	45.4	19.8
Temiskaming Shores CY	4,860	49.0	1,470	30.2	14.8
males	2,440	51.7	390	16.0	8.3
females	2,410	46.3	1,085	45.0	20.8
Cobalt T	470	41.8	100	21.3	8.9
males	250	45.0	35	14.0	6.3
females	225	39.1	75	33.3	13

Source: See Table Notes and Data Sources Table 6.1 for 2016.

The table also shows the level of public sector employment for the cities and selected communities within the district. Along with increased centralization of hospitals, schools, and other public services, the larger population centres usually have larger shares of public employment. For communities that have experienced substantial private sector decline, such as through mine or mill closures, the importance of public employment can reach higher levels than those in the district's largest centre. For example, in Algoma District, the City of Elliot Lake has a much higher public employment share (36.8%) than in the largest centre, Sault Ste. Marie (31.0%). Another example of this, in the Cochrane District, is where the public employment share in Iroquois Falls (36.2%) is much higher than the district's largest centre, Timmins (26.9%). Future research could explore factors affecting the relatively greater or lesser importance of public employment and services in particular communities. The key point here is that for Northern Ontario, the overall level of public employment is much higher, especially for females, and this has an importance for income levels in the region.

In order to draw together some of the distributional issues raised in this study, we turn now to discuss key labour market comparisons for Northern Ontario (Table 7.4) as well as aspects of the resulting employment income and total income distributions (Table 7.5).

To begin, Table 7.4 highlights four major observations. First, compared to the average of Ontario working-age employment (66.5%), the levels were lower in both Northeast Ontario (61.8%) and Northwest Ontario (63.9%). The disparity was large for both males and females, but especially for males in Northeast Ontario. Compared to the average working-age employment for Ontario males (70.8%), Northeast Ontario males had 5.4 percentage points less (65.4%) and Northwest Ontario males had 4.5 percentage points less (66.3%). For females, the overall Ontario level of 62.5% was 8.3 percentage points lower than the overall male level for Ontario. In Northeast Ontario, females at 58.4% had a level 12.4 percentage points below the average male level

Table 7.4. Labour market comparisons for Northeast Ontario and Northwest Ontario economic regions, for 2015.

	Canada	Ontario	Toronto CMA	Ottawa CMA (ON)	Northeast ER	Northwest ER
Work activity during 2015						
Persons 15+ reporting work activity	19,361,010	7,342,205	3,286,350	559,350	282,135	119,905
% males	52.0	51.5	51.4	50.8	51.9	51.3
% females	48.0	48.5	48.6	49.2	48.1	48.7
% of working-age population (15+)	67.6	66.5	67.4	69.3	61.8	63.9
males % of working-age males	71.9	70.8	72.1	72.8	65.4	66.3
females % of working-age females	63.5	62.5	63.0	66.0	58.4	61.5
Persons who worked full year, full time	9,626,010	3,873,565	1,694,705	305,870	140,180	58,375
FYFT % all who worked	49.7	52.8	51.6	54.7	49.7	48.7
FYFT males % of males who worked	53.7	56.8	55.7	58.5	53.2	51.5
FYFT females % of females who worked	45.4	47.4	47.2	50.7	45.9	45.8
Persons who worked part year and/or part time	9,735,005	3,504,645	1,591,645	253,480	141,960	61,535
PYPT % all who worked	50.3	47.7	48.4	45.3	50.3	51.3
PYPT males % of males who worked	46.3	43.2	44.3	41.5	46.8	48.6
PYPT females % of females who worked	54.6	52.6	52.8	49.3	54.1	54.2
Average weeks worked	42.4	42.9	42.6	43.4	42.1	41.5
Males	42.9	43.4	43.3	43.8	42.1	41.2
Females	42.0	42.3	41.9	42.9	42.1	41.8

	Canada	Ontario	Toronto CMA	Ottawa CMA (ON)	Northeast ER	Northwest ER
FYFT employment income during 2015						
Median FTFY employment income ($)	55,121	53,431	56,454	65,140	54,558	53,793
males ($)	60,345	59,326	60,974	70,402	63,143	60,751
females ($)	49,713	47,420	51,880	60,342	46,410	47,462
Average FTFY employment income ($)	65,997	68,628	74,722	74,515	62,401	60,960
males ($)	74,289	76,536	84,081	81,525	70,674	68,218
females ($)	55,510	58,676	63,161	66,283	52,181	52,425
Sources of income by % of total income						
Employment income, inc. self-empl. (%)	72.0	72.9	76.5	72.9	67.3	68.2
for male recipients (%)	75.2	76.0	79.7	75.1	70.4	70.5
for female recipients (%)	67.7	68.7	72.1	70.1	62.8	65.1
Other private income inc. priv. pension (%)	16.3	16.0	14.4	18.5	16.9	16.6
for male recipients (%)	16.4	16.1	14.2	18.7	17.1	17.5
for female recipients (%)	16.0	16.0	14.7	18.2	16.6	15.4
Government transfers to individuals (%)	11.7	11.1	9.1	8.6	15.8	15.2
for male recipients (%)	8.4	7.9	6.1	6.2	12.5	12.0
for female recipients (%)	16.3	15.3	13.2	11.7	20.6	19.5

Source: See Table Notes and Data Sources Table 5.4 for 2016.

for Ontario, and 4.1 percentage points below the average female level for Ontario. In Northwest Ontario, females at 61.5% had a level 9.3 percentage points below the average male level for Ontario, and 1.0 percentage point below the average female level for Ontario.

Second, for those who had any employment during 2015, there were substantial disparities in levels of FYFT jobs, though the low level of FYFT jobs held in the entire economy is problematic in itself—nearly half of all employment is in part-year part-time jobs, usually without benefits. The average percentage of FYFT jobs held in Ontario was 52.8% while for the Northeast and Northwest it was 49.7% and 48.7% respectively. For males the average was 56.8% for Ontario, while Northeast Ontario males at 53.2% had 3.6 percentage points fewer FYFT jobs and Northwest Ontario males at 51.5% had 5.3 percentage points fewer FYFT jobs, than the provincial average. In Ontario, 47.4% of females held FYFT positions, 9.4 percentage points lower than males. This gender gap is widened in Northern Ontario. In Northeast Ontario, females at 45.9% were at a level 10.9 percentage points below the average male level for Ontario, and 1.5 percentage points below the average female level for Ontario. In Northwest Ontario, meanwhile, females, at 45.8%, were at 11.0 percentage points below the average male level for Ontario and 1.6 percentage point below the average female level for Ontario.

Third, even for the FYFT jobs, there exist major disparities for Northern Ontario, not only for female employment incomes but also for higher-paid jobs. The median employment income represents a mid-point in the range of incomes where half of all other incomes are above and half are below. So the median instead of the average in this context is more useful as an indicator of the highest of the lower half of incomes, while low-income measures and other poverty, ranking, and disparity measures can be more useful for describing and comparing even lower levels of income. As Table 7.4 indicates, compared to the median FYFT income for Ontario ($53,431), the median income for Northeast Ontario was higher ($54,558, or by 2.1%). This is a result of the fact that, compared to the male and female median incomes for Ontario, the male median income is significantly higher (by 6.4%) while the female median income is lower (2.1%). The female–male median income ratio for Ontario was 79.9% while for Northeast Ontario it was 73.5%. This contrasts with 82.4% for Canada, 85.1% for the Toronto CMA, and 85.7% for the Ottawa CMA (Ontario). There is a similar though less divergent pattern in Northwest Ontario, with the Northwest median income ($53,793) being only 0.7% higher than the Ontario median. Again, the Northwest male median ($60,751) was higher than the Ontario median ($59,326), by 2.4%. However, the Northwest female median ($47,462) was approximate to the Ontario female median ($47,420), and the female–male median income ratio in Northwest Ontario (76.8%) was similar to the level for Ontario.

However, when we consider *average* (or mean) FYFT employment incomes, the picture changes dramatically. In terms of average FYFT incomes, Northern Ontario averages are well below the averages for Ontario and even more so below the averages for the Toronto CMA and Ottawa CMA. The average FYFT employment income for Ontario was $68,628. The Northeast Ontario average income of $62,401 was 9.1% lower, while the Northwest Ontario average income of $60,960 was 11.2% lower. Both male and female average incomes in Northern Ontario were lower than for the province. For males, the Ontario average was $76,536 while for Northeast Ontario it was $70,674 (7.7% lower), and for Northwest Ontario it was $68,218 (10.9% lower). For females, the Ontario average was $58,676 and the female–male average income ratio was 76.7%. In Northeast Ontario, the female average income was $52,181 or 11.1% less than the Ontario average; the female–male average income ratio was 73.8% within the Northeast but only 68.2% of the Ontario male average. In Northwest Ontario, the female average income was $52,425 or 10.7% less than the Ontario average, a situation similar to Northeast Ontario; the female–male average income ratio was 76.8% within the Northwest but only 68.5% of the Ontario male average.

Fourth, turning to the main sources of total income of individuals (employment, private investment—including private pensions—and transfers), the situation of Northern Ontario is not surprising. Even given overall lower levels of income in Northern Ontario, both males and females have less employment income, higher levels of transfer income, and similar or slightly higher levels of private pension or investment income. In terms of employment incomes in Ontario, which are higher as a whole than in Northern Ontario, the average received in Ontario is 72.9% of total income. For Northeast Ontario employment incomes are only 67.3% of total income, with males at 70.4% and females 62.8%. Similarly, in Northwest Ontario employment incomes are 68.2%, with males at 70.5% and females at 65.1%. For other private incomes, the levels received are only slightly higher in Northern Ontario than the average for Ontario. While the Ontario average was reported at 16.0%, the average in Northeast Ontario was 16.9% and in Northwest Ontario was 16.6%. In Northeast Ontario both males and females had higher levels; in Northwest Ontario the level was higher for males but slightly lower for females. For transfer incomes, the Ontario average level received was 11.1% while for Northeast Ontario it was 15.8% and for Northwest Ontario 15.2%. The situation of need for transfers is highly gendered through both the labour market and household or non-labour market conditions. For Ontario, transfers averaged about 7.9% of total income for males and 15.3% for females. In Northern Ontario, with its more difficult employment conditions, males received a higher percentage in transfers: 12.5% in Northeast Ontario and 12.0% in Northwest Ontario. When compounded with the disparities of gender, females received 20.6% in Northeast Ontario and 19.5% in Northwest Ontario.

Now we turn in more depth to some distributional expressions of the employment conditions in Northern Ontario, which we can see in Table 7.5. In this and the related appendix tables, employment income includes income from part-year, part-time employment as well as FYFT employment. At the outset, one can see that, even including part-year, part-time employment, Ontario as a whole had more persons receiving income from any employment than did Northern Ontario: 73.8% for the province compared to 70.3% for Northeast Ontario and 71.8% for Northwest Ontario. For males, Ontario had 78.2% reporting at least some employment income, while for Northeast Ontario it was 75.6% and for Northwest Ontario it was 75.0%. For Ontario females, 69.7% had at least some employment income, or 8.5 percentage points below males. The employment income situation for females in Northern Ontario was even more unequal than that for males. Northeast Ontario females had only 65.2% receiving at least some employment income, 13.0 percentage points less than the average for males in Ontario, 10.4 percentage points less than the average for males in Northeast Ontario, and 4.5 percentage points less than for females in Ontario. Northwest Ontario females had 68.8% receiving at least some employment income, 9.4 percentage points less than the average for males in Ontario, 6.2 percentage points less than the average for males in Northeast Ontario, and 0.9 percentage points less than for females in Ontario.

Next we examine employment incomes (as reported by Statistics Canada for 2015) by shares of persons receiving income for income groups in ascending bands of $10,000. In general, compared to the average employment income distribution for Ontario and for Toronto, Northern Ontario reported larger percentages at the lowest income level, smaller percentages at the highest, and more persons overall at lower incomes, especially for females. Perhaps due to Northern Ontario's history of single-industry mining, mill, and rail towns, there exists a common notion that the workforce is characterized by unusually large numbers of highly paid blue-collar males in primary and primary manufacturing industries. But the distributional data shows that the male employment income distribution is more similar to the average for Ontario except at the bottom and top levels. It is notable that the overall employment income distributions for Ontario, as well as those for Northeast and Northeast Ontario, and also Toronto,

Table 7.5. Distributions of employment incomes and total incomes, Ontario and Northern Ontario, for 2015

	Ontario			Toronto CMA			Northeast Ontario ER			Northwest Ontario ER		
	all	males	females	all	males	females	all	males	females	All	males	females
All persons with income	10,556,935	5,115,460	5,441,475	4,631,950	2,227,295	2,404,655	440,775	216,870	223,910	181,180	89,620	91,560
Persons with employment income	7,790,680	3,998,335	3,792,350	3,454,590	1,751,260	1,703,330	309,855	163,975	145,880	130,170	67,180	62,990
% persons with employment income	73.8	78.2	69.7	74.6	78.6	70.8	70.3	75.6	65.2	71.8	75.0	68.8
Distribution of employment income (%)												
Under $10,000 (including loss)	22.2	20.7	23.8	20.8	19.0	22.7	25.5	25.0	26.1	24.1	23.1	25.1
$10,000 to $19,999	13.2	11.6	14.9	13.6	12.6	14.7	12.4	10.0	15.1	12.8	11.1	14.7
$20,000 to $29,999	10.6	9.3	12.0	10.7	9.8	11.8	10.3	8.4	12.5	10.8	9.4	12.2
$30,000 to $39,999	9.9	8.8	11.0	9.7	9.0	10.5	9.6	7.7	11.7	10.1	8.5	11.8
$40,000 to $49,999	9.1	8.5	9.7	9.0	8.4	9.6	8.8	7.7	10.1	9.5	8.0	11.1
$50,000 to $59,999	7.6	7.8	7.3	7.4	7.4	7.4	7.3	7.5	7.2	8.0	8.0	7.9
$60,000 to $69,999	6.0	6.6	5.3	6.0	6.3	5.6	5.6	6.5	4.6	5.9	6.9	4.9
$70,000 to $79,999	4.7	5.5	4.0	4.8	5.4	4.2	4.6	5.5	3.5	4.6	5.6	3.6
$80,000 to $89,999	3.9	4.6	3.3	4.0	4.5	3.4	3.9	4.8	2.9	3.7	4.5	2.9
$90,000 to $99,999	3.6	3.9	3.3	3.5	3.7	3.3	3.8	4.4	3.1	3.4	4.0	2.8
$100,000 and over	9.2	12.7	5.5	10.4	13.9	6.8	8.1	12.5	3.2	7.1	10.9	3.2
Distribution of total income (%)												
Under $10,000 (including loss)	15.3	13.9	16.6	17.6	16.6	18.6	13.0	10.5	15.4	14.0	13.1	14.8
$10,000 to $19,999	17.3	14.5	20.0	17.8	15.7	19.8	18.0	13.9	21.9	16.5	13.1	19.7
$20,000 to $29,999	13.4	11.5	15.1	12.7	11.4	13.9	14.5	12.0	17.0	13.9	11.5	16.2

	Ontario			Toronto CMA			Northeast Ontario ER			Northwest Ontario ER		
	all	males	females	all	males	females	all	males	females	all	males	females
$30,000 to $39,999	10.9	10.2	11.5	10.0	9.4	10.6	12.0	11.6	12.5	12.1	10.9	13.2
$40,000 to $49,999	9.7	9.6	9.8	8.8	8.5	9.1	10.3	10.6	10.1	10.8	10.4	11.2
$50,000 to $59,999	7.7	8.1	7.2	7.0	7.1	6.9	8.0	8.8	7.2	8.7	9.3	8.1
$60,000 to $69,999	6.0	6.8	5.2	5.6	6.0	5.2	5.9	7.2	4.7	6.4	7.8	5.1
$70,000 to $79,999	4.5	5.4	3.7	4.4	5.0	3.8	4.4	5.6	3.2	4.6	5.8	3.5
$80,000 to $89,999	3.6	4.3	2.9	3.5	4.1	3.0	3.4	4.5	2.4	3.4	4.3	2.6
$90,000 to $99,999	3.1	3.6	2.6	3.0	3.3	2.6	3.1	3.8	2.3	2.9	3.6	2.2
$100,000 and over	8.6	12.1	5.4	9.6	12.9	6.5	7.3	11.4	3.3	6.7	10.1	3.4
$100,000 to $149,999	5.7	7.7	3.8	5.9	7.6	4.4	5.6	8.7	2.6	5.1	7.6	2.6
$150,000 and over	2.9	4.3	1.6	3.7	5.4	2.2	1.7	2.7	0.7	1.6	2.5	0.8
Ratio of total income shares: persons												
Under $10,000 to persons $150,000+	5.2	3.2	10.5	4.7	3.1	8.5	7.7	3.9	22.0	8.6	5.3	19.5
Low income (LIM) after tax												
All ages (%)	14.4	13.8	15.0	15.6	15.1	16.0	14.9	13.8	16.0	13.2	12.4	14.0
0–5 years (%)	19.8	19.8	19.7	20.3	20.4	20.2	22.3	22.1	22.5	22.0	21.8	22.3
Average after-tax total income ($)	39,318	45,443	33,564	40,565	47,026	34,582	36,845	43,208	30,694	36,819	41,924	31,829
Median after-tax total income ($)	30,641	35,753	26,585	29,242	33,167	26,233	30,758	37,385	25,084	31,611	37,069	27,189

Source: See Table Notes and Data Sources Table 5.4 for 2016.

follow the pattern of a very steep pyramid except for the highest income category. The largest differences among these distributions are at the low and high income extremes.[5]

Compared to the average for Ontario, both Northeast and Northwest Ontario had much higher percentages of persons at the lowest income level (under $10,000): 22.2% for Ontario compared to 25.5% for Northeast Ontario and 24.1% for Northwest Ontario. For male incomes at the lowest level, Ontario had 20.7% while Northeast Ontario had 25.0% and Northwest Ontario had 23.1%. For female incomes at the lowest level, Ontario had 23.8% while Northeast Ontario had 26.1% and Northwest Ontario had 25.1%. The fact that approximately a quarter of persons employed in Northern Ontario received incomes under $10,000 deserves greater attention and highlights larger disparities, especially for women. The male distributions in Northeast and Northwest Ontario compared to the Ontario average were similar to or somewhat lower in the lower and middle income groups. The one in Northeast Ontario slightly exceeded the Ontario average for the $80,000 and $90,000 income groups but was slightly lower at the highest income group ($100,000). In Northwest Ontario, the male distribution had slightly higher than average shares at $50,000, $60,000, $70,000, and $90,000, and was 1.8 percentage points lower at the highest income group.

For female employment incomes, the pattern is almost relentlessly consistent, in both Northeast and Northwest Ontario. Beginning with the larger percentages in the lowest income group, the Northern shares are larger than the Ontario average in the next lower groups until the $50,000 group in Northeast Ontario and the $60,000 group in Northwest Ontario is reached, at which point the Northern shares fall below the Ontario average all the way up to and including the highest income group. It deserves special note that over half of all female incomes in Ontario were below $30,000, and the incidence was even higher in Northern Ontario. If one adds up the share of all incomes below $30,000, the Ontario average was at 46.0%, made up of 41.6% for males and 50.7% for females. In Northeast Ontario, the total was at 48.3%, made up of 43.4% for males and 53.7% for females. In Northwest Ontario, the total was at 47.6%, made up of 43.6% for males and 52.0% for females.

The next set of distributions in Table 7.5 are for total incomes (before taxes). That is, these income data include not only employment incomes but also private pension and investment incomes, as well as transfer payments such as social assistance, workers' compensation, employment insurance, and Old Age Security (OAS) payments. Thus, these size distributions reflect impacts of the federal and provincial transfer systems. As one would expect given the modestly progressive redistributive effects of the transfer systems, there is a reduction in the percentage of persons in the lowest (under $10,000) income group in all the distributions. Transfers likely account for a portion of persons in the lowest group by employment income being raised into the second-lowest ($10,000–19,999) income group for total income, making this the modal income group for these distributions, except for the distribution for males in Toronto. Above this second-lowest income group, the percentage shares decline with each higher income group, following the pattern of a very steep pyramid, except again for the highest group of $100,000 and over. Here we have included also Statistics Canada's income group of $150,000 and over, to provide both indicators of disparity in income extremes as well as aspects of the regional distribution of the highest incomes.

In terms of federal and provincial personal income transfer systems, one sees larger impacts in Northeast and Northwest Ontario compared to the Ontario average, likely due in large part to the higher share of lower incomes and the consequent larger reliance on transfers in Northern Ontario. This set of distributions for total income covers a larger population than that for employment incomes (for Ontario, 10,556,935 persons with income compared to 73.8% of that for persons with employment income), so these distributions will include a portion of the population who do not have any employment income but receive transfer income, such as retirees who receive OAS. In Ontario, for the under-$10,000 income group the share was 15.3% while for Northeast Ontario it was 13.0% and for Northwest Ontario it was 14.0%. For males, the lowest group averaged 13.9% for Ontario compared to 10.5% in Northeast Ontario and 13.1% in Northwest Ontario. For females, Ontario averaged 16.6% compared to 15.4% in Northeast Ontario and 14.8% in Northwest Ontario. The impact of the transfer systems is also indicated to a higher income level by examining the cumulative shares under $30,000. For Ontario, this was 46.0% of the population receiving any income, while in Northeast Ontario it was 45.5% and in Northwest Ontario it was 44.3%. For males, Ontario averaged 40.0% below $30,000, while in Northeast Ontario it was 36.5% and in Northwest Ontario it was 37.7%. For females, the transfer systems had relatively less effect, especially in Northeast Ontario. While for females Ontario averaged 51.7% below $30,000, in Northeast Ontario females were at 54.2% and in Northwest Ontario at 50.7%.

While the transfer systems had modest effects on the distribution of incomes at lower levels, poverty remained. The LIM-AT shows an overall prevalence for Ontario of 14.4% of persons. Northeast Ontario had a slightly higher level, particularly for females, while Northwest Ontario had a slightly lower level for both males and females. However, the level of child poverty was higher across Ontario, including in Toronto, and even more so in Northern Ontario. For Ontario, the overall prevalence of child poverty was 19.8% and for Toronto it was 20.3%, while for Northeast Ontario it was 22.3% and for Northwest Ontario it was 22.0%. Further, there remained major disparities at the extremes, such as indicated in Table 7.5 by the ratio of the numbers of persons in the lowest income group (under $10,000) to the numbers of persons in the highest income group ($150,000 and over). One can see that disparities were greater in Northern Ontario, even more so for women. In Ontario, the disparity ratio was 5.2, meaning that for every one individual earning over $150,000, more than five individuals earned less than $10,000. In Northeast Ontario, this ratio increased to 7.7 and to 8.6 in Northwest Ontario.

If one includes federal and provincial taxes as well as transfers in total income, for lower income groups, both Northeast and Northwest Ontario still show some modest positive effect on these income shares. This is consistent with the observation that, though Northeast and Northwest Ontario have higher median incomes except for females in Northeast Ontario, *average* incomes are lower than the Ontario average, for both Northeast and Northwest Ontario and for both males and females. Of course, lower average total personal incomes for Northern Ontario means incomes received by persons *residing* in Northern Ontario as measured by Statistics Canada. Lower average personal incomes do not necessarily mean lower per capita GDP or aggregate income from the production of goods and services in Northern Ontario, because a portion of these is received as profits, rents, and other incomes outside the region.

Within the overall context of Northern Ontario there is considerable variation in distributional structures across and within the districts and communities. Eight appendix tables based on 2015 census data are provided covering every district, its largest community, and selected centres reflective of particular industries. It would go beyond the present scope to discuss the many features of each area, but a few can be noted as illustration. For instance, Appendix Table D shows a much greater incidence of lower incomes in the Algoma District even for Northern Ontario. For employment incomes at the lowest income group, Sault Ste. Marie had a higher level for males (29.2%) than females (25.4%) as did Elliot Lake, which had even higher levels for both males (33.4%) and females (32.2%). This situation generally reflects low and declining employment, especially in historically male-dominated industries. By contrast, a community like Hornepayne shows an uncommon distributional feature: the median male after-tax income is slightly higher than the average.[6] As another example, Cochrane District had somewhat higher than average incomes for Northern

Ontario but also extreme income disparities, particularly for women, and extremely high incidences of low income (poverty) for children, in Moosonee.

Nor are districts necessarily protected from major employment disparities or income extremes by being geographically adjacent to higher income populations. The largest city in Northern Ontario, Greater Sudbury, compared to the Northern regions as a whole, has not only higher average and median incomes for both males and females, but also lower disparity ratios (Appendix Table I). Yet outside the city in the Sudbury District, the average and median incomes are much lower, and the disparity measures much higher, especially for females.

Districts also vary in how their average distribution relates to the conditions of their largest cities or towns. Kenora District, for example, had much lower average and median incomes, for both males and females, than those in its largest centre, Kenora, and also those in Dryden and Red Lake (Appendix Table E). Red Lake is an example of a relatively higher income mining centre. With a lower proportion of its population at the lowest incomes and a higher proportion at higher incomes, the disparity ratio of 0.9 for males is among the lowest in Northern Ontario and, while the female disparity ratio of 13.0 is lower than levels generally in Northern Ontario, it is still higher than for Ontario. Manitoulin District had even lower levels of average and median incomes and had among the highest proportions of its population at the lowest employment income level of any district (Appendix Table F). This was coupled with extremely high levels of disparity.

By contrast, Nipissing District had much higher levels of average and median incomes and lower levels of disparity, but higher levels of overall and child low income (poverty). In the case of Rainy River District (Appendix Table H), the district had similar average and median incomes to those of Northwest Ontario, though higher disparity ratios and a higher child poverty level in its largest centre, Fort Frances. Timiskaming District is less typical in that the district, compared to its largest centre, Temiskaming Shores, had both a higher share of persons in the highest employment income groups and a somewhat higher share in the lowest employment income group. The Timiskaming District also has Cobalt, which stands out among historic mining towns in Northern Ontario and Canada. Unfortunately, Cobalt also shows a concentrated community situation of very low average and median incomes, and extreme levels of low income, especially for children.

This chapter has reviewed several current distributional disparities that beset Northern Ontario. The disparities reflect not simply a current conjuncture or generalized notion of capitalism as usual (though these too are present), but the particular conditions and history of a hinterland-colonial region. Those foundational conditions have been reproduced in colonial-racial disparities affecting Indigenous peoples. They include major disparities in employment/population rates, employment rates, unemployment rates, and low-income (or poverty) levels. Northern Ontario's conditions also include higher levels of wage and salary earnership (that is, employee status) and hence greater vulnerability to Northern Ontario's unequal labour market conditions. These labour market conditions include lower employment rates and lower levels of FYFT employment and average incomes. The conditions affect both males and females, but they also widen the gender gap in Ontario.

Such disparities are reflected in patterns of income distribution. Northern Ontario has generally larger percentages at the lowest income levels, smaller percentages at the highest incomes, and overall relatively more persons with lower employment incomes, especially for females. Census data from 2016 indicate that approximately a quarter of persons employed in Northern Ontario received incomes under $10,000. Adverse employment and income conditions have been counteracted to a degree by higher levels of public employment (in health, education, and public administration) and by transfer programs, though these have been vulnerable to and negatively affected by neoliberal policies of the provincial and federal governments.

After-tax and transfer data suggest a moderation of the extent of income polarization in Northern Ontario. However, major disparities at the regional and local levels continue, not least in child poverty. As important as the moderating effects of public employment and transfer initiatives are, they have not overcome continuing hinterland-colonial structural conditions.

NOTES

1. According to Statistics Canada, "the household after-tax income is adjusted by an equivalence scale to take economies of scale into account. This adjustment for different household sizes reflects the fact that a household's needs increase, but at a decreasing rate, as the number of members increases." The following are the LIM-AT thresholds for households using the 2015 income data reported in the 2016 Census: $22,133 (1 person), $31,301 (2 persons), $38,335 (3 persons), $44,266 (4 persons), $49,491 (5 persons), $54,215 (6 persons), $58,558 (7 persons). The adjustment for each household size is determined by finding the one-person household threshold value and multiplying it by the square root of each subsequent household size.

2. The official census date was May 10, 2016. Persons aged 15 and over at the time of the census were asked about any jobs they were in at the time of the census or since January 1, 2015. If there was more than one job, then the reference job was the one held longest. This *experienced labour force* total is somewhat smaller than the usual labour force total because it excludes unemployed persons without employment in the previous 16 months.

3. The 2016 census clarified further that "employee does not include working owners of incorporated businesses even though they may receive wages, salaries, commissions, tips, piece-rates, or payments 'in kind' (payments in goods or services rather than money)" (Statistics Canada 2018b).

4. Another industry, hydroelectricity operations, has had major impacts on development, but once construction has been completed their employment impacts have been quite limited and more dispersed across communities, so they are not used here as illustration.

5. For present purposes, the discussion does not suggest such simplified relative measures of inequality as the Gini coefficient, as this does not measure absolute differences in inequality and understates the importance of, and attention to, income extremes, including extreme poverty.

6. It is sometimes assumed for distributions that the median and the average (or mean) are the same or tend to converge, such as is often depicted in a bell curve

(or normal distribution). This is not the case for income distribution and, even more so, wealth distribution in Canada. The typical situation today reflects a skew or polarization of incomes in which some or all higher incomes (50% above the median income) outweigh the lower incomes, making the average (mean) income higher than the median income. Unlike the average, the median is not affected by extremely high income values. As Statistics Canada (2015, "Analytical concepts") notes: "This is a useful feature of the median, as it allows one to abstract from unusually high values held by relatively few people. Since income distributions are typically skewed to the left - that is, concentrated at the low end of the income scale - median income is usually lower than mean income."

CHAPTER 8

CONCLUSION

The purpose of this book has been to provide an overview and historical statistics of long-term trends in population, employment, social composition, and urban concentration in the colonization and evolution of Northern Ontario. The tables are based primarily on Canadian census data from 1871 to 2021. These census data have much value for scholarship and public policy, but there is need for critical discussion of colonial and racial views that affected official census data collection and reporting. In addition, this book pays special attention to long-term trends in relation to employment–population rates, unemployment, and economic dependency, particularly for recent decades of population and employment decline.

Colonial conditions were foundational to the development of Northern Ontario, which came to include about 793,520 km^2 or 87% of the land area of the province of Ontario. Primary to colonization was the dispossession and segregation of Indigenous peoples into small reserves—forming less than 1% of traditional treaty areas—coupled with the denial of sovereignty and cultural genocide. Further, Northern Ontario has had direct provincial control of most of its lands and resources—over 90% of the land with about 5% of the population categorized as being provincial "unorganized" territories—and a hinterland-colonial economy developed based primarily on resource export and transportation corridors. At no point did Northern Ontario have an autonomous regional, territorial, or provincial structure (such as provincehood in the Prairie provinces) that might have mitigated or to a degree democratized provincial control. In this sense, hinterland or semi-colonial conditions persist for the non-Indigenous population, although as only a fraction of the direct colonial control and oppression faced by Indigenous peoples.

The settler population of Northern Ontario grew most rapidly from the 1870s until the 1920s, then shifted to phases of reduced growth until the 1970s, then from the 1980s on to a phase mostly of decline. From 0.5% of Ontario's population in 1871, Northern Ontario's share reached a peak of 12.0% in 1941, then declined to 5.2% in 2021. By contrast, the Indigenous population, which likely had suffered population declines in the decades before 1871, endured further population stagnation and outright decline under the early decades of colonization, and experienced sustained growth only after the 1940s, especially after 1971. From at least half of Northern Ontario's population in 1871, the Indigenous share fell to less than 4% in 1941 through to 1971. However, by 2016, the Indigenous share of the Northern Ontario population had risen to around 14%.

In terms of source populations, most of the population of Northern Ontario was born in Ontario. In the first three decades, the censuses counted more than 70% as being born in Ontario; during these decades of rapid growth the largest numbers of settlers in Northern Ontario likely came from Southern Ontario. The population share born in Ontario (including Northern Ontario) declined to a low of 57.4% in 1911, but thereafter the share generally grew, to 84.0% in 2021. While initially the largest source outside Ontario was the British Isles, and to a lesser degree the United States, these shares declined and by 1891 were soon overtaken by those born in Quebec and, by 1911, those born in continental European countries.

In Southern Ontario in the period of rapid growth, the share of population born in Ontario was generally higher than in Northern Ontario, though it tended to decline after 1901. By 1961 the Ontario-born share in Northern Ontario started to exceed that in Southern Ontario. Southern Ontario differed also in having generally higher shares of the population born in the British Isles and lower shares born in Quebec, the United States, and continental Europe, particularly during the decades of rapid growth. After the Second World War, Southern Ontario compared to Northern Ontario had larger increases in the share of population from continental Europe and, in recent decades, from Asia, other Americas, and Africa.

Colonization and the gender hierarchy of Euro-Canadian settlers also had effects on sex composition and marital status. For sex, particularly during the period of rapid growth led by transportation, mining, and forestry, the male share of the population in Northern Ontario was much higher than the female share, and higher also relative to Southern Ontario. Between 1871 and 1911, the male share rose from 53.7% to 61.7%, while the female share declined from 46.1% to 38.3%. From the 1911 low point, the female share tended to increase until it reached more than 50% in 1991 and later censuses. By contrast, Southern Ontario had female shares near 50% in 1911 and consistently at or over 50% by 1951.

Examining the sex composition of the population also casts further light on recent decades of population decline in Northern Ontario. In particular, the male population reached a census peak as early as 1971 and decline in most decades thereafter. The female population reached a peak in 1991 before it too declined. The major changes in Northern Ontario from the 1970s to the 1990s, in which the total population plateaued and the female share reached more than 50%, reflected declines in primary sector employment and shifts towards increased public sector and services employment.

National and racial segregation, discrimination, and exclusion had impacts on sex composition. In 1911 the dominant English, Irish, Scottish, and French national settler groups had approximately 40–41% female shares in Northern Ontario compared to 49–51% in Southern Ontario. However, some other settler nationalities such as Italian or Polish had much lower female shares in Northern Ontario and, at the extreme, such as those of Chinese background, were female shares of less than 5%. In contrast, data available on First Nation peoples suggest a more balanced female–male distribution, for example, 49.5% in 1911 in Northern Ontario.

Census statistics on national origin have been among those most affected by colonial and racial views as well as concerns about allegiance and assimilation. Despite the ravages of colonialism, the Indigenous population remained an important presence in Northern Ontario. In terms of national-origins data, after declining relative to the population from around half in 1871 to about 3.6% in 1961, the Indigenous share of the population increased to approximately 19.5% in 2021. In Southern Ontario, the Indigenous share also fell, to a low in 1951 and 1961, then probably increased, but throughout the entire period the share was at or under 1% of the Southern Ontario population, according to official census counts.

In terms of the Northern Ontario settler population, the single largest national origin was French, unless one groups together the English, Irish, Scottish, and Welsh origins. The counts of those with French national origins increased absolutely as well as in relative terms, from 15.8% in 1871 to about 28% from 1951 to 1981. However, if one groups the English, Irish, Scottish, and Welsh, then British Isles origins were the largest reported until 1981, a majority from 1881 to 1921, then declined overall to 43.1% in 1981. In recent decades the British Isles share dropped to 13.5% in 2021. The earlier decades of change were tied to Canadian state policies on settlement and immigration. The latter sharp drop in national share, like that reported for several other national origins, occurred after the census introduced "Canadian" as a valid response for national origin in 1991. As a result, the French-origin share too fell sharply, to 10.2% in 2021. Other European origins rose from around 1% in 1871 to a peak of 28.0% in 1961, then declined overall to 20.0% in 2021.

Compared to Northern Ontario, Southern Ontario has had an even greater dominance of British Isles national origins. The British Isles origins share was much higher, around 80% until 1921, and the decline in share that occurred was to 61.4% in 1971, higher by 20 percentage points than in Northern Ontario, before a more rapid decline to 16.1% in 2011, a level approximate to that in Northern Ontario. By contrast, the share of those in Southern Ontario reporting French origins was lower. Those reporting Other European origins in Southern Ontario was higher in the earlier decades until 1911, when demand for low-wage labour was increasing relatively in Northern Ontario. In recent decades, the share of those reporting other European as well as Asian national origins was much higher in Southern Ontario than in Northern Ontario.

For official languages spoken and mother tongue, the censuses do not have regular and consistent counts until 1931, nor adequate counts of bilingualism or multilingualism, although some estimates can be made for the earlier decades. In 1871, those speaking English were probably about one-third of the census population, those speaking French about one-sixth, and those speaking Indigenous languages about one-half. For Ontario as a whole (including Northern Ontario), it is plausible that those speaking English were more than 80%, French about 5%, and Indigenous languages possibly 1%. By 1931 in Northern Ontario, the share of the population speaking English only was counted at about 70%, and those speaking French (whether unilingual or bilingual) was in the range 18–24%, while Indigenous languages were perhaps 4% or less (using data on national origin).

For the period from 1931 to 2021, for the official languages spoken, the percentage increased for those speaking English only, from 69.9% to 75.4%. It decreased for those speaking French only, from 6.8% to 0.9%, while those speaking both English and French, who have been disproportionately francophone, increased from 17.3% to a peak of 26.4% in 2001 then declined to 23.5% in 2021. This suggests that the population share speaking French might have increased from 24.1% to a peak of 27.9% in 2001, then declined to 24.4% in 2021. During these years the total numbers of those speaking French peaked at 213,840 in 1991 and declined in 2021 to 206,025. In Southern Ontario, English has been more dominant, although the percentage of English-only speakers declined overall between 1931 and 2021, from 92.6% to 87.1%. The French-only percentage has been much smaller and also declined, while the bilingual English-French percentage has increased, from 5.1% to 10.1% and in total numbers to 1,346,770. As a whole, in Southern Ontario, those who reported speaking French increased over the period from 6.4% to 10.3%.

In terms of mother tongue (or maternal language) the picture is quite different, and it poses major questions about assimilation and the reproduction and renewal of Indigenous languages and of French. In Northern Ontario, from 1941 to 2021, those with an English mother tongue increased from 53.6% to 77.6%. In contrast, those with a French mother tongue declined from 22.6% to 15.0%. The decline was even sharper for those with an Indigenous mother tongue, from 3.6% to 1.7%. In Southern Ontario, the share of those with an English mother tongue was much larger, nearly 85% for 1941 and 1951, but by 2011, due to changes in immigration patterns, the share had declined to 69.5%, lower than that in Northern Ontario. The percentage of those with a French mother tongue, lower throughout than in Northern Ontario, also declined, from 5.6% to 3.1%. The percentage of those with Indigenous mother tongues, already below 1%, also probably declined. The dangerously low levels for Indigenous mother tongues are primarily a bitter result of the multigenerational actions of the

Canadian state to eradicate Indigenous languages not least through the residential school system and public schools.

Despite the trend towards assimilation to English over the fifteen decades, there exist important language differences among Northern Ontario districts and municipalities. The largest numbers of anglophones (by mother tongue), a majority, are found in the Thunder Bay, Greater Sudbury, and Algoma census divisions. The largest numbers of francophones are in the Greater Sudbury and Cochrane census divisions. For Indigenous languages the largest numbers are in the Thunder Bay and Kenora census divisions. We also compared different census measures of language use and observe, particularly for French-language use, that communities with high levels of workplace use appear to show less assimilation, as in the case of Hearst.

The present volume has had a focus on the decades following the 1970s marked by decline in population and employment. The general turn towards stagnation and decline in the total Northern Ontario population can be dated from the 1980s. The decline began earlier in some districts (or census divisions) and later in others. Timiskaming had an earlier and persisting decline. Others also had persisting declines, but starting later, like Algoma from 1986 and Thunder Bay from 1996. In some districts the population decreases were interspersed by some increases, but at low levels. Overall, decline in Northern Ontario became more generalized. Only Manitoulin and Kenora have recorded population increases to the present.

The decline described here is long-term—well beyond shorter-term cyclical movements in employment and population related to resource commodity prices and production. Recent efforts in official research to focus one-sidedly on demographic and labour supply factors and to promote immigration as a policy solution deflect analysis away from persisting colonialism, resource-export dependency, gender disparities, and neoliberal policies of the provincial and federal governments. The evidence on population changes since at least 2000 is that net out-migration is the most important factor in population loss, which itself should suggest a greater attention to employment conditions and prospects. Although some studies point to below-replacement-level birth rates as a major reason for population decline in Northern Ontario, we challenge this view with evidence that natural population increase is higher in Northern Ontario than in Southern Ontario. In any case, below-replacement-level birth rates have long existed in both Northern and Southern Ontario, so that alone does not explain the timing of decline. Such population discussions have also been tendentious in ignoring the higher death rates in Northern Ontario and the serious health disparities of the region together with their social determinants. Moreover, discussions of social dependency tied narrowly to population age structure and the present aging of Northern Ontario's population have been more arbitrary, rather than being based on actual employment–population conditions, issues of productivity, and transfer payments analyses and policies.

Employment in Northern Ontario reached a peak in 1991, but for males the employment peak was around 1981 and for females it was later, in 2006. From 10.6% of Ontario's employment in 1951, the Northern Ontario share has fallen to 4.8% in 2021, less than the Northern Ontario population share. Employment peaks were reached in different districts in different periods, particularly for males. Cochrane, Timiskaming, and Manitoulin were at male employment peaks as early as 1951, Rainy River and the Sudbury Regional Municipality in 1971, Algoma, Kenora, Sudbury District, and Thunder Bay in 1981, and Nipissing in 1991. Overall, though, male employment tended to decline after 1981. For female employment, district peaks occurred mostly in 2006 and 2011 and overall female employment declined after 2006. In the early decades of rapid settlement the female share of total employment in Northern Ontario was at a lower level than in Southern Ontario, but at least since the 1950s the female share of total employment grew more rapidly; in 2021, it was 48.0% in Northern Ontario compared to 47.3% in Southern Ontario.

Consequently, declines in employment and population have affected the overall employment-to-population ratio (or percentage), which is an important indicator of employment opportunity and inversely related to economic dependency. In Northern Ontario, the employment–population ratio edged up slowly as female employment increased, even as male employment declined, until it reached a peak in 2006 of 45.8%. However, in all the decades since at least 1971 the employment–population ratio was substantially and persistently lower than the average for Ontario—by around 5 percentage points if not more. In 2021, the Ontario ratio was 48.3%, while for Northern Ontario it was 42.2%. Within Northern Ontario there have also been substantial and persisting disparities by district. Manitoulin, Sudbury (District), and Timiskaming have been persistently below the employment–population average in Northern Ontario, and even further below the average for Ontario. By comparison, the cities of Greater Sudbury and Thunder Bay have been above the Northern Ontario average but still below the Ontario average.

Given these lower employment–population rates it is also not surprising that Northern Ontario has had generally higher unemployment rates for male workers and for female workers. The official numbers of unemployed in Northern Ontario grew through the decades from 1951, reaching a peak in 1996 of 46,185, of whom 44% were females. In terms of the unemployed-to-employed rate (a more realistic indicator than the official unemployment rate), in 1996 the level was 14.2% for males and 13.2% for females in Northern Ontario, compared to the average for Ontario of 9.5% for males and 10.7% for females. In the next two decades, as employment conditions deteriorated and population declined through leaving, the count of unemployed declined but the unemployed rates in Northern Ontario remained higher than the Ontario average, especially for males. In 2016 the male rate was 12.5% and the female rate 8.0% in Northern Ontario, while the Ontario average was 8.1% and 7.9% respectively. The crisis impacts of COVID-19 rapidly altered this pattern so that in 2021 the unemployed rates in Northern Ontario for males were 11.7% but much increased for females to 12.0%; in Southern Ontario the male rates increased to 12.6% and the female even more sharply to 15.5%.

Deteriorating employment conditions are also associated with lower levels of full-time relative to part-time employment. Compared to the Ontario averages, Northern Ontario has generally had less full-time employment relative to part-time employment, particularly for males. Though the levels have varied, full-time employment has declined to where, in Northern Ontario in 2021, only 56.0% of male employment and 52.0% of female employment was full-time, compared to the Ontario average of 59.7% and 50.9% respectively.

This book discusses some implications of these employment and population patterns in Northern Ontario as they are indicated in measures of social dependency. Demographic or age-based dependency ratios deflect from the central importance of employment conditions and reveal less than economic dependency ratios about disparities in Northern Ontario relative to the Ontario average, including colonial-racial disparities. For instance, for 2016, a demographic dependency ratio based on non-dependent population using ages 20–64 gives an Ontario ratio of 1.64, with Northeast Ontario and Northwest Ontario ratios of 1.70. An employment-based economic dependency ratio gives a ratio of 2.03 for Ontario but 2.26 and 2.25 for Northeast and Northwest Ontario respectively. The differences in the realism and policy consequences of the two approaches become even more obvious at subregional or community levels.

An important aspect in the development of Northern Ontario is the role of its urban distribution of population and employment. Contrary to a view that Northern Ontario's rural, but not urban, areas faced population decline, the census data show that Northern Ontario's nine cities also have experienced long-term population decline: since 1996, the latest 25 years, by -4.9% compared to the overall Northern Ontario decline of -5.6%. Further, the cities' share of the Northern Ontario population did not change much between 1971 and 2021, increasing only from about 63.7% to 65.2%. In certain periods, several individual cities actually declined more rapidly than the Northern (including rural) population, such as Sault Ste. Marie, Timmins, Elliot Lake, and Temiskaming Shores.

Special attention is given to examining the cities' employment and unemployment conditions in 2016. Compared to the share of the working-age population of Ontario, Northern Ontario as a whole had lower employment levels, for both males and females, and higher unemployment levels, particularly for males. For the nine Northern cities, which together had about two-thirds of Northern Ontario's working-age population, the cities had a higher share of employment within Northern Ontario and a lower share of the unemployed.

All Northern Ontario's cities had male and overall full-year, full-time employment levels lower than the average for Ontario. But within Northern Ontario itself, median employment incomes were generally higher in the cities than in the Northeast and Northwest economic regions overall. However, in some cities, male median incomes were lower than for the region even for full-year, full-time jobs (North Bay, Elliot Lake, and Temiskaming Shores). Cities with such lower employment, and employment incomes, also had higher levels of transfers than prevailed in Northern Ontario generally. Selected smaller communities showed a wide range of employment, income, transfer, and low-income conditions. An active mining town (such as Red Lake) or rail town (such as Hornepayne) showed higher income levels, lower transfer levels, and lower low-income levels, including for females. Other communities with lower employment and incomes, most severely in First Nation communities, also had higher shares of transfers; however, the actual median dollar level of transfers for both males and females was often comparable to, if not lower than, the levels in communities with much higher employment and income conditions.

Given Northern Ontario's recent context of generally declining population and employment, the study goes further to provide selected district- and community-level comparisons of demographic dependency ratios and economic dependency ratios, along with their components. Typical demographic dependency measures put the Northern Ontario ratios about 3–4% above the Ontario average, whereas an economic dependency ratio suggests a level at least 11% higher. However, at the district and community levels there are substantial differences in magnitudes (and their component factors) in both types of dependency ratios. This reflects local differences in employment decline depending on the specific industry and local labour conditions, including the role of public sector employment and policy.

The serious disparities affecting cities and smaller communities within Northern Ontario are reflected more clearly by economic dependency measures. For instance, both Greater Sudbury (CMA) and Thunder Bay (CMA) appear close to the Ontario level in terms of demographic dependency, whereas their economic dependency ratios are higher (2.11 and 2.14, respectively, compared to 2.03 for Ontario). By contrast, Kenora has a demographic dependency ratio above the Ontario average and close to that for Northern Ontario, but an economic dependency ratio below that for both Ontario and Northern Ontario. There is an even wider range of economic dependency across smaller communities. The mining community of Red Lake in 2016 had a relatively low economic dependency level (1.79), while Marathon (2.02), Schrieber (2.03), and Hearst (2.05) had levels below the Northern Ontario average and approximate to the Ontario average. At a much higher level of economic disadvantage are some resource and transportation communities like Moosonee (2.31), Ignace (2.47), Manitouwadge (2.54), Iroquois Falls (2.69), and First Nations such as Atikameksheng Anishnawbek (2.76) and Asubpeeschoseewagong First Nation (3.75). Demographic dependency ratios do little either to explain or to differentiate underlying causes and consequences of the hinterland-colonial conditions of Northern Ontario.

Lastly, the book discussed key structural features and distributional issues of Northern population and employment in light of the long-term decline in population and employment, in four major areas. First is the continuing colonial-racial divide in Northern Ontario, with its systemic disparities in employment, unemployment, and low incomes (poverty). Second, due to its economic or industrial structure, especially the limited role of agriculture compared to other areas of Ontario, Northern Ontario has a higher level of wage- and salary-earning relative to self-employment and a stronger dependence on labour market conditions in distribution. Third, Northern Ontario has a larger presence of public sector employment, in part to stabilize and at times to compensate for losses in private sector employment. This makes even more clear the importance today of government policy in Northern employment and population conditions.

Fourth, we examined in more detail the structure of income distribution in Northern Ontario, noting particularly its greater reliance on employment incomes and transfer payments as income sources. Census data on incomes reported for 2015 shows that both Northeast and Northwest Ontario had greater shares of earners in the lowest income group (under $10,000) at around a quarter of all earners. After transfers, this lowest income group relative to the Ontario average improved: median total incomes in both Northeast and Northwest Ontario were slightly above the Ontario average. This is reflected too in Northern Ontario compared to Ontario having similar aggregate incidences of low-income (after transfers and taxes) for all ages. But child poverty is another matter: the incidences overall in Northern Ontario and in many communities were much higher than the Ontario average.

When it comes to the full range of employment incomes and total incomes in the distributions, including those above median levels and the highest income groups, Northern Ontario generally had lower shares, especially for the highest income groups and for women. So average incomes in Northern Ontario were much lower than the average for Ontario, for both males and for females. Further, a disparity measure based on a ratio of the numbers of persons in the lowest total income group (under $10,000) to the numbers in the highest total income group ($150,000 and over) shows much higher levels of disparity in Northern Ontario compared to the Ontario average, for males and even more so for females. The tables in the Appendix compare Northern districts, district seats, largest centres, and selected smaller communities. These tables show not only substantial differences among areas within Northern Ontario, as might be expected from earlier discussions of employment conditions, but also that several districts and communities have major concentrations of disparity and low income, including extreme levels for children.

A central conception of this book is that Northern Ontario's hinterland-colonial foundational structures continue to be reproduced, to the detriment of most people living here. The tide of international understanding has turned against colonialism to the point where even the Canadian state, once a fervent proponent of colonial expansion and empire, is now a signatory to the United Nations Declaration on the Rights of Indigenous Peoples. Yet the colonial structures of the Northern Ontario hinterland remain, along with their harmful distributional and developmental consequences in such a massive, rich, and beautiful land. Policies and analyses that do not tackle these hinterland-colonial conditions will fail for a major part of Northern Ontario's population, first and foremost Indigenous peoples, but also for most of the non-Indigenous population. Arguably, they have already failed, many times, as is seen in long-term declining employment and population, out-migration, and aggravated colonial-racial, regional, and local disparities and poverty.

This book has emphasized the need for decolonization of official statistics but also the use of the Canadian censuses—with appropriate caution—as contributing to understanding Northern Ontario as a hinterland-colonial region. The book also questions approaches based narrowly on demography and demographic dependency ratios, which deflect from the deteriorating employment and social conditions in Northern Ontario. Similarly, government policy such as in Ontario's

Growth Plan for Northern Ontario (2011) shows the ongoing problem of "studying a colonial economy without perceiving colonialism." Critical research and policy is much needed in Northern Ontario, in directions from resource extraction to transportation services, to health, education, media, and cultural disparities, to ecology and different forms of future growth, and to more democratic community and regional organization. Such research and policy will have to face along its way the fundamental hinterland-colonial question: the ownership, control, and use of the land and its resources in relation to its peoples.

SUPPLEMENTAL TABLES

Appendix Table A. Census measures compared for official and Indigenous languages, Ontario, Greater Sudbury, and Cochrane District, 2016.

	Ethnic origin	Mother tongue	Knowledge of official languages	First official language spoken	Home language	Work language
Ontario (population base)	13,242,160	12,946,960	13,312,865	13,312,865	12,522,045	7,434,675
Indigenous (% of population)	3.9	0.2			0.1	-
males (% of male population)	3.8	0.2			0.1	-
females (% of female population)	4.0	0.2			0.1	-
English (% of population)	37.0	68.8			82.5	97.2
males (% of male population)	36.8	69.6			83.0	97.5
females (% of female population)	37.2	67.9			82.0	96.9
French (% of population)	10.4	3.8			2.2	1.3
males (% of male population)	10.1	3.7			2.1	0.9
females (% of female population)	10.6	3.9			2.3	1.6
English only (% of population)			86.0	93.1		
males (% of male population)			87.5	93.7		
females (% of female population)			84.7	92.5		
French only (% of population)			0.3	3.8		
males (% of male population)			0.3	3.6		
females (% of female population)			0.3	3.9		
English and French (% of pop.)			11.2	0.7		
males (% of male population)			10.2	0.7		
females (% of female population)			12.1	0.7		
Neither English nor French (% of pop.)			2.5	2.4		
males (% of male population)			2.0	2.0		
females (% of female population)			2.9	2.8		
Census official language minority (%)				4.1		
alternative upper estimate (%)				4.5		

	Ethnic origin	Mother tongue	Knowledge of official languages	First official language spoken	Home language	Work language
Greater Sudbury CD (population base)	158,780	156,180	159,860	159,855	155,525	86,595
Indigenous (% of population)	12.5	0.1			-	-
males (% of male population)	12.6	0.1			-	-
females (% of female population)	12.4	0.2			-	-
English (% of population)	40.2	67.5			84.6	95.1
males (% of male population)	39.9	68.8			85.6	97.4
females (% of ffemale population)	40.6	66.1			83.6	92.6
French (% of population)	38.1	26.2			13.3	4.8
males (% of male population)	37.3	25.1			12.4	2.4
females (% of female population)	38.8	27.3			14.2	7.3
English only (% of population)			60.2	73.9		
males (% of male population)			62.5	75.0		
females (% of female population)			58.0	72.8		
French only (% of population)			0.8	25.3		
males (% of male population)			0.7	24.3		
females (% of female population)			0.9	26.4		
English and French (% of pop.)			38.7	0.5		
males (% of male population)			36.6	0.5		
females (% of female population)			40.7	0.5		
Neither English nor French (% of pop.)			0.2	0.2		
males (% of male population)			0.2	0.2		
females (% of female population)			0.3	0.3		
Census official language minority (%)				25.6		
alternative upper estimate (%)				25.9		

(cont)

Appendix Table A. Census measures compared for official and Indigenous languages, Ontario, Greater Sudbury, and Cochrane District, 2016.

Cochrane CD (population base)	Ethnic origin	Mother tongue	Knowledge of official languages	First official language spoken	Home language	Work language
	78,510	76,890	78,930	78,930	76,365	40,435
Indigenous (% of population)	18.4	2.1			0.8	0.2
males (% of male population)	18.0	1.9			0.7	0.2
females (% of female population)	18.9	2.3			0.8	0.2
English (% of population)	31.3	50.9			66.7	81.2
males (% of male population)	31.3	51.8			67.9	83.3
females (% of female population)	31.3	49.9			65.6	78.9
French (% of population)	37.0	44.1			31.5	18.5
males (% of male population)	36.9	43.4			30.5	16.4
females (% of female population)	37.1	44.8			32.5	20.8
English only (% of population)			42.9	56.4		
males (% of male population)			44.5	57.0		
females (% of female population)			41.3	55.8		
French only (% of population)			4.7	42.9		
males (% of male population)			4.5	42.3		
females (% of female population)			4.8	43.5		
English and French (% of pop.)			52.3	0.6		
males (% of male population)			50.9	0.6		
females (% of female population)			53.7	0.6		
Neither English nor French (% of pop.)			0.2	0.1		
males (% of male population)			0.1	0.1		
females (% of female population)			0.2	0.2		
Census official language minority (%)				43.2		
alternative upper estimate (%)				43.5		

	Ethnic origin	Mother tongue	Knowledge of official languages	First official language spoken	Home language	Work language
Timmins CA (population base)	41,230	40,360	41,480	41,480	39,975	22,620
Indigenous (% of population)	14.1	0.7			0.2	-
males (% of male population)	13.4	0.6			0.2	-
females (% of female population)	14.8	0.9			0.3	-
English (% of population)	37.7	58.6			78.6	92.9
males (% of male population)	38.0	59.9			80.1	95.1
females (% of female population)	37.4	57.4			77.2	90.5
French (% of population)	41.0	36.9			20.0	7.1
males (% of male population)	40.3	36.0			18.8	4.9
females (% of female population)	41.6	37.7			21.3	9.5
English only (% of population)			47.1	63.7		
males (% of male population)			49.1	64.5		
females (% of female population)			45.2	62.9		
French only (% of population)			2.0	35.6		
males (% of male population)			1.9	34.7		
females (% of female population)			2.0	36.4		
English and French (% of pop.)			50.8	0.7		
males (% of male population)			49.0	0.7		
females (% of female population)			52.6	0.6		
Neither English nor French (% of pop.)			0.1	0.1		
males (% of male population)			0.1	0.1		
females (% of female population)			0.2	0.2		
Census official language minority (%)				35.9		
alternative upper estimate (%)				36.2		

(cont)

Appendix Table A. Census measures compared for official and Indigenous languages, Ontario, Greater Sudbury, and Cochrane District, 2016.

	Ethnic origin	Mother tongue	Knowledge of official languages	First official language spoken	Home language	Work language
Hearst T (population base)	4,975	4,885	4,980	4,980	4,860	2,590
Indigenous (% of population)	8.0	0.3			-	-
males (% of male population)	7.3	0.2			-	-
females (% of female population)	8.9	0.4			0.2	-
English (% of population)	9.5	9.9			12.4	20.3
males (% of male population)	9.4	10.2			12.8	22.7
females (% of female population)	9.9	9.7			12.1	17.6
French (% of population)	35.2	88.5			86.7	79.7
males (% of male population)	35.8	88.2			86.4	76.9
females (% of female population)	34.1	88.5			87.0	82.4
English only (% of population)			6.2	11.8		
males (% of male population)			6.5	12.0		
females (% of female population)			5.9	11.7		
French only (% of population)			23.3	87.6		
males (% of male population)			23.3	87.6		
females (% of female population)			23.6	87.9		
English and French (% of pop.)			70.4	0.5		
males (% of male population)			70.6	0.4		
females (% of female population)			70.5	0.4		
Neither English nor French (% of pop.)			-	-		
males (% of male population)			-	-		
females (% of female population)			0.2	-		
Census official language minority (%)				87.9		
alternative upper estimate (%)				88.1		

	Ethnic origin	Mother tongue	Knowledge of official languages	First official language spoken	Home language	Work language
Moonbeam TP (population base)	1,215	1,215	1,230	1,230	1,205	660
Indigenous (% of population)	5.3	0.4			-	-
males (% of male population)	4.0	-			-	-
females (% of female population)	7.6	-			-	-
English (% of population)	15.6	18.9			25.7	53.0
males (% of male population)	16.1	20.0			25.8	57.1
females (% of female population)	15.1	18.6			26.5	48.4
French (% of population)	43.6	79.8			74.3	47.0
males (% of male population)	43.5	79.2			74.2	42.9
females (% of female population)	42.9	80.5			74.4	53.2
English only (% of population)			15.0	19.9		
males (% of male population)			16.5	20.5		
females (% of female population)			13.4	19.2		
French only (% of population)			13.4	79.7		
males (% of male population)			12.6	78.7		
females (% of female population)			14.3	80.0		
English and French (% of pop.)			71.5	0.8		
males (% of male population)			70.1	0.8		
females (% of female population)			73.1	-		
Neither English nor French (% of pop.)			-	-		
males (% of male population)			-	-		
females (% of female population)			-	-		
Census official language minority (%)				79.7		
alternative upper estimate (%)				80.5		

Source: See Table Notes and Data Sources Table 4.7 for 2016.

Appendix Table B. Full-time and part-time employment by district in Northern Ontario, census dates, 1981–2021.

	1981	1986	1991	1996	2001	2006	2011	2016	2021
Northern Ontario	385,920	370,380	394,820	379,670	369,540	366,640	346,445	380,405	394,395
full-time (males)	210,355	121,360	120,635	115,545	110,050	113,255	151,685	103,625	113,935
part-time (males)	24,390	94,540	98,820	90,330	85,870	82,070	26,065	92,745	89,365
full-time (females)	95,040	54,440	70,120	70,355	75,515	84,005	118,570	84,600	99,280
part-time (females)	56,135	100,040	105,245	103,440	98,105	87,310	50,125	99,435	91,815
All employment (%)									
full-time total	79.1	47.5	48.3	49.0	50.2	53.8	78.0	49.5	54.1
part-time total	20.9	52.5	51.7	51.0	49.8	46.2	22.0	50.5	45.9
Male employment (%)									
full-time (males)	89.6	56.2	55.0	56.1	56.2	58.0	85.3	52.8	56.0
part-time (males)	10.4	43.8	45.0	43.9	43.8	42.0	14.7	47.2	44.0
Female employment (%)									
full-time (females)	62.9	35.2	40.0	40.5	43.5	49.0	70.3	46.0	52.0
part-time (females)	37.1	64.8	60.0	59.5	56.5	51.0	29.7	54.0	48.0
Algoma District	66,980	63,195	62,035	57,195	55,625	56,885	52,645	55,880	49,000
full-time (males)	36,920	22,785	16,590	17,280	16,400	16,705	22,720	14,595	14,270
part-time (males)	4,070	14,855	17,880	13,520	12,515	12,390	4,015	14,235	10,965
full-time (females)	15,930	8,820	10,195	10,130	10,895	12,740	17,630	11,945	11,695
part-time (females)	10,060	16,735	17,370	16,265	15,815	15,050	8,280	15,105	12,070
Cochrane District	46,170	44,285	45,735	45,180	41,720	41,465	38,345	42,175	36,140
full-time (males)	26,205	15,225	14,860	14,460	13,080	13,450	17,780	11,750	11,165
part-time (males)	2,785	11,445	11,395	10,565	9,815	8,800	2,365	10,525	7,890
full-time (females)	11,235	6,375	7,945	8,065	8,215	8,950	13,020	8,970	8,865
part-time (females)	5,945	11,240	11,535	12,090	10,610	10,265	5,180	10,930	8,220

	1981	1986	1991	1996	2001	2006	2011	2016	2021
Kenora District	28,840	26,645	29,570	30,530	31,140	31,555	26,170	32,010	27,325
full-time (males)	15,850	8,365	9,325	9,205	9,425	9,485	11,810	8,635	8,915
part-time (males)	1,795	7,335	7,495	7,550	7,275	7,125	1,700	7,915	5,250
full-time (females)	7,255	3,690	4,855	5,890		7,430	9,485	7,590	7,645
part-time (females)	3,940	7,255	7,895	7,885	7,880	7,515	3,175	7,870	5,515
Manitoulin District	4,400	4,170	4,890	5,400	5,640	5,920	5,540	6,190	5,410
full-time (males)	2,315	1,130	1,210	1,370	1,430	1,435	2,290	1,470	1,495
part-time (males)	360	1,260	1,470	1,480	1,395	1,600	405	1,680	1,195
full-time (females)	1,060	535	840	910	1,180	1,140	2,085	1,475	1,490
part-time (females)	665	1,245	1,370	1,640	1,635	1,745	760	1,565	1,230
Nipissing District	38,275	37,180	41,625	39,995	40,025	33,305	40,350	41,940	38,010
full-time (males)	19,910	12,430	13,180	11,720	12,225	12,660	17,500	11,215	11,180
part-time (males)	2,825	8,975	9,430	9,440	8,905	9,160	3,080	10,095	8,200
full-time (females)	9,950	5,830	7,860	7,870	8,560	9,750	13,910	9,555	9,350
part-time (females)	5,590	9,945	11,155	10,965	10,335	1,735	5,860	11,075	9,280
Rainy River District	11,125	11,200	11,350	11,490	11,290	11,125	9,320	10,440	9,025
full-time (males)	5,795	3,275	3,255	3,190	3,290	3,275	4,025	2,505	2,580
part-time (males)	865	3,330	3,090	2,985	2,760	2,590	705	2,755	2,005
full-time (females)	2,895	1,540	1,945	2,040	2,365	2,495	3,265	2,285	2,335
part-time (females)	1,570	3,055	3,060	3,275	2,875	2,765	1,325	2,895	2,105
Sudbury District	12,115	11,340	12,725	11,275	10,585	10,190	9,635	10,775	9,585
full-time (males)	7,065	3,840	4,160	3,540	3,120	2,960	4,475	3,150	2,990
part-time (males)	730	3,085	3,275	2,905	2,910	2,650	630	2,505	2,115
full-time (females)	2,755	1,380	1,890	1,760	1,675	1,900	3,150	2,195	2,235

(cont)

Appendix Table B. Full-time and part-time employment by district in Northern Ontario, census dates, 1981–2021.

	1981	1986	1991	1996	2001	2006	2011	2016	2021
part-time (females)	1,565	3,035	3,400	3,070	2,880	2,680	1,380	2,925	2,245
Sudbury Regional Municipality/ Greater Sudbury	76,350	72,295	83,500	79,555	78,185	81,290	79,215	87,070	82,410
full-time (males)	41,965	22,510	26,915	24,305	22,035	25,255	34,670	25,205	25,535
part-time (males)	4,575	18,060	18,390	18,405	18,625	16,590	5,905	19,670	19,825
full-time (females)	18,655	11,185	15,920	15,050	16,750	18,355	27,760	20,125	20,450
part-time (females)	11,155	20,540	22,275	21,795	20,775	21,090	10,880	22,070	16,600
Thunder Bay District	82,820	81,495	85,080	81,765	79,425	78,610	70,700	77,460	67,830
full-time (males)	44,355	25,750	25,780	25,235	24,195	23,165	29,795	20,520	15,980
part-time (males)	4,905	21,230	21,380	19,325	18,105	17,575	6,105	19,205	15,960
full-time (females)	20,820	12,450	15,720	15,450	16,125	17,630	23,500	16,845	18,615
part-time (females)	12,740	22,065	22,200	21,755	21,000	20,240	11,300	20,890	17,275
Timiskaming District	18,845	18,575	18,310	17,285	15,905	16,295	14,525	16,465	69,660
full-time (males)	9,975	6,050	5,360	5,240	4,850	4,865	6,620	4,580	19,825
part-time (males)	1,480	4,965	5,015	4,155	3,565	3,590	1,155	4,160	15,960
full-time (females)	4,485	2,635	2,950	3,190	3,190	3,615	4,765	3,615	16,600
part-time (females)	2,905	4,925	4,985	4,700	4,300	4,225	1,985	4,110	17,275

Source: Data for 2011 are from the NHS and less consistent. See Table Notes and Data Sources Table 5.7.

Appendix Table C. Distribution of employment and total incomes, Algoma District, Sault Ste. Marie, Elliot Lake, and Hornepayne, for 2015.

	Algoma District			Sault Ste. Marie CA			Elliot Lake CA			Hornepayne TP		
	all	males	females	all	males	females	all	males	females	all	males	females
All persons with income	96,055	46,805	49,245	65,395	31,530	33,855	9,470	4,535	4,940	810	425	380
Persons with employment income	62,715	33,510	29,210	44,505	23,765	20,735	4,345	2,200	2,145	625	355	265
% persons with employment income	65.3	71.6	59.3	68.1	75.4	61.2	45.9	48.5	43.4	77.2	83.5	69.7
Distribution of employment income (%)												
Under $10,000 (including loss)	28.3	29.3	27.1	27.4	29.2	25.4	32.7	33.4	32.2	19.2	15.5	24.5
$10,000 to $19,999	12.8	10.2	15.8	12.8	10.1	15.9	13.9	12.5	15.4	8.8	4.2	17.0
$20,000 to $29,999	10.8	8.6	13.5	10.8	8.6	13.3	11.7	8.4	14.9	7.2	4.2	13.2
$30,000 to $39,999	9.2	7.1	11.6	9.1	7.1	11.6	9.4	8.0	11.2	7.2	4.2	11.3
$40,000 to $49,999	8.4	7.0	9.9	8.4	6.9	10.2	7.5	6.4	8.6	8.8	7.0	13.2
$50,000 to $59,999	6.4	6.6	6.2	6.5	6.5	6.6	5.9	6.4	5.4	8.0	8.5	9.4
$60,000 to $69,999	4.9	5.5	4.1	5.0	5.5	4.4	3.7	4.1	3.0	6.4	8.5	5.7
$70,000 to $79,999	4.9	6.1	3.6	5.3	6.5	3.9	3.1	3.6	2.6	4.0	5.6	1.9
$80,000 to $89,999	4.1	5.4	2.7	4.6	6.0	2.9	2.6	3.0	2.3	6.4	9.9	3.8
$90,000 to $99,999	3.8	4.6	2.9	4.0	4.8	3.0	2.8	3.4	2.3	5.6	7.0	3.8
$100,000 and over	6.3	9.5	2.6	6.0	8.9	2.7	6.6	11.4	1.9	18.4	28.2	3.8
Distribution of total income (%)												
Under $10,000 (including loss)	13.1	10.6	15.4	12.3	10.3	14.3	13.1	10.4	15.5	13.0	6.1	18.1
$10,000 to $19,999	18.6	14.0	23.0	17.7	12.8	22.2	24.6	21.1	27.9	11.0	4.9	18.1
$20,000 to $29,999	15.9	13.2	18.5	15.4	12.2	18.4	21.1	20.2	22.0	9.1	4.9	15.3
$30,000 to $39,999	13.1	13.7	12.6	13.4	14.1	12.8	13.1	14.1	12.3	7.1	6.1	8.3

(suite)

Appendix Table C. Distribution of employment and total incomes, Algoma District, Sault Ste. Marie, Elliot Lake, and Hornepayne, for 2015.

	Algoma District			Sault Ste. Marie CA			Elliot Lake CA			Hornepayne TP		
	all	males	females	all	males	females	all	males	females	all	males	females
$40,000 to $49,999	10.1	10.4	9.8	10.3	10.6	10.1	8.7	9.4	8.1	10.4	9.8	11.1
$50,000 to $59,999	7.3	8.2	6.4	7.5	8.3	6.7	5.4	6.5	4.5	7.8	8.5	8.3
$60,000 to $69,999	5.3	6.4	4.3	5.6	6.7	4.6	3.5	3.9	3.2	8.4	11.0	5.6
$70,000 to $79,999	4.5	5.9	3.1	4.8	6.3	3.4	2.3	2.9	1.9	6.5	9.8	1.4
$80,000 to $89,999	3.5	4.9	2.1	3.9	5.5	2.3	1.9	2.2	1.6	7.1	9.8	2.8
$90,000 to $99,999	3.0	3.9	2.2	3.3	4.3	2.4	1.7	2.4	1.3	4.5	6.1	4.2
$100,000 and over	5.7	8.8	2.7	5.8	8.9	2.8	4.5	7.3	1.8	15.6	25.6	5.6
$100,000 to $149,999	4.5	7.0	2.1	4.6	7.0	2.3	3.4	5.6	1.5	13.0	22.0	4.2
$150,000 and over	1.2	1.9	0.5	1.2	1.9	0.6	1.0	1.8	0.4	2.6	4.9	1.4
Ratio of total income shares												
Persons under $10,000 to persons $150,000+	11.1	5.7	28.3	12.7	5.8	37.3	12.7	5.8	37.3	5.0	1.3	13.0
Low income (LIM) after tax:												
All ages (%)	16.2	14.9	17.4	15.3	13.8	16.8	23.2	22.9	23.4	6.7	4.9	6.7
0–5 years (%)	25.3	25.4	25.3	24.6	24.6	24.5	37.9	39.5	36.4	16.7	12.5	0
Average after-tax total income ($)	34,952	40,625	29,564	35,919	41,649	30,613	30,300	35,795	25,298	45,494	58,189	32,488
Median after-tax total income ($)	29,345	35,197	24,019	30,464	36,398	24,979	23,770	27,520	21,453	43,136	59,072	25,152

Note: Due to rounding, there can be apparent errors in percentage totals, especially for the highest income ranges for small communities.

Source: See Table Notes and Data Sources Table 6.1 for 2016.

Appendix Table D. Distribution of employment and total incomes, Cochrane District, Hearst, Iroquois Falls, and Moosonee, for 2015.

	Cochrane District			Hearst T			Iroquois Falls T			Moosonee T		
	all	Males	females	all	males	females	all	males	females	all	males	females
All persons with income	64,995	32,220	32,770	4,240	2,100	2,140	3,780	1,835	1,945	1,030	485	545
Persons with employment income	46,135	24,600	21,530	2,945	1,560	1,385	2,370	1,245	1,120	730	350	375
% persons with employment income	71.0	76.4	65.7	69.5	74.3	64.7	62.7	67.8	57.6	70.9	72.2	68.8
Distribution of employment income (%)												
Under $10,000 (including loss)	23.4	21.1	26.1	18.2	13.8	22.7	26.6	24.5	28.6	19.9	18.6	18.7
$10,000 to $19,999	11.8	9.2	14.7	12.9	9.9	15.9	13.5	10.4	16.5	8.9	10.0	8.0
$20,000 to $29,999	9.8	7.4	12.6	9.7	7.1	12.6	8.9	7.6	10.7	11.0	11.4	10.7
$30,000 to $39,999	9.2	7.0	11.7	9.8	7.4	12.6	9.3	6.8	12.5	8.9	10.0	9.3
$40,000 to $49,999	8.5	7.2	10.0	9.8	8.3	11.6	9.1	7.2	11.2	9.6	10.0	9.3
$50,000 to $59,999	7.7	7.9	7.5	10.4	11.9	8.7	6.1	6.4	5.8	11.6	8.6	13.3
$60,000 to $69,999	6.3	7.6	4.8	8.7	12.2	4.7	4.9	6.8	2.7	7.5	7.1	8.0
$70,000 to $79,999	5.0	6.4	3.4	6.6	9.3	3.6	5.1	6.4	3.1	4.8	5.7	4.0
$80,000 to $89,999	4.1	5.3	2.7	3.9	5.8	2.2	3.8	4.8	2.7	4.1	4.3	4.0
$90,000 to $99,999	4.4	5.4	3.3	4.4	5.1	3.6	4.9	6.8	2.7	2.7	1.4	4.0
$100,000 and over	9.8	15.5	3.3	6.1	9.3	2.5	8.0	11.6	3.6	11.6	14.3	9.3
Distribution of total income (%)												
Under $10,000 (including loss)	12.7	9.7	15.6	8.8	5.5	12.1	12.6	7.8	17.4	19.3	23.3	16.5
$10,000 to $19,999	17.0	12.6	21.4	18.4	13.0	23.8	16.2	10.1	22.0	12.0	12.2	11.7

(cont)

Appendix Table D. Distribution of employment and total incomes, Cochrane District, Hearst, Iroquois Falls, and Moosonee, for 2015.

	Cochrane District			Hearst T			Iroquois Falls T			Moosonee T		
	all	Males	females	all	males	females	all	males	females	all	males	females
$20,000 to $29,999	14.5	11.9	17.1	15.4	12.8	18.3	13.6	10.1	16.9	13.0	10.0	14.6
$30,000 to $39,999	11.2	9.9	12.5	10.9	10.4	11.6	11.5	10.1	13.1	9.4	8.9	9.7
$40,000 to $49,999	9.8	9.5	10.1	10.2	9.4	10.7	13.8	16.2	11.5	8.9	7.8	9.7
$50,000 to $59,999	8.0	8.7	7.3	9.4	11.1	7.8	8.2	10.1	6.7	9.9	8.9	10.7
$60,000 to $69,999	6.3	7.7	4.9	8.0	10.6	5.2	5.3	7.8	2.9	7.3	7.8	6.8
$70,000 to $79,999	4.8	6.4	3.1	5.9	8.9	2.9	4.5	6.4	2.4	5.2	5.6	5.8
$80,000 to $89,999	3.6	4.9	2.3	3.7	5.3	1.9	3.7	5.3	1.9	3.6	3.3	2.9
$90,000 to $99,999	3.5	4.7	2.4	3.2	3.6	2.4	3.4	5.3	1.9	2.1	2.2	2.9
$100,000 and over	8.7	14.0	3.4	6.2	9.6	2.9	6.8	10.6	2.9	9.4	12.2	7.8
$100,000 to $149,999	6.9	11.0	2.8	4.8	7.2	2.1	5.6	8.7	2.7	7.8	8.9	6.8
$150,000 and over	1.8	3.0	0.6	1.4	2.4	0.5	1.2	2.2	0.3	1.6	3.3	0.0
Ratio of total income shares												
Persons under $10,000 to persons $150,000+	7.1	3.3	26.6	6.2	2.3	25.5	10.2	3.5	65.0	12.3	7.0	n/a
Low income (LIM) after tax												
all ages (%)	14.2	12.5	15.9	13.4	10.8	15.6	12.8	12.2	13.3	24.7	25.0	25.2
0–5 years (%)	21.9	20.7	23.2	17.6	16.7	22.2	17.9	21.4	14.3	39.0	40.9	44.4
Average after-tax total income ($)	38,168	45,485	30,907	38,096	44,647	31,702	36,342	45,215	27,809	40,625	40,475	40,754
Median after-tax total income ($)	31,923	40,610	25,218	33,122	42,773	25,648	32,626	41,788	23,872	34,304	33,451	35,072

Note: Due to rounding, there can be apparent errors in percentage totals, especially for the highest income ranges for small communities.

Source: See Table Notes and Data Sources Table 6.1 for 2016.

Appendix Table E. Distribution of employment and total incomes, Kenora District, Kenora, Dryden, and Red Lake, for 2015.

	Kenora District			Kenora CA			Dryden CY			Red Lake MU		
	all	Males	females	all	males	females	all	males	females	all	males	females
Persons with income	50,235	25,115	25,120	12,375	6,040	6,335	6,425	3,075	3,345	3,310	1,705	1,600
Persons with employment income	34,915	18,160	16,755	9,190	4,635	4,555	4,610	2,365	2,250	2,720	1,450	1,265
% persons with employment income	69.5	72.3	66.7	74.3	76.7	71.9	71.8	76.9	67.3	82.2	85.0	79.1
Distribution of employment income (%)												
Under $10,000 (including loss)	26.1	25.6	26.7	21.8	19.6	23.9	25.7	25.6	25.8	14.0	9.7	19.0
$10,000 to $19,999	13.3	12.2	14.4	12.1	10.9	13.5	11.4	8.2	14.4	10.8	7.9	14.2
$20,000 to $29,999	11.6	10.3	13.0	10.2	9.8	10.6	10.5	8.2	13.1	7.9	6.2	10.3
$30,000 to $39,999	10.5	8.9	12.2	10.1	8.4	12.0	9.1	8.2	10.0	8.8	5.5	12.6
$40,000 to $49,999	9.0	7.6	10.5	10.1	8.5	11.9	9.1	7.2	11.1	8.6	6.2	11.5
$50,000 to $59,999	7.1	6.9	7.4	9.0	9.1	9.0	7.2	7.0	7.1	7.9	7.2	9.1
$60,000 to $69,999	5.5	6.0	4.9	7.1	8.1	6.1	6.3	7.0	5.6	5.9	5.5	6.3
$70,000 to $79,999	4.0	4.7	3.1	4.6	5.5	3.7	5.1	7.0	3.1	4.8	5.2	4.7
$80,000 to $89,999	3.3	4.0	2.5	3.8	4.6	2.7	4.4	5.5	3.3	4.6	5.5	3.6
$90,000 to $99,999	2.9	3.5	2.2	3.7	4.1	3.3	4.1	5.5	2.7	5.0	6.2	3.6
$100,000 and over	6.8	10.3	2.9	7.5	11.4	3.3	7.2	10.8	3.1	21.0	35.2	5.1
Distribution of total income (%)												
Under $10,000 (including loss)	18.0	18.6	17.3	10.8	9.4	12.1	12.0	10.6	13.2	9.7	7.4	12.5
$10,000 to $19,999	16.8	13.9	19.6	15.0	12.0	17.9	15.6	11.0	19.8	11.6	8.0	15.4

(cont)

Appendix Table E. Distribution of employment and total incomes, Kenora District, Kenora, Dryden, and Red Lake, for 2015.

	Kenora District			Kenora CA			Dryden CY			Red Lake MU		
	all	Males	females	all	males	females	all	males	females	all	males	females
$20,000 to $29,999	13.5	11.4	15.6	13.3	10.8	15.5	13.4	9.1	17.4	10.3	6.8	13.8
$30,000 to $39,999	11.7	10.4	13.0	11.7	9.9	13.4	12.3	11.5	13.1	9.6	6.8	12.5
$40,000 to $49,999	10.1	9.2	11.1	11.6	11.4	11.8	11.1	10.6	11.5	9.7	7.1	12.5
$50,000 to $59,999	8.1	8.1	8.0	10.2	11.1	9.3	8.9	9.8	8.1	8.6	8.0	9.0
$60,000 to $69,999	6.1	7.0	5.3	7.6	9.0	6.2	7.3	9.3	5.4	6.8	6.5	7.1
$70,000 to $79,999	4.1	5.0	3.2	5.5	6.8	4.3	5.1	7.1	3.4	5.2	5.4	5.4
$80,000 to $89,999	3.0	3.8	2.2	3.9	5.0	3.0	4.1	5.1	2.9	4.3	5.4	3.2
$90,000 to $99,999	2.5	3.2	1.8	3.2	3.9	2.5	3.7	5.1	2.5	4.3	5.4	3.2
$100,000 and over	6.1	9.4	3.0	7.2	10.7	3.9	6.7	10.5	3.2	19.4	32.7	5.1
$100,000 to $149,999	4.8	7.3	2.3	5.5	8.1	3.1	5.6	8.8	2.6	14.4	23.8	4.2
$150,000 and over	1.3	2.1	0.6	1.6	2.5	0.8	1.1	1.8	0.6	5.1	8.6	1.0
Ratio of total income shares												
Persons under $10,000 to persons $150,000+	13.3	8.9	28.7	6.6	3.7	15.1	10.7	5.8	21.5	1.9	0.9	13.0
Low income (LIM) after tax												
all ages (%)	11.0	10.1	11.9	10.9	9.6	12.1	12.8	11.6	13.7	6.2	5.8	6.6
0–5 years (%)	18.5	16.4	20.6	16.5	13.0	20.2	22.4	21.4	23.3	8.1	9.4	6.7
Average after-tax total income ($)	34,690	38,247	31,168	39,895	45,245	34,811	37,902	44,222	32,075	48,607	59,713	36,695
Median after-tax total income ($)	29,275	33,154	26,390	35,161	40,948	29,966	33,516	41,884	27,072	42,926	56,576	32,288

Note: Due to rounding, there can be apparent errors in percentage totals, especially for the highest income ranges for small communities.
Source: See Table Notes and Data Sources Table 5.4 for 2016.

Appendix Table F. Distribution of employment and total incomes, Manitoulin District, Little Current, Nipissing District, and North Bay, for 2015.

	Manitoulin District			Little Current pop centre			Nipissing District			North Bay CA		
	all	males	females	all	males	females	all	males	females	all	males	females
Persons with income	10,845	5,365	5,485	1,230	585	650	68,995	33,480	35,515	58,240	28,225	30,015
Persons with employment income	6,610	3,475	3,130	785	395	390	45,695	23,530	22,165	39,660	20,355	19,305
% persons with employment income	60.9	64.8	57.1	63.8	67.5	60.0	66.2	70.3	62.4	68.1	72.1	64.3
Distribution of employment income (%)												
Under $10,000 (including loss)	34.7	38.0	31.3	28.7	32.9	24.4	25.4	24.6	26.2	24.4	23.8	25.1
$10,000 to $19,999	13.5	13.8	13.1	14.6	12.7	17.9	12.8	10.8	14.9	12.8	10.9	14.8
$20,000 to $29,999	11.0	10.1	12.0	10.2	10.1	11.5	11.3	9.8	12.9	11.2	9.7	12.9
$30,000 to $39,999	12.1	10.5	13.9	11.5	12.7	10.3	10.4	9.1	11.7	10.1	8.7	11.6
$40,000 to $49,999	8.4	6.9	10.1	10.2	7.6	11.5	9.4	9.3	9.6	9.3	9.2	9.5
$50,000 to $59,999	5.8	5.6	6.2	4.5	5.1	5.1	7.7	8.2	7.2	8.0	8.5	7.4
$60,000 to $69,999	3.7	3.2	4.2	5.1	3.8	5.1	5.6	6.6	4.5	5.8	6.9	4.7
$70,000 to $79,999	2.7	2.9	2.6	2.5	2.5	2.6	4.3	4.8	3.7	4.4	4.9	3.9
$80,000 to $89,999	2.3	2.0	2.7	3.2	3.8	2.6	3.5	4.1	2.9	3.7	4.2	3.2
$90,000 to $99,999	2.1	2.0	2.2	3.8	1.3	5.1	3.4	3.4	3.4	3.6	3.6	3.5
$100,000 and over	3.5	5.0	1.8	4.5	7.6	1.3	6.3	9.3	3.1	6.6	9.6	3.4
Distribution of total income (%)												
Under $10,000 (including loss)	18.4	18.5	18.4	12.4	13.2	11.8	13.1	11.3	14.7	12.6	11.0	14.1
$10,000 to $19,999	20.7	18.5	22.7	19.5	15.8	22.8	19.6	16.1	22.9	18.6	15.6	21.6
$20,000 to $29,999	15.4	14.2	16.5	16.2	13.2	18.9	15.1	13.2	16.9	14.7	12.5	16.8

(cont)

Appendix Table F. Distribution of employment and total incomes, Manitoulin District, Little Current, Nipissing District, and North Bay, for 2015.

	Manitoulin District			Little Current pop centre			Nipissing District			North Bay CA		
	all	males	females	all	males	females	all	males	females	all	males	females
$30,000 to $39,999	12.7	13.0	12.5	14.1	15.8	13.4	12.0	11.9	12.1	11.9	11.4	12.4
$40,000 to $49,999	10.6	10.9	10.1	12.4	13.2	11.8	10.5	11.1	9.9	10.5	10.8	10.3
$50,000 to $59,999	7.1	7.1	7.1	6.6	6.1	7.1	8.0	8.9	7.1	8.4	9.4	7.4
$60,000 to $69,999	4.6	5.2	4.2	5.0	6.1	3.9	6.0	7.3	4.8	6.3	7.7	5.0
$70,000 to $79,999	3.1	3.6	2.5	3.7	4.4	3.9	4.1	4.9	3.4	4.3	5.1	3.6
$80,000 to $89,999	2.2	2.2	2.1	2.5	3.5	1.6	3.1	3.9	2.4	3.3	4.0	2.7
$90,000 to $99,999	1.7	1.7	1.6	2.1	0.9	3.1	2.7	2.9	2.5	3.0	3.2	2.7
$100,000 and over	3.5	4.8	2.3	4.6	5.3	3.1	5.8	8.6	3.2	6.3	9.2	3.5
$100,000 to $149,999	2.9	3.8	1.9	4.1	5.3	3.1	4.3	6.1	2.5	4.6	6.4	2.8
$150,000 and over	0.7	1.1	0.4	0.4	0.9	0.8	1.5	2.5	0.6	1.7	2.8	0.7
Ratio of total income shares												
Persons under $10,000 to persons $150,000+	25.7	17.4	48.5	30.0	15.0	15.0	8.5	4.6	22.9	7.3	3.9	19.0
Low income (LIM) after tax												
All ages (%)	14.8	14.4	15.0	16.4	14.9	17.8	17.2	16.0	18.4	15.7	14.7	16.5
0–5 years (%)	23.2	24.3	21.2	26.7	28.6	28.6	24.9	24.4	25.4	22.6	21.8	23.1
Average after-tax total income ($)	30,816	32,392	29,295	32,532	34,124	31,047	35,328	40,392	30,551	36,571	41,972	31,514
Median after-tax total income ($)	25,277	27,451	23,705	28,416	31,232	26,240	29,168	34,181	24,992	30,243	35,433	26,130

Note: Due to rounding, there can be apparent errors in percentage totals, especially for the highest income ranges for small communities.

Source: See Table Notes and Data Sources Table 5.4 for 2016.

Appendix Table G. Distribution of employment and total incomes, Rainy River District, Fort Frances, Timiskaming District, and Temiskaming Shores, for 2015.

	Rainy River District			Fort Frances T			Timiskaming District			Temiskaming Shores C		
	all	males	Females	all	males	females	all	males	females	all	males	females
Persons with income	16,240	8,005	8,240	6,320	3,015	3,305	26,770	13,290	13,480	8,205	3,875	4,330
Persons with employment income	11,175	5,785	5,395	4,360	2,160	2,195	17,640	9,315	8,325	5,565	2,800	2,760
% persons with employment income	68.8	72.3	65.5	69.0	71.6	66.4	65.9	70.1	61.8	67.8	72.3	63.7
Distribution of employment income (%)												
Under $10,000 (including loss)	26.2	26.0	26.3	23.4	23.6	23.0	24.5	21.6	27.8	23.8	21.3	26.1
$10,000 to $19,999	12.4	10.6	14.3	12.4	11.1	13.9	12.2	9.3	15.5	11.9	8.8	15.0
$20,000 to $29,999	10.7	8.9	12.8	10.9	9.3	12.8	10.1	8.1	12.3	11.1	9.6	12.7
$30,000 to $39,999	11.0	9.0	13.0	11.1	9.0	13.0	9.7	7.3	12.4	11.1	7.9	14.1
$40,000 to $49,999	9.7	8.2	11.2	10.9	9.0	12.8	8.8	7.8	9.8	8.9	8.6	9.2
$50,000 to $59,999	7.5	8.1	6.9	8.5	9.5	7.3	7.6	7.9	7.4	8.3	9.3	7.2
$60,000 to $69,999	5.5	6.4	4.4	5.8	6.0	5.5	6.1	7.6	4.4	6.4	7.7	5.3
$70,000 to $79,999	4.1	5.0	3.1	4.2	5.3	3.2	4.8	6.7	2.8	4.6	6.3	2.7
$80,000 to $89,999	3.3	4.0	2.5	3.2	3.9	2.5	3.5	4.8	2.2	3.1	4.1	2.0
$90,000 to $99,999	3.3	3.9	2.7	3.6	4.2	3.0	4.1	5.0	3.1	3.8	4.1	3.3
$100,000 and over	6.5	9.9	2.8	6.0	9.0	3.0	8.6	14.0	2.6	7.3	12.1	2.5
Distribution of total income (%)												
Under $10,000 (including loss)	14.3	13.0	15.6	11.7	10.6	12.6	13.2	10.2	16.2	12.0	9.7	14.1
$10,000 to $19,999	17.0	13.5	20.4	16.2	12.9	19.3	20.0	16.2	23.8	19.1	14.9	22.8
$20,000 to $29,999	14.0	11.2	16.7	13.9	10.3	17.1	15.3	13.7	16.9	16.2	14.7	17.5

(cont)

Appendix Table G. Distribution of employment and total incomes, Rainy River District, Fort Frances, Timiskaming District, and Temiskaming Shores, for 2015.

	Rainy River District			Fort Frances T			Timiskaming District			Temiskaming Shores C		
	all	males	Females	all	males	females	all	males	females	all	males	females
$30,000 to $39,999	11.8	10.3	13.3	12.5	10.5	14.2	11.3	10.2	12.4	11.9	10.6	13.2
$40,000 to $49,999	11.4	11.3	11.5	12.5	12.2	12.8	9.6	9.1	10.2	10.1	9.7	10.6
$50,000 to $59,999	8.9	10.2	7.5	10.0	12.5	7.5	7.3	7.7	6.8	8.2	9.3	7.1
$60,000 to $69,999	6.3	8.1	4.4	7.0	8.9	5.5	5.9	7.5	4.5	6.3	7.8	4.9
$70,000 to $79,999	4.5	5.8	3.2	4.6	6.2	3.3	4.3	6.0	2.5	4.1	5.6	2.6
$80,000 to $89,999	3.0	3.7	2.2	2.8	3.6	2.2	2.9	4.1	1.7	2.8	3.8	1.8
$90,000 to $99,999	2.8	3.4	2.3	2.9	3.8	2.3	3.1	4.0	2.2	2.8	3.4	2.3
$100,000 and over	6.0	9.4	2.8	5.8	8.7	3.3	7.1	11.4	2.8	6.5	10.6	2.9
$100,000 to $149,999	4.6	7.1	2.2	4.5	6.3	2.8	5.5	8.8	2.2	5.0	8.0	2.1
$150,000 and over	1.4	2.3	0.6	1.2	2.4	0.5	1.5	2.6	0.5	1.5	2.5	0.7
Ratio of total income shares												
Persons under $10,000 to persons $150,000+	10.0	5.6	27.6	9.5	4.4	27.0	8.5	3.9	29.9	8.0	3.8	19.8
Low income (LIM) after tax												
All ages (%)	13.7	13.0	14.5	15.3	14.7	15.8	17.5	16.5	18.4	13.9	12.4	15.5
0-5 years (%)	20.7	20.9	20.4	27.0	27.3	26.7	23.0	23.5	22.0	16.8	15.3	18.5
Average after-tax total income ($)	36,055	41,324	30,969	36,817	41,985	32,177	35,431	42,197	28,672	35,766	41,956	30,204
Median after-tax total income ($)	31,002	37,678	25,870	32,936	39,654	27,960	28,805	35,677	23,670	29,470	35,840	24,890

Note: Due to rounding, there can be apparent errors in percentage totals, especially for the highest income ranges for small communities.

Source: See Table Notes and Data Sources Table 5.4 for 2016.

Appendix Table H. Distribution of employment and total incomes, Sudbury District, Greater Sudbury, Espanola, and Cobalt, for 2015.

	Sudbury District			Greater Sudbury CMA			Espanola T			Cobalt T		
	all	males	females	all	males	females	all	males	females	all	males	females
Persons with income	18,325	9,330	8,995	136,285	66,385	69,900	4,195	2,090	2,100	960	470	485
Persons with employment income	12,065	6,595	5,470	97,195	51,440	45,755	2,810	1,535	1,270	535	280	250
% persons with employment income	65.8	70.7	60.8	71.3	77.5	65.5	67.0	73.4	60.5	55.7	59.6	51.5
Distribution of employment income (%)												
Under $10,000 (including loss)	27.9	26.8	29.2	23.6	23.3	23.9	27.4	27.4	28.0	30.8	28.6	32.0
$10,000 to $19,999	12.9	9.4	17.1	11.7	9.2	14.4	11.4	8.1	15.4	16.8	14.3	20.0
$20,000 to $29,999	9.7	6.9	13.1	9.4	7.5	11.6	9.6	6.5	13.4	13.1	10.7	16.0
$30,000 to $39,999	8.3	6.7	10.3	9.2	7.2	11.5	7.3	5.5	9.4	11.2	10.7	10.0
$40,000 to $49,999	8.3	7.2	9.7	8.9	7.2	10.7	7.8	6.2	10.2	11.2	8.9	12.0
$50,000 to $59,999	7.5	8.6	6.2	7.7	7.3	8.2	6.4	6.5	6.3	4.7	5.4	6.0
$60,000 to $69,999	5.7	6.9	4.2	6.0	6.6	5.2	6.4	7.2	5.5	3.7	7.1	0.0
$70,000 to $79,999	4.7	6.0	3.1	4.7	5.4	3.8	5.7	7.2	3.5	1.9	1.8	2.0
$80,000 to $89,999	3.9	5.2	2.6	4.3	5.2	3.4	5.0	6.8	2.8	1.9	3.6	0.0
$90,000 to $99,999	3.8	4.9	2.4	4.1	4.7	3.3	5.2	6.8	3.5	0.9	1.8	0.0
$100,000 and over	7.3	11.5	2.3	10.5	16.4	3.9	7.5	11.7	2.4	2.8	5.4	0.0
Distribution of total income (%)												
Under $10,000 (including loss)	14.6	9.5	20.0	12.4	9.9	14.8	12.9	11.2	14.5	17.1	15.1	19.1
$10,000 to $19,999	18.2	13.6	23.0	16.0	12.1	19.8	20.8	17.0	24.5	26.2	20.4	30.9
$20,000 to $29,999	13.7	11.3	16.3	12.7	9.5	15.7	14.9	12.8	17.0	18.7	19.4	18.1

(cont)

Appendix Table H. Distribution of employment and total incomes, Sudbury District, Greater Sudbury, Espanola, and Cobalt, for 2015.

	Sudbury District			Greater Sudbury CMA			Espanola T			Cobalt T		
	all	males	females	all	males	females	all	males	females	all	males	females
$30,000 to $39,999	12.0	12.1	11.9	11.6	10.7	12.4	10.7	9.3	11.9	12.8	11.8	13.8
$40,000 to $49,999	10.2	11.2	9.2	10.7	10.9	10.4	8.9	7.2	10.4	10.7	10.8	9.6
$50,000 to $59,999	8.1	9.5	6.5	8.7	9.1	8.3	6.8	6.1	7.5	5.9	7.5	4.3
$60,000 to $69,999	6.2	8.3	4.1	6.4	7.6	5.3	6.0	7.7	4.4	3.2	4.3	2.1
$70,000 to $79,999	4.3	5.9	2.6	4.7	5.8	3.7	4.2	5.8	2.7	2.1	2.2	2.1
$80,000 to $89,999	3.5	4.7	2.3	3.9	4.9	2.9	3.1	4.3	1.7	1.6	2.2	0.0
$90,000 to $99,999	2.9	4.0	1.8	3.5	4.3	2.7	3.7	5.1	2.2	0.5	1.1	0.0
$100,000 and over	6.3	10.0	2.3	9.4	15.2	4.0	6.4	10.6	2.0	1.1	3.2	0.0
$100,000 to $149,999	5.0	8.3	1.6	7.1	11.4	3.0	6.4	10.6	2.4	1.6	2.2	0.0
$150,000 and over	1.2	1.7	0.6	2.3	3.8	0.9	1.7	2.9	0.3	0.0	1.1	0.0
Ratio of total income shares												
Persons under $10,000 to persons $150,000+	12.2	5.5	31.1	5.3	2.6	16.0	13.9	5.5	39.0	n/a	14.0	n/a
Low income (LIM) after tax												
All ages (%)	14.3	13.8	14.9	12.8	11.7	13.8	13.2	11.7	14.5	30.8	27.9	32.5
0–5 years (%)	19.3	20.9	17.6	20.0	20.0	20.0	22.2	22.2	22.2	42.9	50.0	50.0
Average after-tax total income ($)	35,669	42,693	28,225	39,963	47,550	32,733	35,438	43,250	27,128	28,375	33,637	23,168
Median after-tax total income ($)	30,224	38,660	22,470	34,060	41,352	27,273	32,619	41,748	23,588	21,760	24,384	19,904

Note: Due to rounding, there can be apparent errors in percentage totals, especially for the highest income ranges for small communities.

Source: See Table Notes and Data Sources Table 5.4 for 2016.

Appendix Table I. Distribution of employment and total incomes, Thunder Bay, Marathon, and Schreiber, for 2015.

	Thunder Bay District			Thunder Bay CMA			Marathon T			Schreiber TP		
	all	males	females	all	males	females	all	males	females	all	males	females
Persons with income	121,260	59,720	61,545	101,140	49,385	51,760	2,750	1,395	1,350	925	470	450
Persons with employment income	84,080	43,240	40,845	70,270	35,785	34,485	1,995	1,070	925	665	360	295
% persons with employment income	69.3	72.4	66.4	69.5	72.5	66.6	72.5	76.7	68.5	71.9	76.6	65.6
Distribution of employment income (%)												
Under $10,000 (including loss)	22.9	21.6	24.3	22.1	21.0	23.2	21.6	16.4	27.6	24.8	18.1	33.9
$10,000 to $19,999	12.7	10.7	14.8	12.7	10.8	14.5	12.8	7.9	18.4	12.8	9.7	16.9
$20,000 to $29,999	10.4	9.1	11.8	10.6	9.3	11.8	9.8	7.9	11.9	8.3	9.7	8.5
$30,000 to $39,999	9.8	8.2	11.5	10.0	8.5	11.6	6.5	4.2	9.2	8.3	5.6	11.9
$40,000 to $49,999	9.7	8.2	11.3	10.0	8.6	11.6	6.0	4.7	8.1	6.8	5.6	8.5
$50,000 to $59,999	8.4	8.5	8.2	8.7	8.9	8.4	6.0	5.1	7.0	9.0	8.3	8.5
$60,000 to $69,999	6.2	7.3	5.0	6.3	7.4	5.1	4.3	4.7	3.8	9.0	12.5	5.1
$70,000 to $79,999	4.9	6.0	3.8	5.0	6.0	4.0	3.8	4.2	3.2	4.5	6.9	1.7
$80,000 to $89,999	4.0	4.9	3.1	4.0	4.8	3.2	5.0	6.5	3.2	4.5	5.6	3.4
$90,000 to $99,999	3.6	4.3	3.0	3.6	4.2	3.0	5.8	7.0	3.8	3.0	2.8	1.7
$100,000 and over	7.4	11.2	3.3	7.0	10.5	3.4	18.3	30.4	3.8	8.3	13.9	3.4
Distribution of total income (%)												
Under $10,000 (including loss)	12.3	10.9	13.7	11.6	10.5	12.7	13.2	8.1	18.3	14.4	7.4	21.6
$10,000 to $19,999	16.3	12.8	19.7	16.3	12.8	19.6	14.9	8.8	21.0	16.6	11.7	22.7
$20,000 to $29,999	14.0	11.6	16.4	14.1	11.7	16.4	12.7	9.6	16.0	10.5	7.4	13.6

(cont)

Appendix Table I. Distribution of employment and total incomes, Thunder Bay District, Thunder Bay, Marathon, and Schreiber, for 2015.

	Thunder Bay District			Thunder Bay CMA			Marathon T			Schreiber TP		
	all	males	females	all	males	females	all	males	females	all	males	females
$30,000 to $39,999	12.3	11.2	13.3	12.4	11.3	13.4	11.5	9.6	13.6	10.5	7.4	13.6
$40,000 to $49,999	11.0	10.8	11.2	11.2	11.0	11.4	7.8	8.1	7.4	9.9	11.7	8.0
$50,000 to $59,999	9.0	9.7	8.2	9.2	10.0	8.5	7.4	7.7	7.0	8.8	9.6	6.8
$60,000 to $69,999	6.6	8.0	5.1	6.7	8.2	5.3	4.9	5.9	4.3	7.7	11.7	3.4
$70,000 to $79,999	4.9	6.1	3.6	5.0	6.1	3.9	3.8	4.8	2.7	5.0	8.5	2.3
$80,000 to $89,999	3.7	4.6	2.7	3.7	4.6	2.8	4.0	5.1	2.7	5.0	7.4	2.3
$90,000 to $99,999	3.1	3.8	2.4	3.1	3.8	2.4	4.5	6.3	2.7	3.3	4.3	2.3
$100,000 to $149,999	7.0	10.5	3.6	6.8	10.1	3.8	15.1	25.7	3.9	7.7	11.7	3.4
$100,000 to $149,999	5.2	7.8	2.8	5.0	7.3	2.8	12.9	21.3	3.9	6.1	9.6	2.3
$150,000 and over	1.7	2.7	0.8	1.8	2.7	0.9	2.5	4.4	0.4	1.1	2.1	0.0
Ratio of total income shares												
Persons under $10,000 to persons $150,000+	7.0	4.1	16.1	6.4	3.8	13.7	5.4	1.8	47.0	13.0	3.5	n/a
Low income (LIM) after tax												
All ages (%)	13.8	13.1	14.5	13.8	13.0	14.5	11.3	9.3	13.2	11.4	10.0	11.9
0–5 years (%)	23.4	23.7	23.1	23.7	24.2	23.4	18.9	21.1	23.5	18.2	0.0	0.0
Average after-tax total income ($)	37,789	43,517	32,211	38,144	43,704	32,828	41,270	52,073	30,093	36,277	46,707	25,714
Median after-tax total income ($)	32,535	38,442	27,696	32,913	38,484	28,372	34,320	49,376	24,128	33,331	46,016	21,120

Note: Due to rounding, there can be apparent errors in percentage totals, especially for the highest income ranges for small communities.
Source: See Table Notes and Data Sources Table 5,4 for 2016.

Appendix Table J. Distribution of employment and total incomes, Wiikwemkoong Unceded, Asubpeeschoseewagong FN, Atikameksheng Anishnawbek, and Fort Severn FN, for 2015.

	Wiikwemkoong FN			Asubpeeschoseewagong FN			Atikameksheng Anishnawbek			Fort Severn FN		
	all	males	females	all	males	females	all	males	females	all	males	females
Persons with income	1,810	875	930	450	220	225	315	155	160	255	125	130
Persons with employment income	940	450	485	170	80	95	220	105	110	195	95	90
% persons with employment income	51.9	51.4	52.2	37.8	36.4	42.2	69.8	67.7	68.8	76.5	76.0	69.2
Distribution of employment income (%)												
Under $10,000 (including loss)	31.9	36.7	26.8	38.2	43.8	31.6	34.1	42.9	31.8	38.5	36.8	44.4
$10,000 to $19,999	17.0	23.3	11.3	14.7	18.8	15.8	15.9	14.3	18.2	20.5	15.8	22.2
$20,000 to $29,999	11.2	11.1	11.3	17.6	18.8	21.1	11.4	9.5	9.1	10.3	15.8	11.1
$30,000 to $39,999	13.8	10.0	17.5	8.8	6.3	15.8	9.1	4.8	13.6	10.3	10.5	11.1
$40,000 to $49,999	10.1	6.7	13.4	5.9	6.3	5.3	9.1	4.8	13.6	12.8	10.5	16.7
$50,000 to $59,999	8.0	5.6	10.3	8.8	6.3	10.5	9.1	9.5	4.5	2.6	0.0	5.6
$60,000 to $69,999	2.1	1.1	3.1	0.0	0.0	0.0	2.3	0.0	4.5	2.6	0.0	0.0
$70,000 to $79,999	1.6	1.1	2.1	0.0	0.0	0.0	4.5	4.8	0.0	0.0	5.3	0.0
$80,000 to $89,999	1.1	1.1	1.0	0.0	0.0	0.0	2.3	4.8	0.0	2.6	5.3	5.6
$90,000 to $99,999	1.1	1.1	1.0	0.0	0.0	0.0	2.3	0.0	4.5	0.0	0.0	0.0
$100,000 and over	1.1	1.1	1.0	0.0	0.0	0.0	2.3	4.8	0.0	0.0	0.0	0.0
Distribution of total income (%)												
Under $10,000 (including loss)	31.6	36.4	27.0	50.6	61.5	41.5	23.7	24.1	20.0	27.1	30.4	20.0
$10,000 to $19,999	25.4	27.9	23.6	15.2	15.4	14.6	22.0	24.1	20.0	22.9	17.4	28.0
$20,000 to $29,999	12.4	12.1	12.1	13.9	12.8	14.6	16.9	17.2	16.7	16.7	17.4	16.0
$30,000 to $39,999	10.6	9.1	11.5	6.3	2.6	9.8	11.9	10.3	13.3	12.5	17.4	12.0

(cont)

Appendix Table J. Distribution of employment and total incomes, Wiikwemkoong Unceded, Asubpeeschoseewagong First Nation, Atikameksheng Anishnawbek, and Fort Severn First Nation, for 2015.

	Wiikwemkoong FN			Asubpeeschoseewagong FN			Atikameksheng Anishnawbek			Fort Severn FN		
	all	males	females	all	males	females	all	males	females	all	males	females
$40,000 to $49,999	8.0	6.1	10.3	6.3	7.7	7.3	6.8	3.4	6.7	10.4	13.0	8.0
$50,000 to $59,999	5.6	3.6	7.5	5.1	2.6	7.3	8.5	10.3	10.0	2.1	4.3	0.0
$60,000 to $69,999	2.7	1.2	3.4	1.3	0.0	2.4	3.4	3.4	3.3	4.2	4.3	4.0
$70,000 to $79,999	1.2	1.2	1.1	1.3	0.0	2.4	3.4	3.4	3.3	0.0	4.3	4.0
$80,000 to $89,999	0.6	0.6	1.1	0.0	0.0	0.0	1.7	0.0	0.0	2.1	0.0	0.0
$90,000 to $99,999	0.9	0.6	1.1	0.0	0.0	0.0	1.7	3.4	0.0	0.0	4.3	0.0
$100,000 and over	0.9	0.6	1.1	0.0	0.0	0.0	1.7	3.4	0.0	0.0	0.0	0.0
$100,000 to $149,999	0.6	0.6	0.6	0.0	0.0	0.0	1.7	3.4	0.0	0.0	0.0	0.0
$150,000 and over	0.0	0.0	0.0	0.0	0.0	0.0	0.0	0.0	0.0	0.0	0.0	0.0
Ratio of total income shares												
Persons under $10,000 to persons $150,000+	n/a	n/a	n/a	n/a	n/a	n/a	n/a	n/a	n/a	n/a	n/a	n/a
Low income (LIM) after tax												
All ages (%)	n/a	n/a	n/a	n/a	n/a	n/a	n/a	n/a	n/a	n/a	n/a	n/a
0–5 years (%)	n/a	n/a	n/a	n/a	n/a	n/a	n/a	n/a	n/a	n/a	n/a	n/a
Average after-tax total income ($)	23,080	19,499	26,467	16,093	11,616	20,416	27,764	26,085	29,421	24,297	24,038	24,548
Median after-tax total income ($)	17,806	14,320	19,827	9,696	3,307	17,728	21,888	20,672	25,920	19,904	22,080	19,136

Note: Due to rounding, there can be apparent errors in percentage totals, especially for the highest income ranges for small communities.

Source: See Table Notes and Data Sources Table 5.4 for 2016.

TABLE NOTES
AND DATA SOURCES

TABLE 2.1.
TREATY AND RESERVE AREAS IN NORTHERN ONTARIO, 2019

1. Total treaty areas are from the treaty texts of the numbered treaties. These areas included water bodies. Estimates of the areas of the Robinson Huron and Robinson Superior are from Surtees (1986).
2. Areas of the districts in Northern Ontario were obtained from the 2016 Census data and are for land areas. The 2016 Census estimates of land reflect boundaries in effect on January 2, 2016. Land data is derived from the Spatial Data Infrastructure (SDI), which includes a water polygon layer.
3. Areas of reserves are from a combination of information obtained in the Indian Land Registry, the Indigenous and Northern Affairs website, schedules of reserves from 1900 to 1972, and original surveys of reserve area. In addition, individual bands were contacted

to confirm land area, and where applicable the information they provided was used. Any inaccuracies are a result of a lack of information or conflicting information in the sources used.

4. Treaty area of 2,339.86 km² for Manitoulin Island Treaty does not include 426.14 km² as indicated in the 1913 schedules of reserves as land unceded. The treaty area left as reserves on Manitoulin Island does include the Wiikwemkoong Reserve, which is a reserve on unceded land; this reserve is also included in the calculation of reserves as a percentage of treaty and district areas.

5. The Sucker Creek No. 23 land area differs from that shown on the band's website. They have purchased farmland adjacent to the reserve and it is uncertain at this time if that land has official reserve status.

6. The schedule of reserves of 1913 refers to reserves within the Robinson-Superior territory that were never confirmed by the Province of Ontario. These reserves include Michipicoten (178 acres), McIntyre Bay No. 54 (585 acres), Cariboo Island Point No. 56 (135.5 acres), and Jackfish Island No. 57 (362.8 acres).

7. For the Pic River First Nation, the Indigenous and Northern Affairs website shows the size of reserve as 316.6 ha, while the 2016 Census shows the size as 411.0 ha. The Ojibways of Pic River First Nation website shows the area as 332.7 ha. The band is currently in litigation and was unable to release information concerning the actual size of their reserve.

8. The Robinson-Huron Treaty surveyed Lake Timagami Reserve in 1884. However, this reserve was never confirmed by the Province of Ontario (Canada 1913, "Schedule of Reserves").

9. Sandy Lake Reserve is listed as a Treaty 5 reserve in the Indian Bands of Treaties 1 to 11; however, on treaty maps of Ontario, this reserve is shown in the territory of Treaty 9. This table includes the Sandy Lake Reserve in the Treaty 5 area.

10. In 1908, Duncan Campbell Scott of the federal Department of Indian Affairs proposed that all reserves within the new boundaries

of Ontario become part of Treaty 9. However, this did not occur. Sandy Lake Reserve, North Spirit Lake, and Kee-Way-Win are listed as Treaty 5 reserves in the Numbered Treaties, while on Treaty maps of Ontario, these reserves are shown in the territory of Treaty 9. This Table has included these reserves in the Treaty 5 area.

TABLE 2.2.
POPULATION, LAND, AND CENSUS DIVISIONS (CDS) OF ONTARIO, NORTHERN AND SOUTHERN, CENSUS DATES, 1871–2021

1871   Population and land totals for Northern Ontario are based on five census districts: Algoma Centre, Algoma East, Algoma West, Manitoulin, and Nipissing North (Nipissing South subsequently was part of Renfrew). The bordering districts of Muskoka and Parry Sound were then two separate census districts.
Census of Canada, 1870–71, Vol. I, Table I: "Areas, Dwellings, Families, Population, Sexes, Conjugal Condition."

1881   Population and land totals for Northern Ontario are based on the then single consolidated Algoma District (which included Manitoulin). In this census the Parry Sound District was made a part of the Muskoka District.
Census of Canada, 1880–81, Vol. I, Table I: "Areas, Dwellings, Families, Population, Sexes, Conjugal Condition."

1891   Population and land totals for Northern Ontario are based on Algoma District and Nipissing District. The previously consolidated Muskoka District is now called the Muskoka and Parry Sound District.
Census of Canada, 1890–91, Vol. I, Table I: "Areas of Canada by Districts," and Table II: "Population, Families and Dwellings."

A further useful source, suggested by the Statistics Canada Library, is Bulletin No. 2 of the 1891 Census, which includes useful analytical material and a table of "Population by Sub-Districts" for Ontario according to 1882 electoral divisions. In this period, census districts largely corresponded with electoral divisions.

1901   Population and land totals for Northern Ontario are based on Algoma District and Nipissing District. Muskoka and Parry Sound are a single district (Muskoka and Parry Sound District). Conversion of acres: 1 acre = 0.00404686 square kilometres.

Fourth Census of Canada, 1901, Vol. 1, Table 1: "Population of 1871, 1881, 1891, and 1901, compared by Electoral Districts with their present limits (1901)" and Table VII: "Areas, Houses, Families, Population, Sex Conjugal Condition."

1911   Population and land totals for Northern Ontario are based on four census districts: Algoma East, Algoma West, Nipissing, and Thunder Bay and Rainy River. Muskoka and Parry Sound District are now divided into two census districts, Muskoka District and Parry Sound District.

Fifth Census of Canada, 1911, Vol. 1, Table 1: "Area and Population of Canada by Provinces, Districts and Subdistricts in 1911 and Population in 1901."

1921   Population and land totals for Northern Ontario increased to eight census districts: Algoma, Kenora, Manitoulin, Nipissing, Rainy River, Sudbury, Thunder Bay, and Timiskaming.

Sixth Census of Canada, 1921, Vol. 1, Table 27: "Population classified according to principal origins of the people by counties and their subdivisions, 1921."

1931   Population and land totals for Northern Ontario increased to ten census divisions (the term "division" replaced "district"): Algoma, Cochrane, Kenora, Manitoulin, Nipissing, Patricia, Rainy River, Sudbury, Thunder Bay, Timiskaming.

Seventh Census of Canada, 1931, Vol. I, Table 1a: "Population of Canada, by counties or census divisions, 1851–1931," and Table 4a: "Land area, 1931, and density of population per square mile, Canada, by counties or census divisions, 1851–1931."

1941 Population and land totals for Northern Ontario incorporated the District of Patricia with Kenora, so reduced the total number of census divisions to nine: Algoma, Cochrane, Kenora, Manitoulin, Nipissing, Rainy River, Sudbury, Thunder Bay, and Timiskaming.

Eighth Census of Canada, 1941, Vol. II, Table 6: "Area and density of population, for counties and census divisions, 1941 and 1931."

1951 Population and land totals for Northern Ontario include nine census divisions: Algoma, Cochrane, Kenora, Manitoulin, Nipissing, Rainy River, Sudbury, Thunder Bay, and Timiskaming.

Ninth Census of Canada, 1951, Vol. I, Table 2: "Area and density of population, for counties and census divisions, 1931, 1941 and 1931," and Table 6: "Population by census subdivisions."

1956 Population and land totals for Northern Ontario include nine census divisions: Algoma, Cochrane, Kenora, Manitoulin, Nipissing, Rainy River, Sudbury, Thunder Bay, and Timiskaming.

Census of Canada, 1956, Vol. I, Table 2: "Area and density of population, for counties and census divisions, 1956."

1961 Population and land totals for Northern Ontario include nine census divisions: Algoma, Cochrane, Kenora, Manitoulin, Nipissing, Rainy River, Sudbury, Thunder Bay, and Timiskaming.

Census of Canada, 1961, Vol. I, Table 2: "Area and density of population, for counties and census divisions, 1961."

1966   Population and land totals for Northern Ontario include nine census divisions: Algoma, Cochrane, Kenora, Manitoulin, Nipissing, Rainy River, Sudbury, Thunder Bay, and Timiskaming.
Census of Canada, 1966, Vol. 1, Table 2: "Area and density of population, for counties and census divisions, 1966."

1971   Population and land totals for Northern Ontario include nine census divisions: Algoma, Cochrane, Kenora, Manitoulin, Nipissing, Rainy River, Sudbury, Thunder Bay, and Timiskaming.
Census of Canada, 1971, Special Bulletin, Geography, Land Areas and Densities of Statistical Units, Table 2: "Area and Density of Population, for Census Divisions, 1971."

1976   The Sudbury census division was divided into the Sudbury District/CD and the Regional Municipality of Sudbury CD, so that the population and land totals for Northern Ontario now include ten census divisions: Algoma, Cochrane, Kenora, Manitoulin, Nipissing, Rainy River, Sudbury (District/CD), Regional Municipality of Sudbury (CD), Thunder Bay, and Timiskaming.
Census of Canada, 1976, Supplementary Bulletins: Geographic and Demographic, Population, Land Areas and Population Density Census Divisions and Subdivisions, Table: "Population, Land Area and Population Density, for Census Divisions, 1976."

1981   Population and land totals for Northern Ontario include ten census divisions: Algoma, Cochrane, Kenora, Manitoulin, Nipissing, Rainy River, Sudbury (District/CD), Regional Municipality of Sudbury (CD), Thunder Bay, and Timiskaming.
Census of Canada, 1981, Census divisions and subdivisions: population, occupied private dwellings, private households, census families in private households, Table 1: "Selected

Population, Dwelling, Household and Census Family Characteristics, For Census Divisions and Subdivisions, 1981."

1986   Population and land totals for Northern Ontario include ten census divisions: Algoma, Cochrane, Kenora, Manitoulin, Nipissing, Rainy River, Sudbury (District/CD), Regional Municipality of Sudbury (CD), Thunder Bay, and Timiskaming. Census of Canada, 1986, Ontario: Part 1, Profiles: "Selected Characteristics for Census Divisions and Subdivisions, 1986 Census: 100% data."

1991   Population and land totals for Northern Ontario include ten census divisions: Algoma, Cochrane, Kenora, Manitoulin, Nipissing, Rainy River, Sudbury (District/CD), Regional Municipality of Sudbury (CD), Thunder Bay, and Timiskaming. Census of Canada, 1991, Profile of Census Divisions and Subdivisions in Ontario: Part A, Table 1 "Selected Characteristics for Census Divisions and Subdivisions, 1991 Census: 100% data."

1996   Population and land totals for Northern Ontario include ten census divisions: Algoma, Cochrane, Kenora, Manitoulin, Nipissing, Rainy River, Sudbury (District/CD), Regional Municipality of Sudbury (CD), Thunder Bay, and Timiskaming. 1996 Census of Canada, Electronic Areas Profiles, Profile of Census Divisions and Subdivisions, Cat. no. 95F0181XDB96001.

2001   Population and land totals for Northern Ontario include ten census divisions: Algoma, Cochrane, Kenora, Manitoulin, Nipissing, Rainy River, Sudbury (District/CD), Regional Municipality of Sudbury (CD), Thunder Bay, and Timiskaming. 2001 Census of Canada, 2001 Community Profiles, Cat. no. 93F0053XIE.

2006   Population and land totals for Northern Ontario include ten census divisions: Algoma, Cochrane, Kenora, Manitoulin, Nipissing, Rainy River, Sudbury (District/CD), Regional Municipality of Sudbury (CD), Thunder Bay, and Timiskaming.

2006 Census of Canada, 2006 Community Profiles, Cat. no. 92-591-X.

2011   Population and land totals for Northern Ontario include ten census divisions: Algoma, Cochrane, Kenora, Manitoulin, Nipissing, Rainy River, Sudbury (District/CD), Regional Municipality of Sudbury (CD), Thunder Bay, and Timiskaming. 2011 Census of Canada, 2011 *Census Profile*, Cat. no. 98-316-X2011001.

2016   Population and land totals for Northern Ontario include ten census divisions: Algoma, Cochrane, Kenora, Manitoulin, Nipissing, Rainy River, Sudbury (District/CD), Regional Municipality of Sudbury (CD), Thunder Bay, and Timiskaming. 2021 Census of Canada, 2016 *Census Profile*, Cat. no. 98-316-X2016001.

2021   Population and land totals for Northern Ontario include ten census divisions: Algoma, Cochrane, Kenora, Manitoulin, Nipissing, Rainy River, Sudbury (District/CD), Regional Municipality of Sudbury (CD), Thunder Bay, and Timiskaming. 2021 Census of Canada, 2021 *Census Profile*, Cat. no. 98-316-X2021001.

TABLE 2.4.

INDIGENOUS POPULATIONS IN NORTHERN ONTARIO AS ENUMERATED BY CENSUS OF CANADA, CENSUS DATES, 1871, 1881, 1901–1971, 2016

The Census of 1891 did not contain a distinct category on "Origins of the People" (or nationality) as in earlier and later censuses. The category "Indian" used in the census data reported here also included Inuit peoples. In several censuses, the Métis populations were not included as a distinct category. The 2016 data refers to "Aboriginal identity" which is generally a larger category and not strictly comparable to earlier data presented here. Consequently, we did not calculate the average annual change in "Indian" population between 1971 and 2016.

1871   Census of Canada, 1870–71, Vol. I, Table 3: "Origins of the People."

1881   Census of Canada, 1880–81, Vol. I, Table 3: "Origins of the People."

1901   Fourth Census of Canada, 1901, Vol. I, Table XI: "Origins of the People."

1911   Fifth Census of Canada, 1911, Vol. II, Table VIII: "Origins of the People by census districts."

1921   Sixth Census of Canada, 1921, Vol. I, Table 23: "Population in 1921, 1911, and 1901 classified according to principal origins by provinces," and Table 27: "Population classified according to principal origins of the people by counties or census divisions, 1921."

1931   Seventh Census of Canada, 1931, Vol. I, chapter VIII "Racial Origin" including Statement II: "Racial Groups Arranged to Eliminate Incomparability, Canada, 1871, 1881, 1901–1931," and Table 35: "Racial origin of the population, rural and urban, Canada and provinces, 1871, 1881, 1901–1931"; Vol. II, Table 32: "Population, male and female, classified according to racial origin, by counties or census divisions, 1931."

1941   Eighth Census of Canada, 1941, Vol. II, Table 31: "Population by racial origin and sex, for counties and census divisions, total and rural, 1941."

1951   Ninth Census of Canada, 1951, Vol. I, Table 31: "Population by origin for Canada, 1871, 1881, 1901–1951"; Table 32: "Population by origin and sex, for provinces and territories, 1951"; Table 34: "Population by origin and sex, for counties and census divisions, 1951."

1961   Census of Canada, 1961, Cat. no. 92-526: "Population by specified ethnic groups, for census subdivisions, 1961"; Cat. no. 92-545, Table 34: "Population by ethnic groups, for Canada, 1901–1961," and Table 35: "Population by ethnic groups and sex, for provinces and territories, 1961."

1971   Census of Canada, 1971, Cat. no. 92-723, Table 1: "Population by ethnic group and sex, for Canada and provinces, 1971"; Table 2: "Population by ethnic group and sex, for Canada and provinces, 1971"; Table 4: "Population by ethnic group and sex, for census divisions, 1971. "

2016   Statistics Canada. *Census Profile 2016*. For the total populations and census division areas, see also the appendix notes for Table 2.

TABLE 4.1.
BIRTHPLACES OF THE POPULATION IN NORTHERN ONTARIO AND SOUTHERN ONTARIO, DECENNIAL CENSUS DATES, 1871–2021

1871   Census of Canada, 1870–71, Vol. I, Table IV: "Birth Places of the People."

1881   Census of Canada, 1880–81, Vol. I, Table IV: "Birth Places of the People."

1891   Census of Canada, 1890–91, Vol. I, Table V: "Places of Birth."

1901   Fourth Census of Canada, 1901, Vol. I, Table XIII: "Birthplace of the People by Provinces"; Table XIV: "Birthplace of the People by Districts."

1911   Fifth Census of Canada, 1911, Vol. II, Table XVII: "Birthplace of the People by provinces"; Table XV: "Birthplace by districts."

1921   Sixth Census of Canada, 1921, Vol. II, Table 36: "Birthplace of the total population, for provinces and territories, 1921and 1931"; Table 53: "Birthplace of the total population by counties or census divisions, 1921."

1931   Seventh Census of Canada, 1931, Vol. II, Table 46: "Birthplace of the population by counties or census divisions, 1931."

1941   Eighth Census of Canada, 1941, Vol. II, Table 43: "Population by birthplace and sex, for counties and census divisions, 1941."

1951   Ninth Census of Canada, 1951, Vol. I, Table 45: "Population by birthplace and sex, for provinces and territories, 1951"; Table 47: "Population by birthplace and sex, for counties and census divisions, 1951."

1961   Census of Canada, 1961, "Birthplace," Cat. no. 92-547, Table 51: "Population by birthplace and sex, for counties and census divisions, 1961."

1971   Census of Canada, 1971, "Population by Birthplace," Cat. no. 92-760, Table 2: "Population by Birthplace, for Census Divisions, 1971."

1981   Census of Canada, 1981, Vol. 3, Profile series B, Cat. no. 95-942, Table 1: "Selected Population, Dwelling, Household and Family Distributions, Showing Selected Social and Economic Characteristics, for Census Divisions, 1981."

1991   Census of Canada, 1991, Profile of Census Divisions and Subdivisions in Ontario: Part B, Cat. no. 95-338, Table 1: "Selected Characteristics for Census Divisions and Census Subdivisions, 1991 Census (20% sample data)."

2001   Census of Canada, 2001, Community Profiles (Archived), "Profile of Citizenship, Immigration, Birthplace, Generation Status, Ethnic Origin, Visible Minorities and Aboriginal Peoples, for Canada, Provinces, Territories, Census Divisions and Census Subdivisions, 2001 Census," Cat. no. 95F0489X2001001.

2011   Census of Canada, 2011, Data products (Archived), National Household Survey Data tables: "Selected Demographic, Cultural, Educational, Labour Force and Income Characteristics (730), First Official Language Spoken (4), Age Groups (8D) and Sex (3) for the Population of Canada, Provinces, Territories, Census Divisions and Census. Subdivisions, 2011 National Household Survey."

2021   Statistics Canada. Table 98-10-0307-01 "Immigrant status and period of immigration by place of birth: Canada, provinces and territories, census divisions and census subdivisions."

TABLE 4.2.
POPULATION BY SEX IN NORTHERN ONTARIO AND SOUTHERN ONTARIO, DECENNIAL CENSUS DATES, 1871–2021

and

TABLE 4.4.
POPULATION BY MARITAL STATUS AND SEX IN NORTHERN ONTARIO AND SOUTHERN ONTARIO, DECENNIAL CENSUS DATES, 1871–2021

1871   Census of Canada, 1870–71, Vol. I, Table I: "Areas, Dwellings, Families, Population, Sexes, Conjugal Condition."

1881   Census of Canada, 1880–81, Vol. I, Table I: "Areas, Dwellings, Families, Population, Sexes, Conjugal Condition."

1891   Census of Canada, 1890–91, Vol. I, Table III: "Civil Condition."

1901   Fourth Census of Canada, 1901, Vol. I, Table III: "Sex and Conjugal Condition, 1891–1901, compared by Census Districts."

1911   Fifth Census of Canada, 1911, Vol. I, Table II: "Conjugal Condition of the People, classified as single, married, widowed, divorced, legally separated and not given, by districts and sub-districts."

1921   Sixth Census of Canada, 1921, Vol. II, Table 32: "Conjugal condition of the total population by nativity and sex, for counties or census divisions, 1921."

1931   Seventh Census of Canada, 1931, Vol. II, Table 28: "Conjugal condition of the population by sex, for counties or census divisions, 1931."

1941   Eighth Census of Canada, 1941, Vol. II, Table 26: "Population by conjugal condition and sex, for counties and census divisions, 1941."

1951   Ninth Census of Canada, 1951, Vol. I, Table 7: "Population by sex for census subdivisions, 1951"; Table 28: "Population by marital status and sex, for counties and census divisions, 1951."

1961   Census of Canada, 1961, "Marital Status," Cat. no. 92-544, Table 30: "Population by marital status and sex, for counties and census divisions, 1961."

1971   Census of Canada, 1971, "Marital Status," Cat. no. 92-717, Table 19: "Population by Marital Status and Sex, for Census Divisions, 1971."

1981   Census of Canada, 1981, Vol. 3, Profile series A, Cat. no. 95-942, Table 1: "Selected Population, Dwelling, Household and Census Family Characteristics, Showing Selected Social and Economic Characteristics, for Census Divisions, 1981."

1991   Census of Canada, 1991, Profile of Census Divisions and Subdivisions in Ontario – Part A, Cat. no. 95-337, Table 1: "Selected Characteristics for Census Divisions and Census Subdivisions, 1991 Census (100% data)."

2001   Census of Canada, 2001, Community Profiles (Archived), Cat. no. 93F0053XIE.

2011   Census of Canada, 2011, Data products (Archived), *Census Profile.*

2021   Statistics Canada. 2022. (table). *Census Profile.* 2021 Census of Population. Statistics Canada Cat. no. 98-316-X2021001. In the 2021 census Statistics Canada introduced the gender categories "men+" and "woman+" to replace the sex categories of "male" and "female." Statistics Canada does not expect this change to have a significant effect on analyses of historical trends (see Chapter 4).

TABLE 4.5.
POPULATION BY NATIONAL ORIGIN IN NORTHERN ONTARIO AND SOUTHERN ONTARIO, DECENNIAL CENSUS DATES, 1871–2021

Nationality data was not collected in the 1891 census. Blank cells here mean the data is not available due either to not being collected or not being published at the CD level.

From 1981 to 2021, data are for the non-inmate (or non-institutional) population, which was approximately 1% less than the full population. Also, the data here from 1981 to 2021 are for single responses only. For Northern Ontario, this was about 87% of the full population in 1981, falling to about 43% in 2011. As well, in 1991, for the first time, the census allowed for a Canadian-origin response. This broadened in later censuses to sub-Canada national and provincial responses, and responses for American and other responses in North America.

The Indigenous numbers here include Inuit and Métis persons when they were enumerated separately from "Indians." Besides "Indians," the Indigenous totals here include census counts of "Half Breeds" in 1871, 1901, and 1941. For Northern Ontario these numbers were 1871 (1), 1901 (3,614), and 1941 (2,380). For further discussion, see Chapter 2. From 1941 to 1961 the censuses reported "Indian (or Native

Indian) and Eskimo" as a single category. For 1971, the census category reported was "Native Indian." Comparable published census division data are not available for 1981 and 1991. The Indigenous data for 2001 to 2021 are for Aboriginal identity; they include "North American Indian," Métis, and Inuit identifications.

The "Other European" total is from the censuses, when reported, 1921 to 1961. In the censuses, Other European meant other than British Isles origins. In the present table it also excludes French origins. For 1871 to 1911, the totals here are for only the European national origins selected by the census, so the total is likely undercounted. For the present table, some individual European origins are not reported due to small numbers in Northern Ontario and not having published counts for most censuses; regardless, their numbers remain in the Other European totals.

The census counted a "Jewish" origin from 1871 to 1921, then called the origin "Hebrew" for 1921 and 1931, then returned to "Jewish" from 1941 to 1971.

The Russian totals for 1871, 1881, and 1901 include Polish and likely Finnish and Ukrainian (as part of the then Russian empire). For 1911 the Russian total is likely to be mostly Finnish.

Scandinavian includes Danish, Icelandic, Norwegian, and Swedish origins for 1871–1961, but Norwegian and Swedish alone for 2001-2021.

From 1871 to 1901 the censuses counted for an "African" category; this was continued from 1911 to 1961 as "Negro" then disappeared without comment.

The Chinese origin for 1901 and 1921 includes a number counted as Japanese. The Japanese origin was first reported separately in 1901 and when available is included here in "Other Asian."

The Other Asian category also includes persons counted as "Hindoo" in 1871 and "Hindu" in 1911, 753 Syrians in 1921, and East Indian and Filipino origins alone in 2001-2021.

1871   Census of Canada, 1870–71, Vol. I, Table III: "Origins of the People."

1881   Census of Canada, 1880–81, Vol. I, Table III: "Origins of the People."

1901   Fourth Census of Canada, 1901, Vol. I, Table XI: "Origins of the People."

1911   Fifth Census of Canada, 1911, Vol. II, Table VIII: "Origins of the People by districts."

1921   Sixth Census of Canada, 1921, Vol. I, Table 27: "Population classified according to principal origins of the people by counties and their subdivisions, 1921."

1931   Seventh Census of Canada, 1931, Vol. II, Table 32: "Population, male and female, classified according to racial origin, by counties or census divisions, 1931."

1941   Eighth Census of Canada, 1941, Vol. II, Table 31: "Population by racial origin and sex, for counties and census divisions, total and rural, 1941."

1951   Ninth Census of Canada, 1951, Vol. I, Table 34: "Population by origin and sex, for counties and census divisions, 1951."

1961   Census of Canada, 1961, "Ethnic Groups," Cat. no. 92-545, Table 37: "Population by ethnic groups and sex, for counties and census divisions, 1961."

1971   Census of Canada, 1971, "Special Bulletin: Specified Ethnic Groups, Census Divisions and Subdivisions," Cat. no. 92-774, Table 2: "Population by Specified Ethnic Groups, for Census Subdivisions, 1971."

1981   Census of Canada, 1981, Vol. 3, Profile series B, Cat. no. 95-942, Table 1: "Selected Population, Dwelling, Household and Family Distributions, Showing Selected Social and Economic Characteristics, for Census Divisions, 1981."

1991   Census of Canada, 1991, Profile of Census Divisions and Subdivisions in Ontario: Part B, Cat. no. 95-338, Table 1: "Selected Characteristics for Census Divisions and Census Subdivisions, 1991 Census (20% Sample Data)."

2001   Census of Canada, 2001, Community Profiles (Archived), Cat. no. 93F0053XIE.

2011   Census of Canada, 2011, Data products (Archived), National Household Survey Data tables: "Selected Demographic, Cultural, Educational, Labour Force and Income Characteristics (730), First Official Language Spoken (4), Age Groups (8D) and Sex (3) for the Population of Canada, Provinces, Territories, Census Divisions and Census Subdivisions, 2011 National Household Survey."

2021   Census of Canada, 2021. Table 98-10-0357-01: "Ethnic or cultural origin by gender and age: Canada, provinces and territories and census divisions".

TABLE 4.6.
ESTIMATES OF OFFICIAL LANGUAGES SPOKEN IN NORTHERN ONTARIO AND ONTARIO, DECENNIAL CENSUS DATES, 1871–1931

1871   Census of Canada, 1870–71, Vol. I, Table III: "Origins of the People."

1881   Census of Canada, 1880–81, Vol. I, Table III: "Origins of the People."

1891   Census of Canada, 1890–91, Vol. I, Table III: "Civil Condition."

1901   Fourth Census of Canada, 1901, Vol. I, Table XI: "Origins of the People"; Vol. IV, Table XIII: "Educational status of persons five years old and over."

1911   Fifth Census of Canada, 1911, Vol. II, Table VIII: "Origins of the People by districts."

1921   Sixth Census of Canada, 1921, Vol. I, Table 23: "Population in 1921, 1911, and 1901 classified according to principal origins by provinces" and Table 27: "Population classified according to principal origins of the people by counties and their subdivisions, 1921"; Vol. II, Table 78: "Language spoken by the population 10 years of age and over resident in Canada June 1, 1921 classified according to racial origin and sex, for provinces and territories."

1931   Seventh Census of Canada, 1931, Vol. I, Chapter VIII, "Racial Origin" including Statement II: "Racial Groups Arranged to Eliminate Incomparability, Canada, 1871, 1881, 1901–1931," and Table 35: "Racial origin of the population, rural and urban, Canada and provinces, 1871, 1881, 1901–1931"; Vol. II, Table 32: "Population, male and female, classified according to racial origin, by counties or census divisions, 1931"; Vol. II, Table 57: "Population speaking one or both of the official languages of Canada, by counties or census divisions, 1931 (persons under 5 years of age classed as speaking the language of their home)." For the total populations and census division areas, see also the Table Notes and Data and Sources for Table 2.

TABLE 4.7.
OFFICIAL LANGUAGES SPOKEN IN NORTHERN ONTARIO AND SOUTHERN ONTARIO, DECENNIAL CENSUS DATES, 1931–2021

The 1931 census did not provide mother tongue data by district/census division. The percentage data provided here are for all Ontario. This includes the percentage of Indigenous languages, which is estimated based on the 10+ years of data for mother tongue of "Indian" and "Eskimo" persons in Vol IV, Table 56.

From 1941 to 1971, the census included "Indian and Eskimo" among mother tongues.

In 1981, Statistics Canada introduced a category of Amerindian languages, including Cree and Ojibway, but for Ontario (15,930) not for census divisions.

In 1991, for mother tongues, the census provided a count for Cree and Inuktitut but not for Ojibway, hence, the numbers here are much lower than actual.

In 2001, Indigenous languages add Statistics Canada's counts for Cree, Inuktitut, and Ojibway.

In 2011, Indigenous languages add Statistics Canada's counts for Cree (not otherwise specified), Inuktitut, Ojibway, and Oji-Cree.

1931   Seventh Census of Canada, 1931, Vol. II, Table 57: "Population speaking one or both of the official languages of Canada, by counties or census divisions, 1931 (persons under 5 years of age classed as speaking the language of their home)"; Vol. II, Table 58: "Mother tongue of the total population by sex, for provinces, 1931 (persons under 5 years of age classed as speaking the language of the home)."

1941   Eighth Census of Canada, 1941, Vol. II, Table 52: "Population by official language spoken and sex, for counties and census divisions, 1941"; Vol. II, Table 54: "Population by mother tongue and sex, for counties and census divisions, 1941."

1951   Ninth Census of Canada, 1951, Vol. I, Table 56: "Population by (a) official language and sex, and (b) mother tongue and sex, for counties and census divisions, 1951."

1961   Census of Canada, 1961, Cat. no. 92-549, Table 66: "Population by (a) official language and sex, and (b) mother tongue and sex, for counties and census divisions, 1961."

1971   Census of Canada, 1971, Vol. I, Pt. 3, Cat. no. 92-725, Table 20: "Population by mother tongue and sex, for census divisions, 1971"; Cat. no. 92-726, Table 28: "Population by (a) official language, (b) language most often spoken at home, and sex, for census divisions, 1971."

1981   Census of Canada, 1981, Vol. 3, Profile series A, Cat. no. 95-902, Table 1: "Selected population, dwelling, household and census family characteristics, for census divisions, 1981"; Vol. 3, Profile series B, Cat. no. 95-942, Table 1: "Selected population, dwelling, household and family distributions, showing selected social and economic characteristics, for census divisions, 1981."

1991   Census of Canada, 1991, Profile of Census Divisions and Subdivisions in Ontario – Part A, Cat. no. 95-337, Table 1: "Selected characteristics for census divisions and census subdivisions, 1991 Census (100% data)"; Profile of Census Divisions and Subdivisions in Ontario: Part B, Cat. no. 95-338, Table 1: "Selected characteristics for census divisions and census subdivisions, 1991 Census (20% sample data)."

2001   Census of Canada, 2001, Data products (Archived): "Detailed Mother Tongue (80), Knowledge of Official Languages (5) and Sex (3) for Population, for Canada, Provinces, Territories, Census Divisions, Census Subdivisions and Dissemination Areas, 2001 Census - 20% Sample Data - Cat. no. 95F0339XCB2001001."

2011   Census of Canada, 2011, Topic-Based Tabulations (Archived): "Detailed Mother Tongue (232), Knowledge of Official Languages (5), Age Groups (17A) and Sex (3) for the Population Excluding Institutional Residents of Canada, Provinces, Territories, Census Divisions and Census Subdivisions, 2011 Census, Cat. no. 98-314-XCB2011033".

2021   Statistics Canada. 2022. *Census Profile*. 2021 Census of Population. Statistics Canada Catalogue no. 98-316-X2021001.

TABLE 5.4.

EMPLOYMENT BY SEX IN NORTHERN ONTARIO
DISTRICTS, WITH EMPLOYMENT PEAKS, CENSUS DATES,
1951–2021

1951   Dominion Bureau of Statistics, 1953. "Population, 14 Years of
        Age and Over, by Activity During the Week Ending June 2,
        1951, and Sex, for Counties or Census Divisions, Rural Farm,
        Rural Non-Farm, and Urban" (table). Ninth Census of Canada
        1951: *Volume V: Labour Force*. Statistics Canada Cat. no. 94-1951.
        https://archive.org/stream/1951981951FV51953engfra (accessed
        July 27, 2016).

1961   Dominion Bureau of Statistics. 1964. "Population, 15 Years of
        Age and Over, by Employment Status and Sex, for Counties or
        Census Subdivisions, 1961" (table). Labour Force: Employment
        Status by Sex. 1961 Census. Statistics Canada Cat. no. 94-533.
        https://archive.org/stream/1961945331964engfra (accessed July
        27, 2016).

1971   https://archive.org/stream/1971947901974engfra#page/n9/
        mode/2up.

1981   https://archive.org/stream/1981939661984engfra#page/n31/
        mode/2up.

1986   https://archive.org/details/1986941121988engfra.

1991   https://archive.org/details/1991953381994engfra.

1996   http://www12.statcan.ca/english/census96/data/profiles/
        index-eng.cfm.

2001   http://www12.statcan.ca/english/profil01/CP01/Search/List/
        Page.cfm?Lang=E&GeoCode=35&Letter=T.

2006   http://www12.statcan.gc.ca/census-recensem-
        ent/2006/dp-pd/prof/92-591/search-recherche/lst/page.
        cfm?Lang=E&GeoCode=35.

2011   https://www12.statcan.gc.ca/nhs-enm/2011/dp-pd/prof/ search-recherche/1st/page.cfm?Lang=E&TABID=1& GEOCODE=35.

2016   Statistics Canada. 2017. *Census Profile*. 2016 Census. Statistics Canada Cat. no. 98-316-X2016001. Ottawa.

2021   Statistics Canada. 2022. *Census Profile*. 2021 Census of Population. Statistics Canada Cat. no. 98-316-X2021001. Ottawa. Released December 15, 2022.

TABLE 5.6.
UNEMPLOYMENT AND UNEMPLOYED RATES BY SEX IN ONTARIO, NORTHERN ONTARIO AND NORTHERN DISTRICTS, CENSUS DATES, 1951–2021

For an introduction to the definition of the unemployed, see Statistics Canada's 2016 Census Dictionary entry: "The 'Unemployed' category consists of persons who, during the week of May 1 to May 7, 2016, were without paid work, were available for work and had actively looked for paid work in the past four weeks." In previous censuses, the reference week prior to the census data would vary within the spring of the census year according to the specific reference date established for each census. The count of the unemployed was less restrictive prior to the 1981 census in that those not searching because they believed no work was available in their area ("inactive searchers") were still counted as unemployed. In 1951, the unemployed included those 14 years of age and older; in later censuses, the age was 15 years and over.

1951   Unemployment and unemployed rates for Northern Ontario include nine census divisions: Algoma, Cochrane, Kenora, Manitoulin, Nipissing, Rainy River, Sudbury, Thunder Bay, and Timiskaming. Dominion Bureau of Statistics 1953. "Population, 14 Years of Age and Over, by Activity During the Week Ending June 2, 1951, and Sex, for Counties or Census Divisions, Rural Farm, Rural Non-Farm, and Urban."

1961   Unemployment and unemployed rates for Northern Ontario include nine census divisions: Algoma, Cochrane, Kenora, Manitoulin, Nipissing, Rainy River, Sudbury, Thunder Bay, and Timiskaming. Census of Canada, 1961, Vol. III, Table 2: "Population, 15 years of age and over, by employment status and sex, for Canada, 1961."

1971   Unemployment and unemployed rates for Northern Ontario include nine census divisions: Algoma, Cochrane, Kenora, Manitoulin, Nipissing, Rainy River, Sudbury, Thunder Bay, and Timiskaming. Census of Canada, 1971, Advance Bulletin, Table 1: "Population 15 Years and Over, by Labour Fore Activity, 1971."

1976   The Sudbury census division was divided into the Sudbury District/CD and the Regional Municipal of Sudbury CD, so that the population and land totals for Northern Ontario now include ten census divisions: Algoma, Cochrane, Kenora, Manitoulin, Nipissing, Rainy River, Sudbury (District/CD), Regional Municipality of Sudbury (CD), Thunder Bay, and Timiskaming. Census of Canada, 1976, Labour Force Activity by Sex, "Population, 15 years and over by sex, showing labour force activity, for Census Divisions, 1976."

1981   Census of Canada, 1981, Census divisions and subdivisions: population, occupied private dwellings, private households, census families in private households, Table 1: "Labour Force Activity of Population, 15 Years and Over Sex, Age Group and Marital Status, For Census Divisions, 1981."

1986   Census of Canada, 1986, Ontario: Part 2, Profiles: "Selected Characteristics for Census Divisions and Subdivisions, 1986 Census – 20% Sample Data."

1991   Census of Canada, 1991, Profile of Census Divisions and Subdivisions in Ontario: Part B, Table 1: "Selected Characteristics for Census Divisions and Subdivisions, 1991 Census – 20% data."

1996   1996 Census of Canada, Electronic Areas Profiles, Profile of Census Divisions and Subdivisions, Cat. no. 95F0181XDB96001.

2001   2001 Census of Canada, 2001 Community Profiles, Cat. no. 93F0053X1E.

2006   2006 Census of Canada, 2006 Community Profiles, Cat. no. 92-591-X.

2011   2011 Census of Canada, 2011 NHS Profile, Catalogue no. 99-004-XWE.

2016   Statistics Canada. 2017. *Census Profile*. 2016 Census. Statistics Canada Cat. no. 98-316-X2016001. Ottawa.

2021   Statistics Canada. 2022. *Census Profile*. 2021 Census of Population. Statistics Canada Cat. no. 98-316-X2021001. Ottawa. Released December 15, 2022.

TABLE 5.7.
FULL-TIME AND PART-TIME EMPLOYMENT BY SEX IN NORTHERN ONTARIO AND ONTARIO, 1981–2021

Full-time refers to 30 hours per week or more, while part-time is where the interviewee did "any work at all" but fewer than 30 hours. See Statistics Canada's 2016 Census Dictionary: "Refers to whether the weeks worked during the reference year were full-time weeks (30 hours or more per week) or not, on the basis of all jobs held. Persons with a part-time job for part of the year and a full-time job for another part of the year were to report the information for the job at which they worked the most weeks." (The reference year refers to the calendar year prior to the census date; for example, 2015 for the 2016 census.) The target populations exclude inmates of institutions.

1981   Census of Canada, 1981, Population, Economic Characteristics, Ontario, Table 6: "Population, 15 Years and Over who Worked in 1980 by Number of Weeks Worked in 1980, and Whether These Weeks Were Mostly Full-time/Part-time by Sex and Age Groups, For Census Divisions, 1981." Cat 93-966 (Vol. 2, Provincial Series). Full-time or part-time reported for the most weeks respondents worked full-time or part-time.

1986   Census of Canada, 1986, Census of Population. Ontario: Part 2, Profiles: "Selected Characteristics for Census Divisions and Subdivisions, 1986 Census – 20% Sample Data." Cat. no. 97-570-X1986003. Part-time data includes part-year or (and) part-time. Full-time is defined as full-year and full-time: "Worked 49–52 weeks in 1985, mostly full time." Part-time here counts: "Worked 49–52 weeks in 1985, mostly part time, or worked less than 49 weeks."

1991   Census of Canada, 1991, Census of Population, Profile of Census Divisions and Subdivisions in Ontario – Part B, Table 1: "Selected Characteristics for Census Divisions and Subdivisions, 1991 Census – 20% data." Cat. no. 95F0170X. Full-time and part-time defined as in 1986.

1996   1996 Census of Canada, Census of Population. Electronic Areas Profiles, Profile of Census Divisions and Subdivisions, Cat. no. 95F0181XDB96001. Full-time and part-time defined as in 1986.

2001   2001 Census of Canada. Profile of Census Divisions and Subdivisions in Ontario. Cat. no. 95-220-XPB. Table 1: "Selected Characteristics for Census Divisions and Census Subdivisions, 2001 Census – 100% data and 20% Sample Data." Full-time and part-time defined as in 1986.

2006   2006 Census of Population. 2006 Census Area Profiles. "Profile for Canada, Provinces, Territories, Census Divisions and Census Subdivisions, 2006 Census." Cat. no.94-581-XCB2006001. Full-time and part-time defined as in 1986.

2011   2011 Census of Canada, 2011 NHS Profile, Cat. no. 99-004-XWE. Full-time or part-time reported for the most weeks respondents worked full-time or part-time.

2016   Statistics Canada. 2017. *Census Profile.* 2016 Census. Cat. no. 98-316-X2016001. Ottawa. Full-time and part-time defined as in 1986.

2021   Statistics Canada. 2022. *Census Profile.* 2021 Census of Population. Statistics Canada Cat. no. 98-316-X2021001. Ottawa. Released December 15, 2022. Full-time and part-time defined as in 1986.

TABLE 6.1.
NORTHERN ONTARIO CITY POPULATIONS AND CHANGES, CENSUS DATES, 1971–2021

Sudbury: On January 1, 1973, the Province of Ontario made a forced amalgamation of the City of Sudbury and several surrounding towns and unincorporated areas into the two-tier Regional Municipality of Sudbury (RMS). The RMS lasted until 2001 when the province made a forced amalgamation of the RMS and its then seven incorporated lower-tier municipalities into the single-tier City of Greater Sudbury. The population data for the Greater Sudbury CD are those approximately consistent with the RMS and the City of Greater Sudbury for the whole period.

Thunder Bay: On January 1, 1970, the City of Thunder Bay was formed by the forced amalgamation of the City of Fort William, the City of Port Arthur, and the townships of Neebing and McIntyre. The population figures for 1971 and later are for the amalgamated city of Thunder Bay.

Sault Ste. Marie: In 1965 the City of Sault Ste. Marie amalgamated with the townships of Korah and Tarentorus. The population figures for 1971 and later are for the area corresponding to the amalgamated city of Sault Ste. Marie.

North Bay: In January 1968 the City of North Bay grew through an amalgamation with the townships of West Ferris and Widdifield. The population figures for 1971 and on are for the area corresponding to the amalgamated city of North Bay.

Timmins: The City of Timmins was formed on January 1, 1973, as a forced amalgamation of the Town of Timmins, the townships of Mountjoy, Tisdale, and Whitney, and about 31 surrounding unincorporated townships. The Tisdale township included the communities of Schumacher and South Porcupine, and the Whitney township included the community of Porcupine. The 1971 population figure is taken from the 1976 Census, which is consistent with post-amalgamation boundaries.

Temiskaming Shores: The City of Temiskaming Shores was formed on January 1, 2004, as an amalgamation of the Town of New Liskeard, the Town of Haileybury, and the township of Dymond. Hence, for census years prior to 2006, the population estimate for the City of Temiskaming Shores is the sum of the census populations for the two towns and the township.

Dryden: On January 1, 1998, the City of Dryden was formed by the amalgamation of the Town of Dryden and the township of Barclay. For census years prior to 2001, the population estimate for the City of Dryden is equal to the sum of the census populations for the town and the township.

Kenora: On January 1, 2000, the City of Kenora was formed by the
1991   amalgamation of the Town of Kenora, the Town of Keewatin,
and the Town of Jaffray Melick. For census years prior to 2001
the population estimate for the City of Kenora is equal to the
sum of the census populations for the three towns.

See, for the source of data:

1971   Census of Canada, 1971, Cat. no. 92-706, Table 6: "Population
by sex, for census subdivisions, 1971."

1976   Census of Canada, 1976, Cat. no. 92-804, Table 3: "Population
for census divisions and subdivisions, 1971 and 1976."

1981   Census of Canada, 1981, Cat. no. 94-905: "Census subdivisions
in decreasing population order."

1986,   Statistics Canada. *1991 Census Area Profiles.* "Profile of Census
Divisions and Subdivisions - Part A." Cat. no. 95F0168X.

1996   1996 Census of Canada, Electronic Areas Profiles, Profile of
Census Divisions and Subdivisions, Cat. no. 95F0181XDB96001.

2001   2001 Census of Canada, 2001 Community Profiles,
Cat. no. 93F0053X1E.

2006   2006 Census of Canada, 2006 Community Profiles,
Cat. no. 92-591-X.

2011   2011 Census of Canada, 2011 NHS Profile, Catalogue
no. 99-004-XWE.

2016   Statistics Canada. 2017. *Census Profile.* 2016 Census. Statistics
Canada Cat. no. 98-316-X2016001. Ottawa.

2021   Statistics Canada. 2022. *Census Profile.* 2021 Census of
Population. Statistics Canada Cat. no. 98-316-X2021001.
Ottawa. Released December 15, 2022.

Bibliography

Adams, Howard. 1989. Prison of Glass: Canada from a Native Point of View. First edition 1975. Saskatoon: Fifth House.

Anderson, Benedict. 1983. *Imagined Communities: Reflections on the Origin and Spread of Nationalism.* London, UK: Verso.

Andreae, Christopher. 1997. *Lines of Country: An Atlas of Railway and Waterway History in Canada.* Erin, ON: Boston Mills Press.

Anghie, Antony. 2005. *Imperialism, Sovereignty and the Making of International Law.* Cambridge: Cambridge University Press.

Archives of Ontario. 2012-23. "The Evolution of Ontario's Boundaries, 1774–1912." http://www.archives.gov.on.ca/en/maps/ontario-boundaries.aspx#1880.

Beaud, J.-P., and J.-G. Prévost. 1993. "La Statistique des origines raciales au Canada, 1921–1941." Note de recherche no. 45. L'Université du Québec à Montréal.

Bélanger, Alain. 2006. *Report on the Demographic Situation in Canada 2001.* Cat. no. 91-209-XIE. Ottawa: Statistics Canada.

Bishop, Charles A. 1994. "Northern Algonquians, 1550–1760." In *Aboriginal Ontario: Historical Perspectives on the First Nations*, edited by Edward S. Rogers and Donald B. Smith. Toronto: Dundurn Press.

Blaut, J. M., 1993. *The Colonizer's Model of the World: Geographical Diffusionism and Eurocentric History.* New York: Guilford Press.

Bouchard, Michel, Sébastien Malette, Guillaume Marcotte, and Siomonn Pulla. 2020. "We Need a Wider, More Nuanced View of Métis Diversity." University Affairs / Affaires Universitaires. May 4. https://www.universityaffairs.ca/opinion/in-my-opinion/we-need-a-wider-more-nuanced-view-of-metis-diversity/.

Bouchard, Pierre, Mélanie Girard, and Simon Laflamme. 2013. "Les Jeunes et Le Nord : Un Parcours à Découvrir / Youth and the North: A Path to Discover." Sudbury and Hearst: Laurentian University and Université de Hearst. http://www.fnetb.com/wp-content/uploads/2015/08/Youth-and-the-North-PowerPoint-Presentation-AGM-2013.pdf.

Boyd, Monica. 1993. "Measuring Ethnicity in the Future: Population, Policies, Politics and Social Science Research." In *Challenges of Measuring an Ethnic World: Science, Politics and Reality*, edited by Gustave Goldmann and Nampeo McKenney. Ottawa and Washington, DC: Statistics Canada and the United States Bureau of the Census.

Boyd, Monica, Gustave Goldmann, and Pamela White. 2000. "Race in the Canadian Census." In *Race and Racism: Canada's Challenge*, edited by Leo Driedger and Shiva S. Halli, 33–54. Published for Carleton University by McGill-Queen's University Press, Kingston and Montreal.

Bruce, Graeme. 2022. "A Visual Look at How Canadians Relocated during the Pandemic." *CBC News, October 26.*

Campbell, Maria. 1973. *Halfbreed.* Toronto: McClelland and Stewart.

Cardinal, Harold. 1969. *Unjust Society: The Tragedy of Canada's Indians.* Edmonton: M.G. Hurtig.

Canada. Department of Indian Affairs. 1913. "Schedule of Indian Reserves in the Dominion." Ottawa: Government Printing Bureau.

Canada. 2018. "Pre-1975 Treaties (Historic Treaties), Post-1975 Treaties (Modern Treaties)." Ottawa: Crown-Indigenous Relations and Northern Affairs Canada. https://open.canada.ca/data/en/dataset.

Chapagain, Tejendra. 2017. "Farming in Northern Ontario: Untapped Potential for the Future." *Agronomy* 7 (3): 59.

Chute, Janet E. 1998. *The Legacy of Shingwaukonse: A Century of Native Leadership.* Toronto: University of Toronto Press.

Cirtwill, Charles. "Does Northern Ontario Need More People?" Northern Policy Institute. 2015. https://www.northernpolicy.ca/article/does-northern-ontario-need-more-people---1974.asp.

Clatworthy, Stewart, and Mary Jane Norris. 2014. "Aboriginal Mobility and Migration in Canada: Trends, Patterns, and Implications, 1971 to 2006." In *Aboriginal Populations: Social, Demographic, and Epidemiological Perspectives*, edited by Frank Trovato and Anatole Romaniuk. Edmonton: University of Alberta Press.

Conteh, Charles. 2017. "Economic Zones of Northern Ontario: City-Regions and Industrial Corridors." Thunder Bay: Northern Policy Institute. https://www.northernpolicy.ca/economiczones.

Coulthard, Glen Sean. 2014. *Red Skin, White Masks: Rejecting the Colonial Politics of Recognition.* Minneapolis: University of Minnesota Press.

Coven, Joshua, Arpit Gupta, and Iris Yao. 2023. "Urban Flight Seeded the COVID-19 Pandemic Across the United States." *Journal of Urban Economics* 133, January: 1–11.

Curtis, Bruce. 2001. *The Politics of Population: State Formation, Statistics, and the Census of Canada, 1840–1875.* Toronto: University of Toronto Press.

Czyzewski, Karina. 2011. "Colonialism as a Broader Social Determinant of Health." *International Indigenous Policy Journal* 2 (1), Article 5.

Daschuk, James W. 2013. *Clearing the Plains: Disease, Politics of Starvation and the Loss of Aboriginal Life.* Regina: University of Regina Press.

Davis, Erin Nicole. 2022. "Interprovincial Migration Peaked during the Pandemic." *Storeys Real Estate News*, March 17.

Desormeaux, Marc. 2022. "A Sudden Move: Understanding Interprovincial Migration Our of Ontario." *Scotiabank Provincial Analysis*, March 17.

Devereaux, Mary S. 1992. "Alternative Measures of Unemployment." *Perspectives on Labour and Income* 5 (4): 35–43. https://www150.statcan.gc.ca/n1/en/pub/75-001-x/1992004/article/140-eng.pdf?st=cgxaPaj_.

Dickason, Olive Patricia. 2006. *A Concise History of Canada's First Nations.* Adapted by Moira Jean Calder. Toronto: Oxford University Press.

Dominion Bureau of Statistics (DBS). 1919. "First Annual Report of the Dominion Statistician." Ottawa: King's Printer.

——— 1929. *Origin, Birthplace, Nationality and Language of the Canadian People: A Census Study Based on the Census of 1921 and Supplementary Data.* Ottawa: Dominion Bureau of Statistics.

Dunbar-Ortiz, Roxanne. 2014. *An Indigenous Peoples' History of the United States.* Boston, MA: Beacon Press.

El-Assal, Kareem, and Sam Goucher. 2017. "Immigration to Atlantic Canada: Toward a Prosperous Future." Ottawa. https://www.conferenceboard.ca/temp/1032b2b0-f636-4b75-bea0-50c87bc552d1/9138_Immigration to Atlantic Canada_RPT.pdf.

FedNor. 2017. *Prosperity and Growth Strategy for Northern Ontario.* Ottawa: Government of Canada. https://fednor.gc.ca/eic/site/fednor-fednor.nsf/eng/h_fn04509.html.

Filippova, Elena, and France Guérin-Pace. 2013. "Le recensement: miroir ou prescripteur?" *Socio* 02 (November): 229–271.

Fine, Sean. 2015. "Chief Justice Says Canada Attempted 'Cultural Genocide' on Aboriginals." *Globe and Mail*, May 28, 2015.

Fisch, Jörg. 2015. *The Right of Self-Determination of Peoples: The Domestication of an Illusion.* New York: Cambridge University Press.

Frey, William H. 2022. "New Census Data Shows a Huge Spike in Movement Out of Big Metro Areas during the Pandemic." *The Avenue*, April 14. Washington, DC: Brookings.

Goldmann, Gustave J., and Senada Delic. 2014. "Counting Aboriginal Peoples in Canada." In *Aboriginal Populations: Social, Demographic, and Epidemiological Perspectives*, edited by Frank Trovato and Anatole Romaniuk. Edmonton: University of Alberta Press.

Goldscheider, Calvin. 2004. "Ethnic Categorizations in Censuses: Comparative Observations from Israel, Canada, and the United States." In *Census and Identity: The Politics of Race, Ethnicity and Language in National Censuses*, edited by David I. Kertzer and Dominique Arel. New York: Cambridge University Press.

Greer, Allan, and Ian W. Radforth, eds. 1992. *Colonial Leviathan: State Formation in Mid-Nineteenth-Century Canada*. Toronto: University of Toronto Press.

Habib, Irfan. 1984. "Studying a Colonial Economy – Without Perceiving Colonialism." *Social Scientist* 12 (12), December: 3–27.

Hall, Anthony J. 2003. *The American Empire and the Fourth World*. Kingston and Montreal: McGill-Queen's University Press.

Hallsworth, Gwenda. 1985. "Towns in Northern Ontario: Some Aspects of their Municipal History." *Laurentian University Review* 17 (2), February: 103–112.

Hamilton, Michelle A., Wendy Mitchinson, and Dominique Marshall. 2007. "'Anyone Not on the List Might as Well Be Dead': Aboriginal Peoples and the Censuses of Canada, 1851–1916." *Journal of the Canadian Historical Association* 18 (1): 57–79.

Haque, Eve. 2012. *Multiculturalism within a Bilingual Framework: Language, Race, and Belonging in Canada*. Toronto: University of Toronto Press.

Heffernan, C., G. Ferrara, and R. Long. 2022. "Reflecting on the Relationship between Residential Schools and TB in Canada." *International Journal of Tuberculosis and Lung Disease* 26 (9): 811–813.

Henderson, James (Sa'ke'j) Youngblood. 2008. *Indigenous Diplomacy and the Rights of Peoples: Achieving UN Recognition*. Saskatoon: Purich Publishing.

Herberg, Edward N. 1990. "The Ethno-Racial Socioeconomic Hierarchy in Canada: Theory and Analysis of the New Vertical Mosaic." *International Journal of Comparative Sociology* 31 (3–4): 206–221.

Hick, Sarah. 2019. "The Enduring Plague: How Tuberculosis in Canadian Indigenous Communities is Emblematic of a Greater Failure in Healthcare Equality." *Journal of Epidemiology and Global Health* 9 (2), June: 89–92.

Hobsbawm, E. J. 1990. *Nations and Nationalism since 1780: Programme, Myth, Reality.* Cambridge: Cambridge University Press.

Hoeppner, Vernon H., and Darcy D. Marciniuk. 2000. "Tuberculosis in Aboriginal Canadians." *Canadian Respiratory Journal* 7 (2), March/April: 141–146.

Howard-Hassmann, Rhoda E. 1999. "'Canadian' as an Ethnic Category: Implications for Multiculturalism and National Unity." *Canadian Public Policy* 25 (4) December: 523–537.

Kerr, Don, Eric Guimond, and Mary Jane Norris. 2003. "Perils and Pitfalls of Aboriginal Demography: Lessons Learned from the RCAP Projections." In *Aboriginal Conditions: Research as a Foundation for Public Policy*, edited by Jerry P. White, Paul S. Maxim, and Dan Beavon. Vancouver: UBC Press.

King, Thomas. 2012. *An Inconvenient Indian: A Curious Account of Native People in North America*. Toronto: Doubleday.

Leadbeater, D. 1997. "Increased Transfer Dependency in the Elliot Lake and North Shore Communities." In *ELTAS Analysis Series #1A6*. Sudbury. http://inord.laurentian.ca/pdf/1a6.PDF.

———. 1999. "Increased Transfer Dependency in the Elliot Lake and North Shore Communities." In *Boom Town Blues: Collapse and Revival in a Single Industry Community*, edited by Anne-Marie Mawhiney and Jane Pitblado. Toronto: Dundurn Press. https://epdf.pub/boom-town-blues-elliot-lake.html.

———. 2008. "Sudbury's Crisis of Development and Democracy." In *Mining Town Crisis: Globalization, Labour and Resistance in Sudbury*, edited by David Leadbeater. Halifax: Fernwood Publishing.

———. 2014. "Metropolitanism and Hinterland Decline." In *Resources, Empire and Labour: Crises, Lessons and Alternatives*, edited by David Leadbeater. Halifax: Fernwood Publishing.

———. 2018. "Northern Ontario and the Crisis of Development and Democracy." In *Divided Province: Ontario Politics in the Age of Neoliberalism*, edited by Greg Albo and Bryan M. Evans. Kingston and Montreal: McGill-Queen's University Press.

Long, John S. 2010. *Treaty No. 9: Making the Agreement to Share the Land in Far Northern Ontario in 1905*. Kingston and Montreal: McGill-Queen's University Press.

MacDonald, David. 2015. "Five Reasons the TRC Chose 'Cultural Genocide.'" *Globe and Mail*, July 6, 2015. https://www.theglobeandmail.com/opinion/five-reasons-the-trc-chose-cultural-genocide/article25311423/.

MacLean, M. C., A. H. Neveu, W. C. Tedford, and N. Keyfitz. 1942. "Unemployment." In 1931 Census of Canada, Vol. 13. Ottawa: Dominion Bureau of Statistics.

Malenfant, Éric Caron, Anne Milan, Mathieu Charron, and Alain Bélanger. 2007. "Demographic Changes in Canada from 1971 to 2001 Across an Urban-to-Rural Gradient." Cat. no. 91F0015MWE. Ottawa; Statistics Canada. https://www150.statcan.gc.ca/n1/pub/91f0015m/91f0015m2007008-eng.htm.

Manuel, Arthur, and Ronald M. Derrickson. 2017. *The Reconciliation Manifesto: Recovering the Land, Rebuilding the Economy*. Toronto: James Lorimer.

Manuel, George, and Michael Posluns. 2019. *The Fourth World: An Indian Reality*. With a new Introduction by Glen Sean Coulthard. First published 1974. Minneapolis: University of Minnesota Press.

Marlatt, Michael. 2004. "The Calamity of the Initial Reserve Surveys under the Robinson Treaties." Papers of the Thirty-Fifth Algonquian Conference, edited by H. C. Wolfart. Winnipeg: University of Manitoba.

Marsh, Leonard. 1940. *Canadians In and Out of Work*. Toronto: Oxford University Press for McGill University.

Métis Nation of Ontario. 2020. "Historic Métis Communities in Ontario." Métis Nation of Ontario. https://www.metisnation.org/registry/citizenship/historic-metis-communities-in-ontario/.

Moazzami, Bakhtiar. 2015. "It's What You Know (and Where You Can Go): Human Capital and Agglomeration Effects on Demographic Trends in Northern Ontario." Thunder Bay: Northern Policy Institute. https://www.northernpolicy.ca/itswhatyouknow.

Morency, Jean-Dominique, Éric Caron-Malenfant, and David Daignault. 2018. "Fertility of Aboriginal People in Canada: An Overview of Trends at the Turn of the 21st Century." *Aboriginal Policy Studies* 7 (1): 34–61.

Morrison, James. 1986. "Treaty Research Report - Treaty No. 9 (1905–1906)." Ottawa. https://www.rcaanc-cirnac.gc.ca/eng/1100100028859/1564415209671.

Nagarajan, K. V. 2008. "Some Aspects of Health and Health Care in the Sudbury Area." In *Mining Town Crisis: Globalization, Labour and Resistance in Sudbury*, edited by David Leadbeater. Halifax: Fernwood Publishing.

Ness, Immanuel, and Zack Cope, eds. 2016. *Palgrave Encyclopedia of Imperialism and Anti-Imperialism*. New York: Palgrave Macmillan.

Neu, Dean, and Richard Therrien. 2003. *Accounting for Genocide: Canada's Bureaucratic Assault on Aboriginal People*. Halifax: Fernwood Publishing.

Nickerson, Dean. 1992. "Issues in the Unorganized Areas of Northern Ontario." Western University Local Government Program, MPA major research paper 8-25-1992. London, ON: Western University.

Nicolson, Norman L. 1953. "Some Aspects of the Political Geography of the District of Keewatin." *Canadian Geographer*, January: 73–83. https://doi.org/10.1111/j.1541-0064.1953.tb01728.x.

Nkrumah, Kwame. 1965. *Neo-Colonialism, the Last Stage of Imperialism*. Nelson.

Ontario. 2005. *Places to Grow Act*. https://www.ontario.ca/laws/regulation/050416.

———. 2011. Places to Grow: Growth Plan for Northern Ontario, 2011. Toronto: Ministry of Infrastructure and Ministry of Northern Development, Mines and Forestry. https://www.ontario.ca/document/growth-plan-northern-ontario.

Ontario Ministry of Finance. 2018. "Ontario Population Projections Update, 2017–2041." Toronto: Queen's Printer for Ontario.

———. 2020. "Ontario Population Projections Update, 2019–2046." Toronto: Queen's Printer for Ontario.

———. 2023. "Ontario Population Projections Update, 2022–2046." Toronto: Queen's Printer for Ontario. https://www.ontario.ca/page/ontario-population-projections.

Pepperell, Caitlin S. et al. 2011. "Dispersal of *Mycobacterium tuberculosis Via the Canadian Fur Trade.*" PNAS 108 (16), April 19: 6526–6531.

Potvin, Mayse. 2005. "Le rôle des statistiques sur l'origine ethnique et la 'race' dans le dispositif de lutte contre les discriminations au Canada." *Revue internationale des sciences sociales* 183:31–48.

Robichaud, André. 2013. "Youth Attraction and Retention in Northeastern Ontario: A Regional Strategy." Papers in Canadian Economic Development 13: 66–88. https:// https://openjournals.uwaterloo.ca/index.php/pced/article/view/3891.

Romaniuk, Anatole. 2014. "Canada's Aboriginal Population: From Encounter of Civilizations to Rival and Growth." In *Aboriginal Populations: Social, Demographic, and Epidemiological Perspectives*, edited by Frank Trovato and Anatole Romaniuk. Edmonton: University of Alberta Press.

Rothwell, Neil, Ray D. Bollman, Juno Tremblay, and Jeff Marshall. 2002. "Recent Migration Patterns in Rural and Small Town Canada." Ottawa. https://www150.statcan.gc.ca/n1/en/pub/21-601-m/21-601-m2002055-eng.pdf?st=izrSHvHP.

Royal Commission on Aboriginal Peoples. 1996. "Report of the Royal Commission on Aboriginal Peoples." Ottawa. https://www.bac-lac.gc.ca/eng/discover/aboriginal-heritage/royal-commission-aboriginal-peoples/Pages/final-report.aspx.

Saarinen, Oiva. 1985. "Municipal Government in Northern Ontario: An Overview." *Laurentian University Review* 17 (2): 5–25.

Said, Edward W. 1994. *Culture and Imperialism.* New York: Vintage Books.

Schwartz, Sharon P. 2022. "Bruce Mines, Ontario, Canada." https://www.cousinjacksworld.com/destinations/cornish_bruce_mines_canada/.

Shepard, Todd. 2015. *Voices of Decolonization: A Brief History with Documents.* Boston: Bedford/St. Martin's.

Simon, Patrick. 1997. "La statistique des origines: 'Race' et ethnicité aux États-Unis, Canada, et Grande-Bretagne." *Sociétés Contemporaines* 26:11–44.

Slack, Enid, Larry Bourne, and Meric Gertler. 2003. "Small, Rural, and Remote Communities: The Anatomy of Risk." Paper prepared for the Panel on the Role of Government (Ontario). https://collections.ola.org/mon/8000/244176.pdf.

Southcott, Chris. 2002. "Youth Out-Migration in Northern Ontario." Thunder Bay. https://youthrex.com/wp-content/uploads/2019/02/outmigration_report_final2_-_youth_out-migration_in_northern_ontario_october_2002.pdf.

Southern Chiefs' Organization. 2018. "Treaty Maps." *Southern Chiefs' Organization Inc.* https://scoinc.mb.ca/about/treaties/.

Statistics Canada. 1983. *Historical Statistics of Canada. Cat. no. 11-518-X.* Ottawa: Statistics Canada.

———. 2000. "Introduction to Censuses of Canada 1665 to 1871: Aboriginal Peoples." Cat. no. 98-187-X. Ottawa: Statistics Canada. https://www150. statcan.gc.ca/n1/pub/98-187-x/4151278-eng.htm. See also Census of Canada 1871, Vol IV.

Statistics Canada. Table 17-10-0039-01 Estimates of population, by sex and age group, census divisions and census metropolitan areas, 2001 Census boundaries. doi: https://doi.org/10.25318/1710003901-eng

———. 2012. "Canada's Rural Population since 1851." Cat. no. 98-310-X2011003. Ottawa: Statistics Canada. https://www12.statcan.gc.ca/census-recensement/2011/as-sa/98-310-x/98-310-x2011003_2-eng.pdf.

———. 2013. "Guide to the Labour Force Survey." Cat. no. 71-543-G. Ottawa: Statistics Canada. https://www150.statcan.gc.ca/n1/en/pub/71-543-g/71-543-g2013001-eng.pdf?st=-h4XPVHZ.

———. 2015. Survey of Labour and Income Dynamics (SLID): A 2010 Survey Overview. Cat. no. 75F0011X. Ottawa: Statistics Canada.

———. 2016a. "Ethnic and Cultural Origins of Canadians: Portrait of a Rich Heritage." Cat. no. 98-200-X2016016. Ottawa: Statistics Canada.

———. 2016b. "Standard Geographical Classification (SGC) 2016, Vol. I, 'Economic Regions - Variant of SGC 2016.'" Ottawa: Statistics Canada.

———. 2017. "GeoSuite, Census Year 2016." Ottawa: Statistics Canada.

———. 2018a. "Aboriginal Population Profile, 2016 Census." Ottawa: Statistics Canada. Cat. no. 98-510-X201600. https://www12.statcan.gc.ca/census-recensement/2016/dp-pd/abpopprof/index.cfm?Lang=E.

———. 2018b. "Dictionary, Census of Population, 2016." Ottawa: Statistics Canada. https://www12.statcan.gc.ca/census-recensement/2016/ref/dict/index-eng.cfm.

———. 2018c. Table 17-10-0082-01: "Components of population growth by economic region, age group and sex, annual, based on the Standard Geographical Classification (SGC) 2011, inactive."

———. 2019a. "Labour Force Survey: Detailed Information for November 2019." Ottawa: Statistics Canada.

———. 2019b. "Life expectancy, at birth and at age 65, by sex, three-year average, Canada, provinces, territories, health regions and peer groups." Table 13-10-0389-01. Ottawa: Statistics Canada.

———. 2020a. "Ethnic or Cultural Origins: Technical Report on Changes for the 2021 Census." Cat. no. 98-20-0002. Ottawa: Statistics Canada. https://www12.statcan.gc.ca/census-recensement/2021/ref/98-20-0002/982000022020001-eng.pdf.

———. 2020b. "Sex at Birth and Gender: Technical Report on Changes for the 2021 Census." Cat. no. 98-20-0002. Ottawa: Statistics Canada.

———. 2021. "Dictionary, Census of Population, 2021." Ottawa: Statistics Canada. 2021. https://www12.statcan.gc.ca/census-recensement/2021/ref/dict/index-eng.cfm.

———. 2022a. "Age, Sex at Birth and Gender Reference Guide." Cat. no. 98-500-X. Ottawa: Statistics Canada.

———. 2022b. "Understanding Sex at Birth and Gender of People in Canada." *The Daily* (Cat. no. 11-001-X), September 14.

———. 2023. "Guide to the Census of Population, 2021." Cat. no. 98-304-X. Ottawa: Statistics Canada.

Sylvestre, Paul-François. 2019. *L'Ontario français: quatre siècles d'histoire*. Édition revue et augmentée. Ottawa: Les Éditions David.

Truth and Reconciliation Commission of Canada. 2015. "Honouring the Truth, Reconciling for the Future: Summary of the Final Report of the Truth and Reconciliation Commission of Canada." http://www.publications.gc.ca/site/eng/9.800288/publication.html.

Tuck, Eve, and K. Wayne Yang. 2012. "Decolonization Is Not a Metaphor." *Decolonization: Indigeneity, Education & Society* 1 (1): 1–40.

UBC First Nations and Indigenous Studies. 2009. "Powley Case." https://indigenousfoundations.arts.ubc.ca/powley_case/.

United Nations. 2008. United Nations Declaration on the Rights of Indigenous Peoples (UNDRIP). New York: United Nations. https://www.un.org/esa/socdev/unpfii/documents/DRIPS_en.pdf.

Uppal, Sharanjit, and Sébastien LaRochelle-Côté. 2015. "Changes in Wealth across the Income Distribution." Cat. no. 75-006-X. *Insights on Canadian Society*. Ottawa. https://www150.statcan.gc.ca/n1/en/pub/75-006-x/2015001/article/14194-eng.pdf?st=l3JMYHyZ.

Verma, Ravi B. P. 2014. "Population Projections for the Aboriginal Population in Canada: A Review of Past, Present, and Future Prospects, 1991 to 2017." In *Aboriginal Populations: Social, Demographic, and Epidemiological Perspectives*, edited by Frank Trovato and Anatole Romaniuk. Edmonton: University of Alberta Press.

Wargon, Sylvia T. 2000. "Historical and Political Reflections on Race." In *Race and Racism: Canada's Challenge*, edited by Leo Driedger and Shiva S. Halli. Kingston and Montreal: McGill-Queen's University Press.

Weller, Geoffrey R. 1980. "The Evolution of Local Government in Northern Ontario." Paper prepared for the annual meetings of the Canadian Political Science Association, Montreal, June 2–5. Thunder Bay: n.p. (Lakehead University Library).

White, Pamela M., Jane Badets, and Viviane Renaud. 1993. "Measuring Ethnicity in Canadian Censuses." In *Challenges of Measuring an Ethnic World: Science, Politics and Reality: Proceedings of the Joint Canada–United States Conference on the Measurement of Ethnicity, April 1–3, 1992*. Cat. no. CS91-515-1993. Ottawa: Statistics Canada.

Yoshida, Yoko, and Howard Ramos. 2013. "Destination Rural Canada: An Overview of Recent Immigrants to Rural Small Towns." In *Social Transformation in Rural Canada: Community, Cultures, and Collective Action*, edited by John R. Parkins and Maureen G. Reed. Vancouver: UBC Press.

Zefi, Christina. 2018. "The Northern Attraction Series Exploring the Need for a Northern Newcomer Strategy." Thunder Bay: Northern Policy Institute. http://www.northernpolicy.ca/upload/documents/publications/commentaries-new/zefi_northern-attraction-1-en-18.10.09.pdf.

INDEX

Canadian Studies

Series editor: Pierre Anctil

The Canadian Studies collection touches upon all aspects of Canadian society in all disciplines with a special focus on Canadian women, cultural and religious minorities, and First Nations. The collection is also devoted to regional studies, local communities, and the unique characteristics of Canadian society. Among the topics privileged in this collection are all contemporary issues, especially in the domain of the environment, with regards to large urban centres and new forms of art and communications.

Previous titles in the *Canadian Studies* Series

Simon-Pierre Lacasse, *Les Juifs de la Révolution tranquille : regards d'une minorité religieuse sur le Québec de 1945 à 1976*, 2022.

Winfried Siemerling, *Les écritures noires du Canada : l'Atlantique noir et la présence du passé*, traduit de l'anglais par Patricia Godbout, 2022.

Pierre Anctil, *History of the Jews in Quebec*, 2021.

Geneviève Bonin-Labelle, ed., *Women in Radio: Unfiltered Voices from Canada*, 2020.

Francis Mus, *The Demons of Leonard Cohen*, 2020.

Pierre Anctil, *A Reluctant Welcome for Jewish People: Voices in Le Devoir's Editorials*, 1910–1947, 2019.

Le Mawiomi Mi'gmawei de Gesp'gewa'gi, *Nta'tugwaqanminen – Notre histoire : l'évolution des Mi'gmaqs de Gespe'gewa'gi*, 2018.

Pierre Anctil, *Jacob Isaac Segal: A Montreal Yiddish Poet and His Milieu*, 2017.

Hughes Théorêt, *The Blue Shirts: Adrien Arcand and Fascist Anti-Semitism in Canada*, 2017.

For a complete list of the University of Ottawa Press titles, please visit:
www.Press.uOttawa.ca

Printed in August 2024
at Imprimerie Gauvin,
Gatineau (Quebec), Canada.